TEXTUAL AND VISUAL SELVES

TEXTUAL & VISUAL

SELVES

PHOTOGRAPHY, FILM, AND COMIC ART

IN FRENCH AUTOBIOGRAPHY

Edited by Natalie Edwards, Amy L. Hubbell, and Ann Miller

UNIVERSITY OF NEBRASKA PRESS · LINCOLN AND LONDON

Chapter 3 was previously published as
"Photography and Autobiography in
Hélène Cixous's *Photos de racines* and
Annie Ernaux and Marc Marie's *L'Usage de
la photo*," *French Review* 84.4 (2011). Used
with permission of the American Association of Teachers of French; permission
conveyed through Copyright Clearance
Center, Inc.

A different version of chapter 5 was
previously published in *Women in French
Studies* 17 (2009).

Set in Chaparral.
Designed by Nathan Putens.

Library of Congress
Cataloging-in-Publication Data
Textual and visual selves: photography,
film, and comic art in French autobiography / edited by Natalie Edwards, Amy L.
Hubbell, and Ann Miller. p. cm. Includes
bibliographical references and index.
ISBN 978-0-8032-3631-8 (pbk.: alk. paper)
1. French prose literature—History and
criticism. 2. Authors, French—Biography—History and criticism. 3. Art in
literature. 4. Autobiography—Authorship. 5. Visual perception in literature.
6. Literature and photography—France.
7. Self in literature. I. Edwards, Natalie.
II. Hubbell, Amy L. III. Miller, Ann, 1949
Sept. 1–   PQ771.T49 2011
840.9'35—dc23   2011020265

CONTENTS

List of Illustrations vii

Acknowledgments ix

Introduction:
Textual and Visual Selves 1
*Natalie Edwards, Amy L. Hubbell,
and Ann Miller*

1 Beyond Autobiography 29
   Véronique Montémont

2 Chronicles of Intimacy: Photography in
   Autobiographical Projects 51
   Shirley Jordan

3 The Absent Body: Photography and
   Autobiography in Hélène Cixous's
   Photos de racines and Annie Ernaux and
   Marc Marie's *L'Usage de la photo* 79
   Natalie Edwards

4 The Photobiographical Today: Signs of
   an Identity Crisis? 99
   Floriane Place-Verghnes

5 Reclaiming the Void: The Cinematogra-
   phic Aesthetic of Marguerite Duras's
   Autobiographical Novels 115
   Erica L. Johnson

6   Illustration Revisited: Phototextual
    Exchange and Resistance in Sophie
    Calle's *Suite vénitienne* 139
    Johnnie Gratton

7   Viewing the Past through a
    "Nostalgeric" Lens: Pied-Noir
    Photodocumentaries 167
    Amy L. Hubbell

8   Georges Perec, Memory, and
    Photography 189
    Peter Wagstaff

9   The Self-Portrait in French Cinema:
    Reflections on Theory and on Agnès
    Varda's *Les Glaneurs et la glaneuse* 209
    Agnès Calatayud

10 Autobiography in *Bande Dessinée* 235
    Ann Miller

    Contributors 263

    Index 267

ILLUSTRATIONS

1   Anne Brochet includes this photograph with no caption 38

2   Harboring shadows of others 58

3   Dis-locating the autobiographical self in Marie NDiaye 62

4   A degree zero of photographic evidence 68

5   Image of the girl leaning on the railing of the steamship 128

6   Original view of the girl leaning on the ferry railing 129

7   The mistake in the tile in Jacques Derrida's house in El Biar, Algeria 181

8   Italian child finds first penny, 1926, Ellis Island 205

9   The artist in the mirror 214

10 I'm an animal I don't recognize 229

11 The fading of memory 247

12 The proliferation of the self within the panel 252

13 The graphiator deplores the need to exhibit himself as character 255

ACKNOWLEDGMENTS

This book is the product of discussions and debates initiated at two conferences, one in Leicester, England (November 2007), and the other in Buffalo, New York (April 2008). The editors would like to thank all colleagues who were involved, including several who were present at both. Particular thanks are due to Professor Susan Hayward for her valuable input at the Leicester conference, and to Dr. Elizabeth Jones, the co-organizer. For the Buffalo conference, thanks are due to the Northeast Modern Languages Association and, from Amy Hubbell and Ann Miller, to Natalie Edwards, who convened the Textual Visual Selves panel. We are grateful to the *French Review*, which originally published chapter 3 by Natalie Edwards, and to *Women in French Studies*, which originally published chapter 5 by Erica L. Johnson. We much appreciate the careful guidance we have received from Kirsten A. Elias Rowley and her colleagues at the University of Nebraska Press, and we would also like to express our gratitude to Christopher Hogarth, Malcolm Hope, Douglas Powell, and Sorenne Powell for their support and patience.

TEXTUAL AND VISUAL SELVES

INTRODUCTION

TEXTUAL AND VISUAL SELVES

Natalie Edwards, Amy L. Hubbell, and Ann Miller

Autobiography in France has taken a decidedly visual turn in
recent years. Photographs, shown or withheld, have featured
in narratives of the self, offered as evidence or as metaphor of
what was, what might have been, or what cannot be said. At
the same time, French-speaking photographers, filmmakers,
and cartoonists have embarked on projects that explore issues
of identity, personal and collective. This book presents essays
in which the intersection of textual and visual autobiographies
is examined from a variety of theoretical perspectives. We
begin by briefly surveying some of the debates upon which
contributors aim to build.

THE AUTOBIOGRAPHICAL SELF

Some of the issues raised by the inclusion of images in life writing, and particularly those bearing on notions of reference, authenticity, and the autobiographical self as indeterminate and resistant to objectification, can be found in existing critical writing on textual autobiography. The genre of autobiography itself underwent radical change in the middle of the twentieth century, as the canonical affirmation of unique selfhood, stable across time, gave way to the more fractured subjectivity exemplified by Roland Barthes's *Roland Barthes par Roland Barthes* [*Roland Barthes by Roland Barthes*] in 1975. Barthes declares that he does not set out to restore the "truth" of a former self, to achieve what his autobiographical predecessors would have called "authenticity," or to describe his present self, confining himself to saying, "I am writing a text and I call it R.B." He poses the rhetorical question: "Do I not know that in the field of the subject, there is no referent?" (56). His elusiveness is accentuated by the alternation between first- and third-person pronouns and the insistence that the text be read as an account of a fictional character (123).

The theorist Philippe Lejeune, writing in the same year in *Le Pacte autobiographique* [*The Autobiographical Pact*], founded the referential credentials of autobiography on his famous pact between author and reader as to the nominal identity between narrator, extratextual author, and textual self (15), an identity that he distinguishes from resemblance. The pact does not suppose the kind of verifiable resemblance between the textual subject ("sujet de l'énoncé" [enunciated subject], in Lejeune's terms) and the extratextual model in his or her past or present incarnation that would be expected of a biography (35). Lejeune situates authenticity in the relationship of the first-person narrator (or "sujet de l'énonciation" [subject of the enunciation]) to the narrating process, and argues that it admits deformation, forgetfulness, or even lying (39), although, by definition, it would clearly not accommodate Barthes's personal pronoun ruse.

Two years later Lejeune's pact was challenged when the writer and academic Serge Doubrovsky coined the term "auto-fiction" to designate his own life-writing practice, alerting readers to the fact that the appearance of a textual character bearing the same name as the extratextual author does not preclude the reimagining or embellishment of real-life events, or indeed the inclusion of wholly fictional episodes. Doubrovsky's brilliant word play tends in any case to send the reader spinning off along the signifying chain to a realm where referential truth seems hardly relevant. As he has said in an interview, "[A]utofiction is defined by the adventure of language" (qtd. in Contat 120). The term "autofiction" has since gained considerable critical currency (see Jones).

Michael Sheringham, in his seminal text *French Autobiography: Devices and Desires; Rousseau to Perec*, sees advantages to Lejeune's pact, which "is referential but only to the extent that it refers to the extra-textual existence of the author present as a name on the cover," without implying "any specific kind of relationship" between the textual "I" and its extratextual counterpart (20). A textual self selectively extracted from the flux of an inner and outer life, constructed in language and shaped into narrative, must, he asserts, inevitably sacrifice authenticity. The production of the self as a textual construct is, then, a form of othering (viii). It must, in addition, negotiate with preexisting texts with the beliefs about the nature of selfhood that they promote and, crucially, with the Other that is the reader (ix). The transaction between the autobiographical desire and these multiple forms of otherness is carried out, Sheringham contends, by the various kinds of "devices" that are the subject of his book. These include diagrams (Stendhal), the figure of the devil (Gide), the juxtaposition of two narratives (Perec), and many more (ix). The subject of autobiography is "a hybrid, a fusion of past and present, self and other, document and desire, referential and textual, *énoncé* and *énonciation*—not a product but a process" (21).

Feminist theorists of autobiography have brought a particular perspective to the question of "othering" by drawing attention to the exclusion of women from traditional autobiographies, which served, they point out, to legitimize the individual self of the white male subject, and so to consign others to the margins. Françoise Lionnet, in the preface to her book *Autobiographical Voices: Race, Gender, Self-Portraiture*, advocates a Nietzschean perspective on "writing as an enabling force in the creation of a plural self, one that thrives on multiplicity and ambiguity," in order to combat "polarized and polarizing notions of identity, culture, race or gender" (16), while Sidonie Smith notes that, for women, autobiography has played a role in a politics of resistance, a means of both confronting and refusing the fixed identities assigned to them (434–35). Claire Boyle, writing about four twentieth-century French autobiographers, both male and female, stresses the concern of the autobiographer to avoid reification of the self as "an object that others may possess" (1). Nancy K. Miller, in a memoir of her own life, argues that, far from being about "terminal moi-ism," autobiography necessarily mingles the selves of the writer and of others, in a set of specific techniques that multiplies the narrative voice in order better to represent the self (3).

PHOTOGRAPHY AND AUTOBIOGRAPHY

The autobiographical "device," in Sheringham's term, that we are concerned with in this volume is the inclusion of images: photographic, filmic, or drawn. If it is the photography-autobiography combination that has attracted the most critical ink, this is undoubtedly because of the impact of Barthes's *La Chambre claire* [*Camera Lucida*], written shortly before his death in 1980, which has acquired the status of foundational text. As an autobiographical work containing photographs that is at the same time a theorization of the power and poignancy of the photographic image, it has to a large extent set the terms of the debate on reference. Where in *Roland Barthes par Roland Barthes*, a preface had carefully dissociated the self constructed in the text from Barthes the "individu civil" (6) ["individual with a private life" (4)], the later book declares that photography authenticates the existence of its subject (*La Chambre* 166). He explores the ontology of the photographic image from the standpoint of his own experience as a spectator, asserting its necessary attachment to its referent (16–18), contemplating its link with death (in photographs of himself, Barthes sees not just an other but death in person) (31), and analyzing its impact on the spectator through the elaboration of the distinction between "studium" (encoded social meaning) and "punctum" (the detail that escapes coding, whose impact "wounds" the spectator) (47–49). When he turns to the photograph of his mother as a child that forms the basis of his meditation in the second half of the book, these reflections take on a highly personal meaning. What he holds in his hand is "literally an emanation from the referent" (*Camera* 80), "the treasury of rays that emanated from [his] mother as a child" (82) on that day, but in this photograph, time is the punctum (*La Chambre* 148). The image simultaneously represents the indubitable "cela-a-été" (150) ["this-has-been" (*Camera* 107)] and the future anterior of the fact that she would go on to die (*La Chambre* 150). Indeed, the photograph itself is destined to perish (145). Film, Barthes argues, has a different relationship with both reference and time: it has a referent, but not one that feels like a ghost. Whereas a photograph immobilizes time, the cinematic image is pulled into the future, "protensif" [extensive in time], not melancholic (140).

Although Barthes, concerned to analyze his own reactions as a spectator, demonstrates little interest in the role of the photographer, Gilles Mora invents the term "photobiographie" to describe the work of a group of French photographers who began in the 1980s to use the medium in a more subjective way than hitherto. In a 1999 article, he sets out to define the genre that he has christened. He discusses the limit case of autobiographies consisting essentially of photographs, with the verbal element supplied only by captions. He is happy to agree with Barthes that the photograph has a constitutive connection with the real and so can be categorized as an index in the terms established by the semiotician Charles Peirce (185). However, the photograph alone is condemned to be only a fragment of the real. Echoing an argument elaborated by Elizabeth Bruss in 1980 in relation to film (which will be discussed later in this introduction), Mora claims that a photograph, lacking the enunciative apparatus of language, such as the pronoun system, is unable without the aid of a text to undertake the autobiographical enterprise of reconstruction of the real. A photograph can have a "point of view" only in the spatial sense, and is not of itself capable of introspection (186). Certain photographers have nonetheless attempted to use photographs with autobiographical intent, but Mora maintains that the results are always problematic. He excludes from the category of photobiography examples where photographs are used simply to illustrate a text (as in the work of Raymond Depardon) or to suggest intimacy through the portrayal of the photographer's domestic life or those that turn private life into an object of voyeuristic consumption (like those of American documentary photographer Nan Goldin, in his view)

(187). He argues that the difficulty for a photographer who wishes to move beyond the fragment to create meaning is that of establishing a context. Mora suggests that photomontage can bring a certain sense of perspective but maintains that in the case of a photographer like Robert Frank, it was the addition of a verbal text to his visual autobiography, *The Lines of My Hand*, that brought out the sense of time passing (187–88). Ultimately, Mora claims, photobiography will not achieve its introspective ambitions if it contents itself with stringing together images without text. His example of the accomplishment of a genuine meditation on time is Denis Roche's *Photolalies* [Photolalias], which uses the "mixed format" of photographs and texts to bring past and present together. Whereas for Barthes a photograph is haunted by the future demise of its subject, photobiography, for Mora, is situated at the heart of life's resistance to death (189).

Timothy Dow Adams, in *Light Writing and Life Writing*, structures his book along the continuum from autobiographers like Barthes, who describe or include photographs, to photographers who, like Mora's French group, make the move into autobiography. As the "and" of his title suggests, Adams does not share Mora's concern with defining a new hybrid genre and delimiting its boundaries. What preoccupies him is the additional complication brought to the question of reference when "life" and "light" writing become intertwined. He begins by arguing that "the history of referentiality in photography has run almost a parallel course to autobiography" (xvi), going on to retrace this history. If, for its inventors, photography was a chemical and physical process that gave Nature "the power to reproduce herself" (Louis Daguerre, qtd. in Adams 5), the supposed truthfulness of the photographic image has long been challenged. Adams rehearses the arguments: photographs may be staged—indeed, all posed photographs may be regarded as fictional (3). They may be cropped, enlarged, hand colored, or retouched, and their purported direct physical link with their subject is further complicated by changes in focus, angles, use of filters, and many other techniques. Moreover, Adams emphasizes that before the advent of digital manipulation, similar effects were achievable through craft methods (4–5). Nonetheless, he acknowledges that a sophisticated awareness of the potential for fakery has not diminished the persistence of "an inherent belief about the photograph's direct connection to the real" (3–4), a conviction that he finds in the works of writers such as Barthes, Susan Sontag, and Rosalind Krauss, who could hardly be accused of naïveté (xv). He alludes to the work of the autobiography theorist Paul John Eakin, who highlights the contrast between the post-structuralist dismissal of the self as referent set out in *Roland Barthes par Roland Barthes* and the conviction asserted in *La Chambre claire* that the photograph testifies to the existence of the referent. In Eakin's striking phrase, "When the austere tenets of post-structuralist theory about the subject came into conflict with the urgent demands of private experience, Barthes turned for solace to [. . .] photography" (Eakin 11). For Adams, though, the power of photography arises not out of its referentiality but rather out of "the indeterminacy of its sense of reference to the world" (15), an indeterminacy that it shares with autobiography. When the two forms occur together, neither can act as guarantor of the veracity of the other: on the contrary, the combination of photographs with life writing "may intensify rather than reduce the complexity and ambiguity of each taken separately" (xxi).

Competing conceptions of photography, as referential or as indeterminate, are central to an essay by Alex Hughes in *Phototextualities*, an edited volume that contains analyses of the role of photographic images in many different kinds of narrative. Hughes's chapter explores the reflections of Hervé Guibert, a gifted photographer, in *L'Image fantôme* [Ghost Image], published in 1981, on how photography may provide a model for the narrative of a life, although his book contains no actual photographs. Hughes contrasts Guibert's initial estimation of the potential of photography to offer "intimate perceptual access to its referent," as in the case of Barthes's photograph of his mother (170), with blurred or out-of-focus images that "fail to afford their viewer a sense that she or he can use them to achieve a possessive, penetrating grip on the real of the referent" (173). Corresponding to these ways of imagining photography are "different autobiographical desires" (172), and Guibert's chosen mode of self-portraiture is the "phantom image" of the title, indexical but shadowy and nonmimetic, emblematized within the text as he evokes photographs that failed to come out or that were of such poor quality as to be unreadable (175–77). Hughes contends that the exclusion of photographs from Guibert's narrative guards against the ever-present temptation to find in them the autobiographical referent that may elude us in the text (177). However, her essay ends by finding referentiality elsewhere: the evocation of certain photographs and related episodes has a "metanarrative referentiality," foreshadowing themes that will surface in Guibert's subsequent life writing (178).

Linda Haverty Rugg, writing in *Picturing Ourselves* on the use of photographs by four literary autobiographers, calls for a more direct reaffirmation of referentiality as a kind of strategic self-objectification (14), a move that recalls the intervention by feminists into theories of autobiography, to which Rugg explicitly alludes, emphasizing the concern of women and minority groups to combat dominant cultural definitions (10). Rugg notes the association of the medium with surveillance, a threat that impels two of her chosen authors, Walter Benjamin and Christa Wolf, not to display the photographs around which they structure their autobiographical accounts. She acknowledges that this offers a way of preempting readings imposed from without (18–19). It is, however, not the only strategy. Rugg argues that "naïve" and "sophisticated" readings of photographs can be brought together with empowering effect. As she says, "[T]he presence of photographs in autobiography cuts both ways: it offers a visualization of the decentred, culturally constructed self; and it asserts the presence of a living body through the power of referentiality" (19). The introduction of photographs into an autobiography seems to locate the self in the author's body, but this does not imply either biological essentialism or loss of agency. On the contrary, "the trick," as she says, "is seeing both the material body and its cultural construction at the same time" (20). For Rugg it is this trick that affords the possibility of self-construction.

In their introductory chapter to *Interfaces: Women, Autobiography, Image, Performance*, Sidonie Smith and Julia Watson, like Rugg, aim to show how women can escape a history in which they have been "an object of speculation and specularization" (5). Their book takes in the autobiographical work of women working across a number of visual arts, but photography is strongly featured. The key term for them is not referentiality, though, but performativity: women's self-representation is "a performative act constituting subjectivity in the interplay of memory, experience, identity, embodiment and agency" (4). They argue that the past is not just a repository but is created by acts of remembering, located in bodies and in the objects that make up our experiential history. Identities materialize within collectivities but, they insist, it is possible for autobiographical subjects to assume agency and rewrite existing cultural scripts, a form of resistance that may involve the "strategic deployment of narcissism" (10). This implies a critique rather than a simple replication of the masculinist tradition of representation, and the authors see visual-textual interfaces in particular as sites that promote engagement with issues around gendered subjectivity and artistic production (11–16). Much of their first chapter is taken up with a model for reading this gendered interface which, they suggest, may be configured relationally, contextually, spatially, or sequentially. The relationship between juxtaposed textual and visual elements allows them to play off and interrogate each other through parallels or contradiction (22–25); the textual may situate the visual in a cultural surround that makes explicit taken-for-granted official histories (25–28) or "reworks the nation's official memory of a group as devalued or invisible" (28); the spatialization of visual representation allows for images and words to be layered over each other, or visual elements framed by a paratext (28–29); in a sequential presentation, serial versions of the self will dispel the possibility of any definitive or "truthful" self-portrait, while the collapsing together of different time frames can counter the gaps and absences in personal and collective narratives (28–35).

CINEMA AND AUTOBIOGRAPHY

There is a growing body of critical literature about film and life writing, some of which, like Robert Rosenstone's edited collection *Revisioning History: Film and the Construction of a New Past*, focuses on the capacity of the medium to reconfigure the national past in accordance with, or in opposition to, official histories. Other critics, like Elizabeth Bruss, have looked at the ontology of cinema. Bruss argued in 1980 that the medium is ontologically unsuitable as a vehicle for autobiographical narratives on three main grounds. The first of these is truth-value (film captures a global image and does not have the enunciative resources for sincerity). The second is act value (there is not a single source but a disparate group of individuals involved at all stages; moreover, any attempt to stamp "subjectivity" on the image will produce unacceptable distortions of reality). The third is identity value (the person on the screen cannot simultaneously be perceiving the image through the camera lens) (301–08). However, Bruss goes on to argue that while film cannot produce the old self-knowledge of classical autobiography, it has other ways of representing the self. The image of the body becomes the locus of identity rather than its mask and does not have to be the illusory whole of Lacan's mirror stage: it can be a new assemblage. Subjectivity is released from the ostensible temporal and spatial unity of the speaking subject in the same way that, in *Roland Barthes par Roland Barthes*, Barthes looks at the power of autobiographical text to extend and transform the person of its author (319).

Seven years after Bruss's work, Lejeune produced an article on cinema and autobiography in which he noted that the terminology of autobiography was increasingly being used in relation not only to photography but also to film, a development that, he felt, gave rise to a number of complications (7). For example, autobiographical cinema has a problem with authenticity: whereas the signifier in language has no relationship with the referent, and any written account of the past is necessarily a reconstruction (which does not prevent it from being read as truthful), film is capable of recording the real directly. When, therefore, the filmmaker restages scenes that took place in the past, their inauthenticity will be immediately obvious. The difficulty can, Lejeune suggests, be overcome by filming scenes in the present but filming the past only in the form of traces, such as photographs. A voice-over, which has the resources of verbal language, can then make the link to the past (9). Lejeune gives examples of films that have moved him, such as Depardon's *Les Années-déclics* [The Click Years], which includes the author's commentary on his own photographs and on extracts from his films (12). Lejeune also acknowledges Bruss's point about the inability of the cinematic apparatus to find an equivalent of the fusion of the enunciating and enunciated "I": even if the person shown in front of the camera is in fact responsible for the images, the spectators will not be aware of this unless it is made explicit in a verbal paratext. The image that we see has nothing intrinsically first person about it (10). Lejeune's rather surprising conclusion is that autobiographical cinema exists but is founded on the conditions of viewing, in the underground circuit whereby the filmmaker who has represented his or her own life is present at the screening.

Raymond Bellour, writing in 1988, responds both to Bruss and to Lejeune. He suggests that when filmmakers use photographs from the past, the split temporality can be unsettling. In one way the pact is more direct: the autobiographical subject says, "I am me and that was me," but in another way the previous self seems unconnected to the present self, even if the voice-over tempers the effect of rupture. The photographs fragment the subject, he says, and make it intermittent, a series of "small snapshot-deaths" (338). He argues that video may lend itself better to self-portrayal than film: the electronic image is continuous and gives a sense of immersion in real time. Moreover, the author may more readily include his or her own body in the image, since the address to camera seems less transgressive than in film. Furthermore, it is easier to transform the electronic image, which does not arouse the same expectations of documentary truth as the film image:

Bruss's dichotomy between the expression of subjectivity and the need for filmed reality to remain "objective" is therefore less striking (344–45).

Wendy Everett, in 1995, counters Bruss's claim that film precludes the subjective self-awareness of autobiography: on the contrary, she claims that "film constitutes a privileged medium for the expression of autobiographical memory" (4), often motivated by the desire to explore personal and national guilt. It has the capacity for the reconstruction of past worlds reimagined and realized not in accordance with historical veracity but with memory, often interwoven with fantasy. The apparent surface realism is in fact a personal vision, a "memory realism," in which objects and settings serve as triggers in a process of self-discovery and reevaluation of the past (5–6). At the same time, the ability of the camera to create multiple viewpoints allows for distancing irony or judgment.

André Gardies, in an introduction to a series of essays that explore autobiographical and autofictional film, published in 2006, also raises the question of subjectivity in film. He argues that although some critics have looked for subjectivity in the image in the form of the decisions that the filmmaker necessarily makes (focal length, framing, lighting, and so on), the locus of affect is the film's reception by the spectator, whose subjective investment the film may succeed in arousing (9–11). Whether or not it does so is, according to Gardies, a function of the film's discourse as a whole, implying the coexistence and "arrangement" of a number of elements (18): a close-up of domestic objects will be read as subjective if the objects have been singled out by a voice-over (or some other device, such as the reading of a journal) and associated with the former life of a family member; empty places filmed in the present can be accompanied by a verbal commentary that reactivates the past and the people associated with it; the inclusion of archive film brings the collective past into the present and underlines temporal distance through its contrast with the "now" of the filming (14–18). Gardies affirms the significance of the autobiographical pact in shaping the reception of the film: such images will be felt as subjective if the terms of the pact have been met through a voice-over that uses first-person pronouns and affirms the identity of the speaker with the character seen on the screen (including not only the past incarnations of that character in home movies but also its other incarnations, where it may in fact be played by an actor) and with the extratextual filmmaker, usually through use of his or her name (18–21). The pivot, according to Gardies, is the narrative voice-over: identified with the character but not visibly uttered by him or her, it allows the spectator to slip into the space where the film's subjectivity will resonate with his or her own (21–23).

COMIC ART AND AUTOBIOGRAPHY

Autobiography has appeared relatively recently in French-language comic art, and most critical writing has focused on the work of American artists, who have been producing autobiographical work since the underground movement of the 1970s. Charles Hatfield argues that the issue of truth or falsity "remains a live one for the as-yet little-studied genre of autobiographical comics, in which ideologically fraught claims to truth collide with an anxious distrust of referentiality" (114). He introduces the idea of "ironic authentification" (125): a subversion of the pact that cements it by making demands on the reader's sophistication. By admitting that his or her core identity cannot be represented, the artist asserts him- or herself as truthful. Visual-verbal tension allows for conflicting viewpoints to exist simultaneously, and multiple selves, inherent in the comics format, challenge the notion of an unchanging self. The compact between the reader and the artist is thus constantly renegotiated (126–27).

READING THE SELF IN TEXTUAL VISUAL NARRATIVE

Each chapter in this volume discusses textual and visual self-representation in specific French-language autobiographic works. These encompass books offering only verbal descriptions of photographs, some of which may never have been taken; books that intersperse photographs through the text; films in which a voice-over is combined with moving images that may linger for some time on photographs and paintings or incorporate extracts from other films; and comic art, in which text enters the image in the form of narrative boxes and dialogue.

A number of shared themes emerge. The ambiguity and indeterminacy of the "iconotextual object," as it is defined in the opening chapter, are often exacerbated in the works discussed, and contributors explore what happens when the pact is pushed beyond breaking point. Attachment to the referent is shown to be less important than emotional force, often achieved through silence and absence, as in the work of Anne Brochet, Annie Ernaux, and Camille Laurens. Images of objects or people may not function straightforwardly as attestation of what has been, but rather serve as the repository of an inner life and as an inscription of what might have been, an imagined rather than a lived past. This evasiveness characterizes Georges Perec's displacement of the search for vestiges of his own past onto that of others a continent away and may also be found in the willfully partial backward vision of Pieds-Noirs or the artful fakery of Sophie Calle. Places may represent individual or collective memories or mythologies and, simultaneously, roads not taken or still open to exploration.

The desire to escape objectification is, unsurprisingly, a recurring theme, particularly in the work of the women who feature in this volume, but the techniques deployed and analyzed are remarkably diverse, from outright refusal of the camera's normalizing and fetishizing gaze (Marie NDiaye) through audacious preempting of that gaze (Marguerite Duras) to the exuberant doublings of Agnès Varda, who substitutes herself for the subjects of canonical works of art, and the multiple textual selves produced by comics artists, the newest entrants into the autobiographical domain.

Barthes's Winter Garden snapshot, the invisible emblem of photography's power to prefigure death, is evoked in several chapters, and a number of contributors return to a group of writers whose works memorialize loss or abandonment (Brochet, Hélène Cixous, Ernaux, Laurens, Perec, and Varda, for example). It is suggested, though, that complex textual strategies can ultimately produce an affirmation of life.

The first of the studies in this book, "Beyond Autobiography" by Véronique Montémont, surveys a range of issues raised by the autobiographic turn taken by photography and the photographic turn taken by autobiography. Montémont summarizes aesthetic and philosophical debates about referentialism, including the contention that the photograph offers immediate access to the referent, of which it is a trace, as against the insistence that its reception is determined by social and anthropological codes on the part of both photographer and spectator. She emphasizes that photobiographers have tended nonetheless to regard the connection with the real as inherent to their work. She goes on to consider how relations between image and text can be analyzed, arguing that a photograph is never merely an addition. She discusses a range of possible interactions between visual and verbal elements of autobiography, from the attempt by the text to determine the interpretation of images to the flagrant lack of coincidence between photographs and the words surrounding them. In a number of cases that she considers, it is what is not said or what is not shown that works to powerful effect. She finally examines the applicability of Lejeune's pact to photographs, noting the difficulty of allowing that a photo can say "I," particularly in view of the sense of otherness that it provokes in its own subject. But Montémont concludes that the issue of enunciation may be less important to the reader than the sense that a photograph is part of the author's self, as memory or symbol.

Shirley Jordan, in "Chronicles of Intimacy: Photography in Autobiographical Projects," focuses on four photobiographies that offer an unsettling intimacy with their subjects, threatening the boundaries between private and public. At the same time, all emphasize the elusiveness of the autobiographical self, and all offer a meditation on the photograph as a trace in unresolved narratives of loss and pain. Camille Laurens, in *Cet absent-là* [That Missing One], and Marie NDiaye, in *Autoportrait en vert* [Self-Portrait in Green], repeat Barthes's ekphrastic gesture of referring within the text to photographs that are withheld from the reader, displaying only photographs that portray people unknown to them, a strategy of concealment, suggests Jordan, and of avoidance of the fixity that the camera seeks to impose on its subject. The blurred quality of many of them emblematizes the unreliability of visual evidence and works to figure the autobiographical act itself. In apparent contrast, both Anne Brochet, in *Trajet d'une amoureuse éconduite* [The Journey of a Woman Dismissed by Her Lover], and Annie Ernaux, in *L'Usage de la photo* [The Use of Photography], cowritten with Marc Marie, include photographs that seem to offer themselves as documents.

However, as Jordan shows, this is problematized, since what they illustrate is above all emptiness and absence. In addition, they raise the issue of how far scenes depicted may have been staged for the camera, thus casting further doubt on the veracity of the accounts as a whole. Jordan suggests that the work of Serge Tisseron can be used to show how photographs such as these, assuredly marked by the death and wounding that Barthes associates with the medium, can nonetheless be part of a healing process.

Natalie Edwards also discusses *L'Usage de la photo* by Ernaux and Marie, along with Hélène Cixous's *Photos de racines* [*Rootprints*], drawing out the implications of the absence of the body of the female writer from both of these works. Edwards refers to the debate among theorists of feminist autobiography about the importance of visibility for women: life writing offers them the possibility of achieving embodiment on their own terms, refusing objectification. Why then, Edwards asks, do these two women choose images that evoke death (Cixous's comparison of her family album to a cemetery, Ernaux's description of her photographs of discarded clothes as a "nature morte") over the portrayal of living bodies? She argues that both refuse the immobility implied by images of the body. The trauma of the present time (the pain of not belonging or of illness) can be escaped, whether through the spectral presence of Cixous's ancestors or the perspective extended by Ernaux through to a future in which the traces represented by the photographs will be remembered. Moreover, through writing, they attain a timelessness that perpetuates the self beyond its bodily presence. Edwards looks also at the interweaving of other voices in these texts: Ernaux's is coauthored, and Cixous adopts the voice of her grandfather at one point, displacing the autobiographical self in a plurivocal narrative that emphasizes movement and evolution. Again, photobiography proves to thematize concealment and the play between the preservation and the repression of memories.

Floriane Place-Verghnes contrasts the belief of twentieth-century photojournalists, such as Cartier-Bresson, that they could capture the "decisive moment" with the tendency of current photobiographers to focus on the everyday, on what seems unimportant. She argues that this rejection of traditional notions of what is significant is a manifestation of the crisis of universalizing discourses, contending that in recent years photobiography has been the most apt genre both for giving form to the resulting sense of the indeterminacy of identity and for negotiating the tension between the self and the Other. In her analysis of five texts, Place-Verghnes does not focus on photographs as traces, emphasizing instead the erosion of faith in the capacity of photography to offer a transcription of the real, quoting Fredric Jameson's assertion that photographers now seek to achieve an internal vision with no external equivalent. She finds this exemplified in Ernaux and Marie's mysterious transformation of their experience and in Laurens's belief that it is love that makes things visible. Moreover, she maintains that the fragmentation evident in the work of photobiographers can be a way of giving access to an understanding of the history of an individual as imbricated in that of others: in Raymond Depardon's *Errances* [Restless Wandering], the self and other seem to fuse; in Claire Legendre and Jérôme Bonnetto's *Photobiographies*, the boundaries of identity are fluid; and in *Journal de mes Algéries en France* [Journal of My Algerias in France], Leïla Sebbar makes a detour through life stories recovered from the diaspora to construct a postcolonial identity.

Erica L. Johnson brings a number of theorists of feminist autobiography to support the view that women tend to use just such nonlinear accounts, offering multiple viewpoints, to embed ambiguous, decentered self-portraits. Johnson contrasts Marguerite Duras's novel about her childhood in French colonial Indochina, *L'Amant* [*The Lover*], with the film adaptation by Jean-Jacques Annaud. Duras uses a pair of photographs, one "real" and one that was never taken, to present her autobiographical subject retrospectively, in a highly cinematic way, through the imagined gaze of others. The photographs are available to the reader only through ekphrastic description, a move that masks the autobiographical referent and stresses its unverifiability. However, Johnson argues that Annaud's film version closes the gap between image and referent, substituting "authenticity," based on the nostalgic re-creation of colonial settings, for Duras's complex account of artistic self-discovery. Johnson goes on to recount Duras's riposte to the film, a second text, *L'Amant de la Chine du Nord* [*The North China Lover*], consisting of dialogue and directorial notes, in which the autobiographical subject becomes far more elusive, and images, including some taken from Annaud's film, are textualized in a way that opens up their indeterminacy, thereby sabotaging "authenticity." Johnson notes that Duras's text stresses the importance of the self-aware, self-reflexive look of her textual self, by no means the simple object of the gaze displayed by the film. Furthermore, the characters, including the colonized subjects, are given agency through Duras's instruction for the camera to focus on their own look at what lies beyond the frame.

In "Illustration Revisited: Phototextual Exchange and Resistance in Sophie Calle's *Suite vénitienne*," Johnnie Gratton revisits debates about the staging of photographs, which he formulates in terms of a new prototype of "illustration." He begins by returning to the established meaning of the term, long stigmatized as subordinating image to text (even if in some cases it worked creatively against the text), arguing that photographs do not fit this prototype, given that they tend not to be custom-made and often predate the text. A new prototype therefore distinguishes "illustrative" photographs (contrived and posed and/or digitally altered) from "documentary" photographs, witnesses to the event of which they bear the indexical trace. In this new prototype, the failure to authenticate the documentary writing that they accompany can, however, be seen as a virtue of photographic "illustration." The chapter goes on to offer an analysis of the text/photo relations in Sophie Calle's *Suite vénitienne* in order to demonstrate how certain photographs that appear to document the artist's project are in fact best understood as illustrations of the project. Gratton shows how this change of status stems from the fact that the published versions of Calle's activities in Venice include photographs taken in the course of both an original "following" project and a subsequent "follow-up" project. But he also offers reasons explaining why it might be shortsighted to conclude that the inclusion of illustrative photos simply subverts the documentary value of the work as a whole: the notion of performance may be prized over that of index and artistic integrity over "authenticity."

Amy L. Hubbell considers the use of photobiographies, often in the form of coffee-table photodocumentary books, to construct a highly selective collective memory for Pieds-Noirs. She cites in particular Marie Cardinal's *Les Pieds-Noirs* [The Pieds-Noirs], in which the author's photographs represent the experiences of the whole community. Hubbell points out that nostalgic accounts of the communal past began as early as 1962, and that "nostalgérie," which aims to re-create the homeland in an unchanging state, has survived scholarly research and revelations about conditions and events before and during the Algerian War. Hubbell notes that images that do not accord with the collective vision are often disregarded. Although in recent years the images have migrated to the Internet, their importance to Pied-Noir life stories has not diminished, with cemeteries in particular functioning as key sites marking both loss and the attempt to preserve memories. She argues that the engagement of intellectuals in this mythologizing enterprise is more ambivalent: in 1998, for example, the prominent scholar Benjamin Stora published his chronicle of a return to the homeland, *Impressions de voyage* [Travel Impressions], complete with the usual iconic images of the colonial past, including cemeteries, in the same volume as *Algérie: Formation d'une nation* [Algeria: The Building of a Nation]. By including in the latter photographs in which he poses with anticolonial militants, he writes his own story into the history of Algerian nationhood. Jacques Derrida, on the other hand, watches the filmed return made on his behalf by cinematographer Safaa Fathy and stresses the sense of displacement occasioned by the images. Hubbell suggests that, ultimately, Pied-Noir Internet communities risk deconstructing the very past that they attempt to unify.

Peter Wagstaff discusses a book and a film by Georges Perec, a writer similarly preoccupied with the problem of memory and its role in the construction of identity. It is the absence of memory that Perec seeks to articulate: that of his migrant Polish family and of a wider Jewish cultural inheritance rooted in the Europe of World War II and the Holocaust. Faced with the crisis of representation occasioned by the inadequacy of language and the ethical obstacles to giving artistic expression to the Holocaust, Perec rejects direct representation in favor of the allusive and the indirect. *W ou le souvenir d'enfance* [*W or the Memory of Childhood*] makes detailed reference to (unseen) photographs of his family and childhood, attempting to construct meaning in the present from the fragmentary visual remnants of the past, whilst casting doubt on their indexicality by querying his own earlier descriptions of them. Later, he scripts a documentary film, *Récits d'Ellis Island: Histoires d'errance et d'espoir* [*Ellis Island: Tales of Vagrancy and Hope*], which focuses on the dilapidated Ellis Island reception center for immigrants, a metaphor, suggests Wagstaff, for the human experience of loss and the centrality of memory in the creation of identity. The film includes traces of the past in the form of photographs of family groups and of the present in Perec's visit to the now-empty space. Wagstaff draws on the work of the philosopher Vilém Flusser, who holds that photographs disrupt the linear progression of the historical narrative. Rather than using photographs as evidence, argues Wagstaff, Perec can find in them the possibility of escape into a utopian alternative, a defense against the inexorability of his own family story, and meaning in the face of death.

Agnès Calatayud discusses the recent development of self-portraiture, once believed to be impossible in film, into a film genre in its own right, embracing miscellaneous practices including documentaries, home movies, travel diaries, and personal essays. Calatayud looks at issues raised by Jean-Luc Godard, one of the earliest practitioners of the genre with *JLG/JLG—Autoportrait de décembre* [JLG/JLG—Self-Portrait in December] in 1995, including the distinction between autobiography and self-portrait: for Godard, the latter is fragmented rather than continuous and eschews intimate revelations, even if making the self public is inevitably painful. Calatayud goes on to consider various strategies employed by filmmakers to represent the embodied self on-screen, including the use of mirrors and doubles as well as a frequent desire to represent their professional selves through metacinematic reflections and quotations. She notes a concern with the passing of time and with loss, themes particularly in evidence in the work of

Agnès Varda, whose *Les Glaneurs et la glaneuse* [The Gleaners and I] (2000) Calatayud analyzes in detail. She argues that Varda offers a self-portrait as puzzle, the elements of which include not only the filming of parts of her own body, like her aging hands, but also found objects, music (a rap with her voice on the soundtrack), and the insertion of herself into famous paintings and into the history of cinema, through an encounter with a descendent of Etienne-Jules Marey. Calatayud contends that for Varda the filmic image, in which she shows herself in motion, contrasts with the death-mask-like still photo: the film may show the irreparable effects of time, but it is on the side of life.

Ann Miller looks at the recent emergence of autobiography as a key genre in *bande dessinée*, or French-language comic art. She notes that the genre came to prominence in the work of *bande dessinée* artists associated with the independent publishing collectives that have been founded since the 1990s, which emphasize the claims of the medium to be considered as an art form rather than as mass-cultural pulp. She considers comic strip autobiography in relation to the terms of Lejeune's pact and, notably, the significance for comic strip autobiographies of his distinction between identity and resemblance. She admits that the question of physical resemblance to the subject becomes more salient in a visual medium but argues that comic strip, freed from the ontological relationship to the real that is fundamental to cinema, works through metonymy and tends to eschew documentarism in its pursuit of emotional truth. She goes on to assess the capacity of comic strip for the expression of subjectivity. Its resources include the facility with which the graphic line can introduce elements of inner life into the external world, the temporal indeterminacy of the interframe space, which can be used to powerful effect, and the built-in proliferation of the drawn self, which works against any sense of a fixed identity. The essay concludes by focusing on the extratextual consequences for artists whose life narratives include a portrayal of their milieu and by responding to the charge that this autobiographical turn represents a retreat into narcissism.

The project of this volume is, then, to engage with and extend the debate on textual visual selves through the analysis of a collection of extraordinary French-language works in a range of media. The chapters "Beyond Autobiography" by Véronique Montémont and "The Photobiographical Today: Signs of an Identity Crisis?" by Floriane Place-Verghnes were translated into English by Ann Miller. Translations of citations into English come from published editions as available or are provided by the individual contributors unless otherwise noted. The contributions arose out of two conferences: one held in Buffalo, New York, and one in Leicester in the United Kingdom. It is hoped that some sense of the productive dialogues initiated on those occasions will emerge from the bringing together of the work of scholars who offer different perspectives on these texts, and that the book will serve to generate continuing dialogue.

WORKS CITED

Adams, Timothy Dow. *Light Writing and Life Writing: Photography in Autobiography*. Chapel Hill: University of North Carolina Press, 2000.

Barthes, Roland. *La Chambre claire*. Paris: Gallimard Seuil, Cahiers du Cinéma, 1980. (*Camera Lucida*. Trans. Richard Howard. London: Jonathan Cape, 1982.)

———. *Roland Barthes par Roland Barthes*. Paris: Seuil, 1975. (*Roland Barthes by Roland Barthes*. Trans. Richard Howard. London: Macmillan, 1977.)

Bellour, Raymond. "Autoportraits." *Communications* 48 (1988): 327–88.

Boyle, Claire. *Consuming Autobiographies: Reading and Writing the Self in Post-war France*. London: Legenda, 2007.

Bruss, Elizabeth. "Eye for I: Making and Unmaking Autobiography in Film." *Autobiography: Essays Theoretical and Critical*. Ed. James Olney. Princeton NJ: Princeton University Press, 1980. 296–320.

Contat, Michel. "Quand je n'écris pas, je ne suis pas un écrivain." *Genesis* 16 (2001): 119–35.

Doubrovsky, Serge. *Fils*. Paris: Gallimard, 1977.

Eakin, Paul John. *Touching the World: Reference in Autobiography*. Princeton NJ: Princeton University Press, 1992.

Everett, Wendy. "The Autobiographical Eye in European Cinema." *Europa: An International Journal of Art, Language and Culture* 2.1 (1995): 3–10.

Frank, Robert. *The Lines of My Hand*. New York: Lustrum, 1972.

Gardies, André. "Le Spectateur en quête du je (et réciproquement)." *Le Je à l'écran*. Ed. Jean-Pierre Esquenazi and André Gardies. Paris: L'Harmattan, 2006. 9–23.

Hatfield, Charles. *Alternative Comics: An Emerging Literature*. Jackson: University of Mississippi Press, 2005.

Hughes, Alex. "Hervé Guibert's Photographic Autobiography: Self-Portraiture in *L'Image fantôme*." *Phototextualities: Intersections of Photography and Narrative*. Ed. Alex Hughes and Andrea Noble. Albuquerque: New Mexico University Press, 2003. 167–81.

Jones, Elizabeth H. "Autofiction: A Brief History of a Neologism." *Life Writing*. Ed. Richard Bradford. Basingstoke UK: Palgrave Macmillan, 2009. 174–84.

Lejeune, Philippe. "Cinéma et autobiographie: Problèmes de vocabulaire." *Revue belge du cinéma* 19 (Spring 1987): 7–12.

———. *Le Pacte autobiographique*. Paris: Seuil, 1975.

Lionnet, Françoise. *Autobiographical Voices: Race, Gender, Self-Portraiture*. Ithaca NY: Cornell University Press, 1989.

Miller, Nancy K. *But Enough about Me: Why We Read Other People's Lives*. New York: Columbia University Press, 2002.

Mora, Gilles. "La Photobiographie: Une forme d'autobiographie?" *Cahiers RITM* 20 (1999): 183–89.

Roche, Denis. *Photolalies*. Paris: Argraphies, 1988.

Rosenstone, Robert, ed. *Revisioning History: Film and the Construction of a New Past.* Princeton NJ: Princeton University Press, 1995.

Rugg, Linda Haverty. *Picturing Ourselves: Photography and Autobiography.* Chicago: University of Chicago Press, 1997.

Sheringham, Michael. *French Autobiography: Devices and Desires: Rousseau to Perec.* Oxford: Clarendon, 1993.

Smith, Sidonie. "Autobiographical Manifestos." *Women, Autobiography, Theory: A Reader.* Ed. Sidonie Smith and Julia Watson. Madison: University of Wisconsin Press, 1998. 433–40.

Smith, Sidonie, and Julia Watson. "Mapping Women's Self-Representation at Visual/Textual Interfaces." *Interfaces: Women, Autobiography, Image, Performance.* Ed. Sidonie Smith and Julia Watson. Ann Arbor: University of Michigan, 2002. 1–44.

1

BEYOND AUTOBIOGRAPHY

Véronique Montémont

The 1970s saw the first signs of a new way of thinking about photography in France. This was underpinned by a two-way movement in artistic practice and its theorization, with names like Raymond Depardon, Gilles Mora, Claude Nori, Bernard Plossu, and Denis Roche in the forefront. A unifying thesis for these artists and theorists was the conviction that photography and life are intimately linked, a premise that could form the basis of a new visual language. This is why they appealed for what Cécile Camart calls "autobiographical investment in the photographic act" (375), which resulted in the publication in 1983 of the dazzling *Manifeste photobiographique* [Manifesto for

Photography]. This text, written by Mora and Nori, is resolutely confident in the vitality of the newborn genre and conceptualizes writing and photography as a single act of creation: "And so photography can enable us to live our lives over again. It is essentially a biographical witness. We will give it new impetus by putting it at the heart of our autobiographical project, to the point where we no longer know whether to live for taking photographs or the opposite" (103). Twenty years on, Mora has stated that his wish was not fulfilled, even if the founders of the movement, particularly Roche and Depardon, have produced an extraordinary body of photobiographic work ("Pour en finir" 116). However, despite the fact that photography and autobiography have not become as interwoven as Mora had hoped, it is clear that contemporary French literature has taken a photographic turn, given the increasing recourse to photographic material in autobiography and autofiction.

Following on from writers such as Roland Barthes and Georges Perec and from artists such as Sophie Calle and Christian Boltanski, a number of artists, many of them distinguished, have introduced visual material into their texts: Hélène Cixous (*Photos de racines*, 1994) [*Rootprints*]; J. M. G. Le Clézio (*L'Africain*, 2004) [The African]; Annie Ernaux and Marc Marie (*L'Usage de la photo*, 2005) [The Use of Photography]; Roger Grenier (*Andrélie*, 2005); Marie Desplechin (*L'Album vert*, 2007) [The Green Album]. Others do not actually include photographs but base their narratives on absent or fantasmatic images: François Bon (*Mécanique*, 2001) [Mechanical]; Antoinette Dilasser (*Les Vraies images*, 2007) [The Real Images]; and of course Hervé Guibert, who describes photographs that he has not been able to take but that are etched into his imagination (*L'Image fantôme*, 1981) [Ghost Image]. These texts form a heterogeneous collection; however, since the presence of photographs (whether real or brought into being by description) has a different effect on their relation to biographical reality according to whether they are icons (based on resemblance) or indexes (based on the material trace left by an object) (Peirce 140), there is need to put forward a few possible theoretical frameworks in order to gain a better understanding of the interactions at work between the text and the image in autobiography.

PHOTO-TEXT RELATIONS

Photography and autobiographical discourse meet in a range of different ways. Just as Jean-Marie Schaeffer (68–74) describes photography as a complex system, it could be argued that photobiography is neither a generic category nor the mechanical adding together of two discourses but a composite system that has three aspects: textual, iconic, and the explicit or implicit relations between the two. The latter determine the perspective that the reader chooses to adopt in decoding the work. An initial approach may be a quantitative assessment of the ratio of image to text in an autobiography. At one end of the scale would be texts containing no images but that use "notional" ekphrasis (Hollander 209). This is a procedure that consists of invoking absent objects, in this case one or more photographs, which become the focal point for descriptions, commentaries, reveries, and readings, on the now-famous model of the Winter Garden photograph in Barthes's *La Chambre claire* [*Camera Lucida*] (106–10). Other examples can be found: Marguerite Yourcenar's *Souvenirs pieux* [*Dear Departed*], which lingers over the deathbed portraits of her mother, Fernande; Perec, in *W ou le souvenir d'enfance* [*W or the Memory of Childhood*], daydreams about childhood photographs depicting him and his mother; Bon's *Mécanique* turns upon the repeated description of a portrait of his father driving an unusual-looking traction engine; Ernaux's *Les Années* [The Years] is rhythmically punctuated by descriptions of photographs of the author at different ages. The use of ekphrasis means that the relationship between image and reader remains abstract and entirely dependent on the descriptive elements filtered through the text. This relationship is, then, in some sense disappointing. But at the same time, it encourages the imagination to play an active role, given that readers are directly invited to fill in the space of these images, left blank from the point of visual representation, with those of their own imagining. Ernaux, for example, justifies in just such a way her decision not to include the photographs mentioned in *Les Années*, making the assumption that readers can substitute their own. She has said to a journalist, "So far, no reader has complained that my photos were missing, and several have told me that as they read [the book], they 'saw' their own" ("Entretien").

In other cases, authors have instead chosen to reproduce images in the book. Depardon, Roche, Barthes, and later Marc Marie and Ernaux in *L'Usage de la photo* offer examples of an integration of the two media, where the strategic relationship between text and image allows the photographic material to be affected by its caption. Indeed, Mora emphasizes, "Photobiography has rarely produced works that could stand on their own without language" ("Photobiographies" 110). And a title like *Légendes de Denis Roche* [Captions by/Legends of Denis Roche] plays on the ideas of commentary and of story by its insistence on the role of the relationship to the text. Within this category, degrees of greater or lesser textualization can be distinguished. Some authors, like Depardon, allow the image to be relatively autonomous: in *La Ferme du Garet* [Garet Farm], the order of the photographs corresponds in general to the chronology of the account of the author's childhood, but this does not preclude repetitions and missing captions. Conversely, Anny Duperey's *Le Voile noir* [The

Black Veil] articulates the images into a logical sequence that is entirely dictated by the text. The book is an investigation into the personality of the author's parents, who died in an accident when she was eight, and is based on photographs taken by her father, Lucien Legras, which are scrutinized and analyzed. As this reconstitution rests on a certain number of hypotheses (most notably the possibility that the accident could have been unconsciously motivated), the images are called upon as evidence. So Duperey deduces, from photographs of misty mornings, that her father was melancholic, and from a faraway look, that her mother suffered from depression. The family structure and the affective links between individuals are similarly resuscitated on the basis of a few snapshots of communal meals. At this point, we no longer look at these images as family photographs or as the work of a particularly talented amateur photographer: they have become clues in the investigation, which is a desperate attempt to fight against amnesia.

At all events, the copresence of text and image necessarily affects the way in which the work as a whole is received. While the text mediates a complex reality that is accessed by the deciphering of signs and then by the intellectual construction of what the signs represent, the photograph—which is no less complex—seems to follow a reverse perceptual process: the representamen is visible in the first instance and is followed by the decoding of the referent to which it relates. It appears on the surface of the page with an immanence that it is tempting to assimilate to a kind of material truth of the thing that is displayed. As Ernaux says, it has a "power to draw you in," a "disturbing reality effect" ("Entretien")—hence the complex and often paradoxical relationship between the photograph and its referent, between autobiography and what it presents as its visual traces.

THE ICONOTEXTUAL OBJECT

Theories of aesthetics and philosophy have greatly clarified the semiological problematic that is attached to the relationship between the photographic image and reality. As Schaeffer emphasizes, the image is in the first instance a matter of physico-chemical data, the trace of the "visual manifestation" (54) of a light source: in other words, the referent. But it is doubly determined on the level of meaning, by the consciousness that produces it (the photographer) and by the consciousness that receives it (the viewer). The referent is therefore but one element in a wider system, which cannot dispense with its presence but which necessarily takes up a distance from it. Moreover, and still according to Schaeffer, social and anthropological codes weigh heavily on and condition our different modes of reading the image. This is why photography cannot be considered to be a kind of legally accredited mechanical sampling of reality. "How could anyone still believe that a photograph offers proof of anything?" François Soulages asks ("Trace" 22). Nonetheless, this is exactly what the photobiography reader wishes to believe, disposed as he or she is to accept the photograph as a memory trace, alternative or complementary to the written text.

Philippe Lejeune has shown that the reader's adherence to an autobiographical text supposes a pact, and that one of the conditions of this, the clause on referentiality, amounts to a commitment by the author to speak "the whole truth, nothing but the truth" (36). Implicitly, these expectations were quickly transferred to the photographic image. This explains why, in spite of the change of perspective introduced by theory, in spite of the awareness that photography is above all an art of transforming a luminous imprint into a visual composition, a notion like "reality" is not easily expelled from the discourse of photobiographers. Lived experience and how they choose to show it are still the essential core of the problematic within which they work. Roche, for example, has declared that "reality [should] enter into the viewfinder and accumulate there, charge itself up until it fills [the photo] right to the edge, until it is complete, definitive, finished: and, therefore, *saturated*" (*Disparition* 184). Mora, for his part, compares photobiography to an imprint and sees it as "a specific type of sign, which manifests a fundamental—and constitutive—connection with reality" ("Photobiographies" 109). But this does not mean that the conjunction of text and photograph should be viewed as a mechanical addition, a superimposition that is supposed to produce more truth or get closer to the truth. On the contrary, this conjunction, which might seem to approach some ideal of veracity in autobiography, introduces a certain play through the way in which the two elements enter into contact with each other and sometimes clash.

Some analysts and artists, following on from the manifestos of the 1980s and 1990s, have shown awareness of the fact that the relationship between text and photo is very far from obvious. "The relationship of photograph to literature cannot be limited to that of a loyal servant" (Soulages, *Esthétique* 238). Christine Delory-Momberger sees in literature "a field of both reference and competition, of dialogue and confrontation" with autobiographical photography (13). And in a text called "L'image parfaite" [The Perfect Image], in *L'Image fantôme*, Guibert contrasts the two modes. For him, photography is "an all-encompassing and forgetful practice" whose material result can end up becoming "foreign" to us, while writing, a "melancholy activity," makes it possible to "go beyond and enrich the immediate photographic transcription" (24). There is, then, an opposition between two media that have different codes and to which not all authors attribute the same properties.

For some, a photo involves a kind of irrecoverable distortion of experience, while for others it is instead the indispensable means of activating the process of memory.

We have seen that on the material level, the degree of textualization can be considerable or negligible; we should add that the relationship between the two elements is necessarily dynamic and sometimes conflictual. Indeed, it is by no means rare for the text to go beyond a purely informative role (date, place, identification of the representamen) to become involved in narrating personal history. Barthes, for example, warns us right at the beginning of *Roland Barthes par Roland Barthes* [*Roland Barthes by Roland Barthes*] that the childhood photographs that we are going to see represent for him "figurations of the body's prehistory: of that body making its way towards the labor and pleasure of writing" (3). To put it another way, the reader is invited to see in this tall skinny boy the future thinker and intellectual who will subsequently be shown in the images of him as an adult (lecturing, at a conference, in his office). Roche, whose captions tend to be merely informative, nonetheless regularly establishes parallels between the date the photo was taken and his activity as a writer: "1960, boulevard Saint-Germain. It was Lise who took the photograph of me. [. . .] I'm writing *Amazon-like Forest*" (*Légendes* 60); "Photos taken, above, by Martine S., and, below, by Lise. *The Centesimal Ideas of Miss Elanize* has gone to press" (64); these notes are a way of reminding the reader that he considers writing to be fundamental in his creative output. Depardon, on the other hand, emphasizes his role as a photographer, even if his living conditions, which were rural and very modest, did not predispose him toward this unexpected choice of profession. And the captions of his images sometimes designate the technical operation just as much as the person who is represented in them: "I took this photograph of Nathalie to try out my new lens, a 35 mm which closes at 22" (208). In all these cases, our perception of the photo is teleologically oriented toward a certain representation: that of a character and his or her ethos, which the language of the text has constructed around the image, aiming to draw its content toward this particular meaning.

The converse is also true: the text is put to the test by the image; if it opts for notional ekphrasis, it remains forever incomplete, integrating absence as a poetic effect, as Barthes suggests: "I cannot reproduce the Winter Garden Photograph. It exists only for me. For you it would be nothing but an indifferent picture, one of the thousand manifestations of the 'ordinary'; [. . .] but in it, for you, no wound" (*Camera Lucida* 73). If, on the other hand, the author chooses to include the photographs in the text, the caption, the commentary, or the ekphrasis risks being confronted with the image. The reader will be able to evaluate descriptive accuracy, fidelity to the subject represented (or at least the perception of it), or possibly the extent to which these texts are fictional. In any case, the reader's attention will have been decentered, and comprehension of the work as a whole can only be the product of a comparative synthesis of both types of discourse and a calculation of the degree of veracity that arises from their copresence. This operation is made more complex by the fact that in many cases where the image might be expected to confirm the text and vice versa, there may be a disjuncture or outright contradiction. To be precise, not all text-image relationships are verbalized; they may fall back on tacit implications to provide additional meaning. When Anne Brochet recounts her abandonment by her lover, she chooses to photograph banal places and objects mentioned in the text: an empty room, a telephone, a cupboard.

1. Anne Brochet includes this photograph with no caption. From *Trajet d'une amoureuse éconduite*. Photograph by Anne Brochet. Photo © Anne Brochet.

No caption, no explanation, and no human face, with the exception of a photo of the author enveloped in plastic wrap. The text is likewise pared down, a bare factual account with only the most desultory mention of emotion. This double minimalism bestows a poignant force upon the photo of a humble telephone or street. It constitutes the desolate proof that the affair is over, that these places and these objects will never again be inhabited or touched by the lover, except through a solitary act of recall. More tragically, Dorothy Allison, in *Two or Three Things I Know for Sure*, shows several photos of herself as a child: a little girl in white or dressed for her first Communion. These are inserted without commentary in an account of her childhood in which Allison describes, among other things, how she was abused by her stepfather (42). The contrast between these two versions is violent and disturbing: it is precisely through this dissonance that the full horror of the situation is conveyed.

In point of fact, the juxtaposition of text and photo turns out to be an excellent way of making an autobiographical text tip over into autofiction, which Philippe Gasparini defines as "all narratives which are designed for a double reading, simultaneously fictional and autobiographical" (14). It may be the case that the two modes, photo and text, which each present themselves as autobiographical, do not entirely match. Put another way, they no longer meet in a relationship of referentiality (identifying, naming, describing, contemplating, reconstructing) but rather hint at gaps, tension, or even conflict between the two media. This dissonance points to the fact that there has been a degree of manipulation, and that, as a result, the search for authenticity in narratives of the self is no longer the first consideration. The case of the French installation artist Boltanski exemplifies this deliberate splitting: Boltanski began his textual output with a series of booklets whose titles invite us to read them as having an underlying autobiographical basis: *Recherche et présentation de tout ce qui reste de mon enfance* [Search for and Presentation of All That Remains of My Childhood] (1969), *L'Album photographique de Christian Boltanski, 1948–1958* [Christian Boltanski's Photograph Album] (1972), *L'Appartement de la rue de Vaugirard* [The Flat in the Rue de Vaugirard] (1973). Part of this material appeared again in *Les Modèles* [The Models] (1979) under the subheading "Five Text-Image Relationships." In each case, the aim is to set up a system of oppositions, or at least of flagrant disjuncture between text and image: photos of an empty flat, described as if the furniture was still there, photographic portraits bearing names and dates ("Christian Boltanski at the age of 7—6 July 1951") as if they were childhood photographs—yet portraying ten different people. "What I wanted to say was that 'Christian Boltanski' wasn't a particular person, but that the name stood for all children. [. . .] Being called 'Proustian' had annoyed me immensely, and in these pieces, I was reacting against the fact that my work had been classified as autobiography" (Boltanski and Grenier 83).

Nonetheless, Boltanski's device necessarily gives rise to just such a question because the wording of the caption draws the work into the domain of autobiography, despite the author's protestations. In this precise case, the photograph has social currency. Boltanski did not, with the *10 Portraits photographiques de C.B.* [10 Photographic Portraits of C.B.], photograph a person but a social practice with its codes and its historicity: the pose, the clothes, the reflection of a collective image of childhood. As a result, the discrepancy in meaning between captions and images does not cancel out the work's status as photobiography but transcends it, relocating it in a narrative of the self as a social being.

The work of Calle is based on constant negotiation between autobiographical material and the procedures of both mise-en-scène and narration that act upon it. The artist's creations always take as their point of departure a lived experience, but one whose contrived or strange nature has a literary appeal: arranging for strangers to be followed, sending her bed to a young man suffering from a broken heart, having stories told to her from the top of the Eiffel Tower, investigating an address book found in the street (*M'as-tu vue?*). According to Yve-Alain Bois, the work as a whole forms a "permanent double game," a "Borgesian frenzy of false appearances" (36). But this frenzy, insofar as it exists, is governed by strict rules of iconographic syntax in a highly effective "dialectic [. . .] between seeing, reading, and the marriage of both" (Soulages, *Esthétique* 242). The interplay between image and text develops incrementally: the text informs the reading of the photographs on which, in turn, the narrative progression of the whole work depends on a macrostructural level. This dynamic is particularly noticeable in *Douleur exquise* [Exquisite Pain]. This book, published in 2003, recounts a failed love affair following a trip to Japan. It makes use of a plethora of documentary material (Polaroids, train tickets, headed notepaper, letter and diary pages) photographed in what purports to be an edited diary. But it soon becomes clear that the process of editing is another way of rewriting the story of a painful breakup by drawing on the standard devices of tragedy. The introduction, the commentaries, the mark of the red inventory stamp on every photo show the successive stages of an unfolding tragedy: Calle will never be like the Japanese bride whose photo she took in Tokyo, and her lover will never see the outfit that she bought at Yamamoto to wear for their reconciliation. Her happy smile in the penultimate photograph ("Only one more day. I've never been so happy. You waited for me" [194]) is a fine example of tragic irony, since the author had revealed at the outset of her work that her lover would fail to show. In *Douleur exquise* the photos are subservient to their captions, which are the stuff of popular fiction (adventure, excitement, coincidence) whose artifice (symmetry, nods and winks, irony) is obvious. Here again, the fictional dimension that arises out of the hijacking of the image by the text is not a negation of autobiography but a transformation of it. A story that is described by the author herself as banal (13) is rewritten, distilled, and so stands for the violence of any breakup, with the photos used as evidence in an unflinching witness statement.

All of these examples serve to demonstrate that the text-image relationship cannot be reduced to a power game between two codes. Out of their copresence emerges a new semiotic object demanding a particular mode of reading that involves giving consideration to the text and image separately but also to their relationship. The reader may then question the accuracy, the relevance, and the ambiguity of this relationship. It is therefore not surprising that theorists and critics should have had to resort to neologisms to refer to these unfamiliar works of art: Soulages uses the term "co-creation," and Michael Nerlich and Alain Montandon speak of an "iconotext." We are now going to assess how far the concept of autobiographical pact elaborated by Philippe Lejeune can be applied to pho-tobiography: to what extent can it take account of images? At what point does it cease to be operational? It is by test-ing its limits that we will best understand the new types of problematics born of the introduction of photographs into autobiography.

A KNOCKOUT BLOW FOR THE PACT?

In an article on Calle, Jean-Paul Guichard points out that "there is not a single mention of images or even photographs in *Le Pacte autobiographique*" (79). There is a good reason for this. This omission is not a blind spot in Lejeune's theory;

it arises out of the structural impossibility of extending to photography one of the key elements of the pact: enunciation. Thus Lejeune proposes that there must be an "identity between the author (whose name refers to a real person) and the narrator" as well as "identity between the narrator and the protagonist." Furthermore, he emphasizes that "the enunciator of the discourse must allow him/herself to be identified within the discourse itself" (15). And the affirmation of this identity requires the use of first-person pronouns along with the citation of the proper name within the text. On this point, photography meets an ontological stumbling block: it possesses no resources, other than linguistic ones, to say "I," and this refers the question of identification back into the textual sphere, which rarely enters into the photographic frame. An exception might be made for name cards of various kinds (in mug shots, at conferences, in group photographs), handwriting, or collage. For example, Alix Cléo Roubaud includes pieces torn from her diary in a photograph called *La Dernière chambre* [The Final Bedroom] (10). Jo Spence has herself photographed by Terry Denett before her breast cancer operation, naked to the waist, with "PROPERTY OF JO SPENCE" written on her diseased breast in felt-tipped pen (157). Classic self-portrait poses in front of a mirror, which feature in the work of Depardon or Roche, might also be considered instances of subjective enunciation, of which the markers would be the presence of the photographer and the camera. The camera, specifically, would act as the equivalent of a shifter. But even in this case, a noun ("self-portrait") is required to link the photo to the author.

A further issue arises: that of the camera operator. In literature it is tacitly assumed that the agent of the creative literary process is the author. In the sphere of literary autobiography, excluding the commercial end of the market, which has seen a rash of celebrity "autobiographies" in the form of "conversations with" this or that journalist, the breaking of the link between author and narrator is theoretically prohibited. Outsourcing to a ghostwriter, fake authorship, and rewriting by an editorial team are still perceived, at least in Europe, as the mark of lightweight production, placing the work outside the boundaries of the field of literature. In contrast, the conception of an image can be unproblematically separated from its realization. By common consent, a "self-portrait" can be attributed to an artist while being technically delegated to an assistant, a technician, or some other intermediary (Bajac and Canguilhem 17). Calle often has her photographs taken by other photographers (particularly by Jean-Baptiste Mondino, whose style is not difficult to detect). Roche, in his *Légendes*, often has himself photographed by his partners, first Lise and then Françoise. The photographs in Boltanski's *Portraits de C.B.* were taken by Annette Messager, and Spence enlisted the collaboration of Denett. But the authenticity of the images is not challenged, especially if the point is to represent the self. It is in fact vital to adopt this wider definition of enunciation, since the alternative would be to exclude a whole swathe of photobiographical material. The childhood photograph, for example, necessarily fails to comply with the identity between "author" (camera operator) and protagonist: it would be impossible to have taken pictures of oneself as a baby or even to have conceived or commissioned them.

Finally, the issue of content needs to be raised. In an autobiography, as long as it is in prose, is retrospective, and fulfills the conditions of the pact, the actual subject matter is neither here nor there, since it is assumed to have an intrinsic link to its narrator. An author may choose to tell his own story, like Pierre Pachet, through the biography of his parents or, as in the case of Bon, by providing a commentary on a photograph of his father. On the other hand, it is very difficult to label the content of an image as autobiographical once it is no longer possible, or less easily possible, to link an act of enunciation with the resulting utterance. The childhood photograph, here again, exemplifies this paradox. It is hard to imagine a more authentic document or one more bound up with the very definition of identity. And yet such photographs are not always acknowledged by their own subjects: Ernaux, Roubaud, and Perec all speak of their feeling of estrangement at the sight of these images and seem to feel the need to relocate this material within a lengthy text in order to regain ownership of it. Photographs ultimately pose the problem of the grasp that individuals have on their own memory, their ability to think of themselves as whole when they are confronted by the otherness that the image presents to them.

As I conclude this essay, I am aware of having raised a number of issues without necessarily providing solutions. The very complex nature of photobiography and the evolving practices associated with it mean that we are not in a position, unlike Philippe Lejeune in the case of autobiography, to put forward a photobiographic pact that would map the boundaries of a new genre. Achieving this would require consideration of issues relating to aesthetics, phenomenology of perception, enunciation, semiology, and transmediality at one and the same time. The diversity of potential approaches is in fact so great that Delory-Momberger opts to make the definition of photobiography a matter of personal decision: for her, given that "we are faced with a variety of individual practices which defy categorization [. . .], it is up to [. . .] the photographer alone to acknowledge the photobiographic dimension in his/her work or the spectator in the reading that s/he makes of it" (27). Mora, for his part, deems that the label "photobio-graphic," which he invented in the French context, has been contaminated by a "commercial instrumentalization" ("Pour en finir" 116), and that his original conception has not lived up to its promise. Does this mean that we must relinquish the idea of perceiving books whose text works in biographical interaction with the images as belonging to a new genre? It seems to me that this would involve giving up all notion of pinning down the uniqueness and the charm of these works, which disrupt our habits in relation to autobiography and force us to appreciate the work of the artist on two levels.

A few methodological points can be systematically noted. Textual elements, from the briefest caption to the longest ekphrasis, come within the province of linguistics and can be analyzed with the tools of Lejeune's pact: proper names and enunciation. It is also possible to investigate the way in which the subject has chosen to represent him- or herself, to see whether he or she operated the camera, and what methods are used to identify what is shown in the photographs as biographic. The presence of an authorial epitext (articles, interviews, theoretical texts) can help us to understand the poetic qualities of the image and the photographic impulse as well as the link that the artist aims to establish between the two media that he or she uses. But what seems essential is to understand the dynamic of the forces at work in the iconotextual dimension because it is out of the points of contact between them that artistic innovation is born: is it a case of saturation, redundancy, ellipsis, dissonance, disjuncture, or contradiction? Are we looking at an integrated work of art, with truly reciprocal interactions, or do the two dimensions remain watertight? On the pragmatic level, what is the effect on the reader? Does the artist equip him or her to make a link, or even a synthesis, between text and photo, or prevent him or her from doing so? At all events, the meeting of the two elements in a single location, autobiography, does not guarantee that an ideal of documentary truth has been reached. It opens up instead a force field of interactions whose energy and relevance provide templates for the auto-biographical process. Ultimately, the reality evoked by the indexical or iconic value of the photos is secondary for the reader, who is rarely familiar with the referents. Nonetheless, what sets photobiography apart is the confirmation by the author, through the text, that it pertains to him or her: as memory, as symbol, as family heritage—and, thereby, as an essential component of autobiography.

WORKS CITED

Allison, Dorothy. *Two or Three Things I Know for Sure*. New York: Plume, 1995.

Bajac, Quentin, and Denis Canguilhem, eds. *Le Photographe photographié: L'autoportrait en France, 1850–1914*. Paris: Paris Musées et Maison Européenne de la Photographie, 2004.

Barthes, Roland. *La Chambre claire: Note sur la photographie*. Paris: Gallimard, Le Seuil, L'Etoile, 1981. (*Camera Lucida*. Trans. Richard Howard. New York: Hill & Wang, 1981.)

———. *Roland Barthes par Roland Barthes*. Paris: Seuil, 1975. (*Roland Barthes by Roland Barthes*. Trans. Richard Howard. London: Macmillan, 1977.)

Bois, Yve-Alain. "La Tigresse de papier." Calle, *M'as-tu vue?* 29–40.

Boltanski, Christian. *L'Album photographique de Christian Boltanski, 1948–1958*. Hamburg: Hossmann, 1972.

———. *L'Appartement de la rue de Vaugirard*. Paris: Association Française d'Action Artistique, 1991.

———. *Les Modèles*. Paris: Cheval d'Attaque, 1979.

———. *Recherche et présentation de tout ce qui reste de mon enfance*. Livre d'Artiste, 1969.

———. *10 Portraits photographiques de C.B.* Paris: Multiplicata, 1972. Rpt. in Boltanski, *Les Modèles*.

Boltanski, Christian, and Catherine Grenier. *La Vie possible de Christian Boltanski*. Paris: Seuil, 2007.

Bon, François. *Mécanique*. Lagrasse: Verdier, 2001.

Brochet, Anne. *Trajet d'une amoureuse éconduite*. Paris: Seuil, 2005.

Calle, Sophie. *Douleur exquise*. Arles: Actes Sud, 2003.

———. *M'as-tu vue?* Paris: Xavier Barral / Centre Georges Pompidou, 2003.

Camart, Cécile. "Les Stratégies éditoriales de Sophie Calle: Livres de photographies, photo-roman, livres d'artistes." *Littérature et photographie*. Ed. Jean-Pierre Montier, Liliane Louvel, Danièle Méaux, and Philippe Ortel. Rennes: Presses Universitaires de Rennes, 2008. 373–89.

Cixous, Hélène, and Mireille Calle-Gruber. *Photos de racines*. Paris: des Femmes, 1994.

Delory-Momberger, Christine, ed. *Photographie et mise en images de soi*. La Rochelle: Association Himéros, 2005.

Depardon, Raymond. *La Ferme du Garet*. Arles: Actes Sud, 1997.

Desplechin, Marie. *L'Album vert*. Paris: Nicolas Chaudun, 2007.

Dilasser, Antoinette. *Les Vraies Images*. Cognac: Le Temps Qu'il Fait, 2007.

Duperey, Anny. *Le Voile noir*. Paris: Seuil, 1992.

Ernaux, Annie. *Les Années*. Paris: Gallimard, 2008.

———. "Entretien avec Marie-Laure Delorme." *Mediapart*. 2 Apr. 2008. (11 Sept. 2009.)

Ernaux, Annie, and Marc Marie. *L'Usage de la photo*. Paris: Seuil, 2005.

Gasparini, Philippe. *Est-il je? Roman autobiographique et autofiction*. Paris: Seuil, 2004.

Grenier, Roger. *Andrélie*. Paris: Mercure de France, 2005.

Guibert, Hervé. *L'Image fantôme*. Paris: Minuit, 1981.

Guichard, Jean-Paul. "Poker menteur: De la photographie comme trace d'existence de Sophie Calle." Méaux and Vray 73–82.

Hollander, John. "The Poetics of *Ekphrasis*." *Word & Image* 4 (1988): 209–19.

Le Clézio, J. M. G. *L'Africain*. Paris: Mercure de France, 2004.

Lejeune, Philippe. *Le Pacte autobiographique*. Paris: Seuil, 1996.

Méaux, Danièle, and Jean-Bernard Vray, eds. *Traces photographiques, traces autobiographiques*. Saint-Etienne: Presses de l'Université de Saint-Etienne, 2004.

Montandon, Alain, ed. *Iconotextes: Actes du Colloque International de Clermont*. Paris: Ophrys-CRDC, 1990.

Mora, Gilles. "Photobiographies." 1999. Rpt. in Méaux and Vray 105–13.

———. "Pour en finir avec la photobiographie." Méaux and Vray 115–17.

Mora, Gilles, and Claude Nori. "Manifeste photobiographique." 1983. Rpt. in Méaux and Vray 103–06.

Nerlich, Michael. "Qu'est-ce qu'un iconotexte? Réflexions sur le rapport texte-image photographique dans *La Femme se découvre*." Montandon 255–302.

Pachet, Pierre. *Autobiographie de mon père*. Paris: Autrement, 1994.

Peirce, Charles S. *Ecrits sur le signe*. Trans. Gérard Deledalle. Paris: Seuil, 1978.

Perec, Georges. *W ou le souvenir d'enfance*. Paris: Denoël, Gallimard, 1975.

Roche, Denis. *La Disparition des Lucioles: Réflexions sur l'acte photographique*. Paris: L'Etoile, 1982.

———. *Légendes de Denis Roche: Essai de photo-autobiographie*. Montpellier: Gris Banal, 1981.

Roubaud, Alix Cléo. *Journal, 1979–1983*. Paris: Seuil, 1984.

Schaeffer, Jean-Marie. *L'Image précaire: Du dispositif photographique*. Paris: Seuil, 1987.

Soulages, François. *Esthétique de la photographie*. Paris: Nathan, 1998.

———. "La trace ombilicale: Photobiographies." Méaux and Vray 17–24.

Spence, Jo. *Putting Myself in the Picture: A Political Personal and Photographic Autobiography*. Seattle: Real Comett, 1988.

Yourcenar, Marguerite. *Souvenirs pieux*. Paris: Gallimard, 1974.

2

CHRONICLES OF INTIMACY

PHOTOGRAPHY IN AUTOBIOGRAPHICAL PROJECTS

Shirley Jordan

We must obtain our own negative
And rather than develop it,
hollow it out.
▪ ROBERTO JUARROZ, *Quinzième poésie verticale*

How do photography and lived experience fold into one
another? Writers of autobiographical narratives have long
experimented with the question, using photographs as catalysts
that raise questions about ontology, identity, memory, and
evidence. Through moments of self-reflection, self-knowledge,
or self-alienation, through the stories and the ekphrastic forays
they generate, photographic images buttress or buffet our
sense of self. As a starting point for this discussion of photography and the autobiographical subject, I want to use the idea,
expressed by Argentine poet Roberto Juarroz and adopted by
Camille Laurens for her phototext *Cet absent-là* [That Missing

One], of hollowing into one's negative. What does this metaphor suggest? A paradoxical insistence on photographic absence; a curiosity about photographic processes; rejection of fixity and finish in favor of the undeveloped; an interest less in seeing the self *in* photography than thinking the self *through* photography. Juarroz's suggestions have a distinctly autofictional resonance consistent with the contemporary urge to use photographs in autobiographical investigations as other than straight "evidence" of self-presence. They prompt us to ask: how close can we get to ourselves through photographs? What good is photography as autobiographical evidence?

This chapter discusses some of the distinctive ways in which autobiographical accounts in French have, in recent years, increasingly been constructed around photographs and ideas of photography. It focuses on a cluster of experiments that not only combine text and image but are saturated in photography, driven or persistently underwritten by its practices and theories. These are Camille Laurens's *Cet absent-là*, Marie NDiaye's *Autoportrait en vert* [Self-Portrait in Green], Anne Brochet's *Trajet d'une amoureuse éconduite* [The Journey of a Woman Dismissed by Her Lover], and Annie Ernaux's and Marc Marie's *L'Usage de la photo* [The Use of Photography]. Each of these authors has produced just one phototext thus far, and the contemporaneous publication of these is indicative of a distinct photographic turn in contemporary life writing in French. Such a turn is evidenced too by recently forged coinages, from "photobiography" to "photoautobiography" or "(phauto)biography" (one is tempted to add "[phauto]fiction"). These four experiments in chronicling lives through photographs and photographic conceits have, as we shall see, much in common and allow us to take a snapshot of the kinds of projects involving photography that were being elaborated in the mainstream at a particular moment.

Before I turn to the texts, I want to address the terms of my title. As "chronicle" suggests, I shall be concerned not with isolated photographs but with series of photographs used to document a specific event, period, or phenomenon. I am also interested in the relationship between the recourse to photography and the emphasis on intimacy in autobiographical and autofictional accounts. As it explores the potential of telling through showing, visual autobiography plays with photography's propensity to position us as intimates, privy to what only those closest to the autobiographical subject would normally see: the grain of the skin, a pile of soiled clothes, the uninspiring contents of a cupboard, a slept-in bed. Serge Tisseron's psychoanalytically driven account of why photography is such an intimate medium is useful here, explaining both the excitement and the unease the medium can generate.

Tisseron argues that photography's fascinating seductiveness, its emotional and sensory appeal, and the dynamic of boundaries and barriers that it raises are bound up with Lacan's mirror stage and with the tension between distance and a presymbolic experience of skin-on-skin parental contact. He suggests that development of the visual is compensatory and emphasizes the privileged appeal to touch of photography: more than painting, it provides the illusion that we really can touch what it shows (132–36). Poised between "representation" and "containment," it is a medium wherein "the 'silky,' the 'velvety,' the 'grainy' are represented in an almost tactile way" (123). Further, the photograph permits a peculiar sense of possession of the photographed subject, the like of which is not provided by textual or filmed accounts. It is transportable, ever available for scrutiny, ever open to the caress of the eye, and each look we cast upon it is latently weighted by the protracted processes of desire and distancing through which we have all been socialized. Diane Arbus's well-known comment that there is something naughty about photography alludes to more than voyeurism: it reminds us that photography threatens established boundaries by promising to get us up close again. Arguably, then, photography as a medium is already especially enmeshed in the dialectics of private and public, proximity and distance, desire and uncertainty that are increasingly foregrounded in contemporary autobiographical and autofictional works.

The four texts on which I focus here narrativize intense relationships, either of romantic and sexual love or of maternal love. They are persistently engaged in drawing their own limits concerning what may be shown and what Tisseron calls "the photographic intimacy 'that cannot be shown'" (135). All of them play on our desire to get close and on the "privileged fusional contact" (139) that locks us in to connections with the photograph's materiality. All also raise the paradoxes of the "intimate" that have been highlighted in recent analyses by Elisabeth Lebovici, Dominique Baqué, and others. As Lebovici puts it, paraphrasing Blanchot, "If 'intimacy is ourselves being ordinary,' we are therefore forced to accept the contradiction of an intimacy which obeys the paradoxical tendency to magnify it in order to represent it" (18). In cutting into the flow of intimate experience, in seeking to externalize and freeze it, perhaps intimacy always escapes us. All the works analyzed here use photography as a compelling way of accessing very private experiences; at the same time, all invite us to explore the boundaries of intimacy and highlight the medium's revelatory limitations.

What else do these phototexts have in common? Photography within them is required to be the bearer of a great deal, since it is harnessed to a swell of unresolved anxiety, pain, or loss that each work chronicles. In other words, they express a collective desire to call upon it as an appropriate device—palliative, cathartic, investigative—for narrating specific sets of circumstances. All are photographic metanarratives in the sense that they give an account of taking photographs and/or encourage reflections on the technologies of photography and the ways in which (predigital) photographic processes and images achieve significance. All are obsessive: with regard to loss and memory; in relation to their fascination with photographic images; and, for Brochet and Ernaux and Marie, in relation to their impulse to take and display such images (Brochet's work includes seventy of her photographs; Ernaux and Marie's gives evidence of a sudden "photographic greed" [91]). All harness the tropes of photographic processes and technologies to account for human experience. All work with photography yet contest and push against it even as they do so. All are excessively engaged with the absence/presence dichotomy inherent in photography and demonstrate a shared fascination with traces (see Méaux and Vray) or with images that, like those described in Hervé Guibert's *L'Image fantôme* [Ghost Image], are "intimate to the point of invisibility" (back cover). Structurally, all observe what Agnès Fayet calls, with reference to Ernaux, "an aesthetic of the fragment" (311), and all manipulate our understanding of how meaning is achieved in one of the most common of photographic narratives: the album. Finally, the critical questions that these phototexts raise are rendered more intractable by a ludic undercurrent that destabilizes our reading of them: emotional intimacy and the sense this can generate, *pace* Roland Barthes, of being "pricked" by images is frequently undercut here by unease about their evidential status.[1]

The texts studied here draw on a range of image types: amateur photography and art photography, experimental portraits, family photographs, and found photographs. Laurens and NDiaye use photographs taken by others; Brochet and Ernaux and Marie take the photographs themselves. It is interesting to note in terms of subject matter that, intimate though they are, these chronicles evacuate the self. Only Anne Brochet includes an image of herself, to which I shall return. Such reticence sets them apart from the self-examination of practiced and ironic exhibitionists such as Sophie Calle. It seems clear, then, that these four projects have enough common features to make it meaningful to read across them. My purpose as I focus on each one in turn will be to draw out selected key features that constitute the text's distinctiveness and that find echoes in one or more of the others.

CET ABSENT-LÀ: PORTRAITS AND PALIMPSESTS

Camille Laurens's autofictional "I" was already a well-honed construct by the time *Cet absent-là* was conceived. The author's interest in subverting generic conventions was also already apparent and, in her investigations of identity, love, desire, sexual difference, and writing, she had frequently drawn analogies between life writing and the visual, especially the cinematic. Laurens plays on the gaze and, as Margaret Andrews comments, not only can her "terse and highly visual writing" evoke that of film scripts, but the interactions she describes are often framed as moments in a film-making process. *Cet absent-là* transfers this interest in the visual to photography and constitutes a remarkably sustained experiment in thinking events and emotions photographically.

Written in the first person, *Cet absent-là* is addressed to Camille's lover and chronicles the period between her meeting and losing him. It does so through its responses to a distinctive collection of nineteen photographic portraits taken by photographer Rémi Vinet and reproduced in Laurens's book. These portraits are of people—men, women, and children of various ages and origins—to whom Vinet is close but who are to Laurens complete strangers. Most striking about these photographs is their obsessively reiterative technique, which renders their subjects simultaneously near (they are insistently close up) and distant (excessive blurring makes them feel remote). Laurens's lover is similarly desired but absent. He is emotionally inaccessible and, since Vinet did not wish to incorporate a portrait of him in the text, he remains invisible. The text's principal absentee, however, "cet absent-là," is Laurens's baby son, Philippe, who died shortly after his birth in 1994, a decade before this text was published. The tropes of photographic practice, and especially of portraiture, offer, then, a vehicle for exploring four things in this text: love, self-identity, insupportable loss, and modes of autobiographical/autofictional self-presentation. Through visual analogy, questions are posed about the degree to which we can seize and know experience and about what residue remains available to us as time passes. What emerges is that by contrast with the cinematic analogies used in Laurens's earlier autofictional writing, photographic fixity endangers her sense of becoming and is associated with autobiographical closure.

In terms of human relationships, Laurens sees an intimate connection between photographic portraiture and the experience of love: "You need love to capture a face, love is what makes things visible" (15). *Cet absent-là* begins with description of a "love at first sight," described as a "flash," whereby Camille suddenly becomes visible, captured in the gaze of the man who is to be her lover: "[I]t's like a flash: someone can see me; someone is seeing me. I bathe in the crowd like light-sensitive paper floating in developing fluid, I leave an impression at the speed of light, time alights upon me momentarily; my body is a snapshot; I capture a gaze" (11). This freezing of the self in the gaze of another's desire is ambiguous: if to "capture a face" is integral to the process of love, it also suggests fixity on somebody else's terms.

The value of Vinet's portraiture for Laurens is precisely that it evokes rather than fixes. She explores its blurriness and the technical procedures through which this is achieved: Vinet develops images, projects them onto a white sheet, then photographs the projection, attentively releasing his subjects into grainy phantom images that he refers to not as portraits but as "figures." Consideration of these "figures" gives rise to a view of a palimpsestic self, in permanent mobility, *insaisissable* [elusive] and harboring shadows of others. In her autofictional *Dans ces bras-là* [In Those Arms], Laurens remarks on the presence in her own face of her father's face (141). Here she sees in it both her father and her child and uses Vinet's photographs similarly to consider resemblance: "And the father in the lover, and the child in the man, and the man in the child, and the one who is missing in the one who is there, so many faces in each one, ghosts" (*Cet absent-là* 37). The "figure," opened to multiple interpretations and identifications, becomes a way of visualizing bonds. It is, as Anne-Marie Garat observes apropos of the anonymous fam-

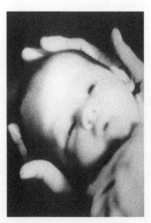

ily photographs she studies, "as if each face called up the memory of another one, the aura of one who wasn't there" (117). Vinet's photographs, then, provide visual intimacy: they have a close-up, private idiom, alluding to the distinctiveness of a gesture, the angle of a head or the quality of a look, and the ways in which these move us. In eschewing fixity and opening up to multiplicity they

2. Harboring shadows of others: "Figures." From *Cet absent-là*. Photograph by Rémi Vinet. Photo © Rémi Vinet, figure 18, 1998.

seem to liberate the photographic subject. At the same time, these cherished images are close to evaporation and underline photography's uneasy intimations of loss.

In terms of the theme of loss in *Cet absent-là*, a process of substitution is at work whereby the photographs we see stand in for photographs that cannot be shown. There is thus an intimate, implied album underlying this one, available only through ekphrasis but evoked by this phototext's core image, Vinet's "figure" of a newborn baby. This picture is ghosted by the never-to-be-looked-at photographs of Philippe that Laurens possesses and has concealed "in an envelope, I know where it is" (43). One of the most powerful of the many metaphoric alliances created in my corpus between photographic processes and human experience is found in Laurens's account of the Polaroid photographs that hospital staff took of her son on the cusp between life and death. In a dramatic inversion, Philippe's life slips away as the picture develops. He becomes the negative of this new image that replaces him, the absence to its presence: "[A]t the moment when the image slowly appears on the paper, life goes away from him at the same rate, it leaves him. It is like Edgar Poe's *The Oval Portrait*. Moreover we say 'to take a photo.' What can anyone take from us, apart from our life?" (92). The loss of Laurens's son somewhere between two Polaroid images perhaps inevitably gives rise to the conclusion not only that photography is a mortuary form but that photography kills: "Any photograph is an acclamation of death, and even provokes it, brings it on: you aim, you press, it kills" (35). It is interesting that the most directly autobiographical of Laurens's works is the 1995 text titled *Philippe*, a raw literary account of her loss. A decade later, this different and more allusive account becomes possible, with the intermediary tropes of photography providing a metaphorical route back into the unspeakable.

To conclude, *Cet absent-là* explores photographic portraiture but rejects it on any other than Vinet's terms. To have one's photo taken is "[to let oneself] be put in a coffin" (99). Only moving images, which cannot be framed or contained in an album, or Vinet's dissolving "figures" are acceptable. Laurens closes her text on a final rejection of photography as a mortuary art, on a confirmation that the self is mobile and multiple, and on a resolution to keep on the (autofictional) move rather than to submit herself to the (autobiographical) lens.

AUTOPORTRAIT EN VERT: PHOTOGRAPHIC GHOSTING

Marie NDiaye's idiosyncratic writings explore exclusion, anxiety, and yearning and deploy fantastic devices to convey the disarray of a central protagonist. These devices, interrupting as they do an otherwise realist mode, also disorientate the reader. The author's major works repeatedly expose the deficient fiber of family ties, revealing family as ambivalent and uncanny, "both absent and too present" (Rabaté 38), and incorporating episodes whose affective impact is generated by the meanings of family photographs. Photographs are displayed, discussed, stolen, ripped, defaced, and on one occasion buried, in fictional demonstrations of the image's power to validate identity.

Prior to the publication of *Autoportrait en vert* NDiaye wrote nothing autobiographical and remained unfashionably resistant to journalistic probing of her private life. When she accepted an invitation to contribute to the recently launched Mercure de France *Traits et portraits* [Features and Portraits] series, whose express purpose is to provide a forum for exploring the visual in autobiographical projects, her aim was to create a self-portrait that would be in tune with her habitual elusiveness.[2] Accordingly, the autofictional "I" of *Autoportrait en vert* makes her a much less available subject than Camille Laurens, and the drift between fact and fantasy that destabilizes her text makes her especially difficult to locate. NDiaye composes her chronicle in the form of a first-person diary that, through dated entries, fragmented chronology, and flashbacks, records selected events in a town beside the Garonne, from an unspecified time in 2000 to December 2003. "Marie," the diary's author, describes her protectiveness toward her children; her contacts with estranged or unknown members of her extended, fragmented family of origin; the unaccountable appearance of a number of spectral "women in green"; and the pregnant fear that the swollen Garonne is about to burst its banks. This anxious voice is that of a *métisse* whose father is Senegalese, who is a well-known writer married to one Jean-Yves, whose parents have separated and remarried, and whose family of origin has become unrecognizable. While much of this detail is autobiographically rooted, any sense of verifiable truth is eroded by the implausible, fabular quality of narrative events.[3] The women in green, the sudden unrecognizability of formerly familiar individuals, and the lurking presence of a fearful dark shape that is intuited rather than seen throw the reliability of evidence—especially visual evidence—into question.

Photographs have a multiple presence in *Autoportrait en vert*. The written text alludes to photographs of family members, revealing on one important occasion their uncomfortably powerful indexical link to the observed subject: when Marie receives from her estranged mother a photograph of a baby half sister, she rushes to bury it in the neighbor's chicken pen (65). A second narrative, ghosting the written one, is achieved through the inclusion of two categories of photograph: found photographs from anonymous family archives that date from the beginning of the last century and art photographs taken in the mid-1990s by photographer Julie Ganzin. These give the work an especially pronounced hybridity, standing in tension with the diary and also with each other. The written text makes no mention of them: they are unaccountable apparitions, or intrusions, which further create enigma by their cloudy or time-damaged quality or their unconventional composition. NDiaye has in common with Laurens, then, a strategic rejection of photography's indexical certainty. She too relies on photographs of strangers and on blurring.

What kind of visual narrative is forged here and in what sense does it feed into NDiaye's "autoportrait"? I shall argue that the photographs that punctuate this text but that are partially decoupled from it serve persistently to dis-locate the autobiographical self, transferring our attention away from NDiaye as a private individual and back to her writing. Take, for instance, the most intimate of these images: the cluster of amateur photographs that represent mother/child ties. These do seem subtly to echo maternal anxieties expressed in the diegesis. The circulation of gazes, the quality of touch or grasp, and the small implicit struggles between mother and infant that are latent within the photographs encapsulate the tension between fusion and separateness with which the narrator/

3. Dis-locating the autobiographical self in Marie NDiaye. From *Autoportrait en vert*. Unknown photographer. Photo © Marie NDiaye.

mother is also preoccupied. It is clear that these pictures are not anchored in NDiaye's personal life, although we are free to imagine that they speak to her experience of motherhood. Instead they are archetypes, alluding to that generic stuff of family that is at stake in all NDiaye's writing and that is so well drawn out in studies of the powerful sharedness of family photography by writers such as Anne-Marie Garat, Marianne Hirsch, and Annette Kuhn.

What of the other category of photograph in this uncanny album? The opening and closing images, both by Julie Ganzin and both titled *Décrire* [Describe] (6, 95), show women alone and absorbed in contemplation. In each case the figure has her back to us, her unavailability a signal that the subject of the photograph is not the woman herself but the activity in which she is engaged. Are these allusions to the figure of the writer? Two further images by Ganzin serve as particularly focused comments on NDiaye's resistance to the autobiographical exercise. The first, a detail from an ambivalent photograph titled *Eco e Narciso* (25), which is suggestive of a woman about to plunge into a lake, is surely a playful comment on autobiography's perils. In the second, taken from a series titled *La Montagne Sainte-Victoire*, the subject faces the camera but remains unavailable (80). On the point of slipping away beyond the left of the frame, she twists her body to gesture toward our interrogating eye and Ganzin's play between blurred and sharp focuses within a single photograph—a recurring tactic in many of those reproduced here—makes it appear as if the subject has cast a web, or thrown a blurring substance in our direction. What we are allowed to see with clarity are just two things: the landscape and the act of blurring. Further, several of these images hint at heat hazes and tricks of the light, keeping us—and sometimes the women who figure in them—hermeneutically challenged as we strain to see.

A further dimension of *Autoportrait en vert* is its placing of unusual stress on the potential meanings of sequencing and structure, and hence on the ways in which we expect images to construct narratives. Just as the written chronicle includes flashbacks and double takes, so we return more than once to photographs and their near doubles. Ultimately, however, there is no predevised code to crack. NDiaye has recently made clear not only that the photographs in *Autoportrait en vert* have no autobiographical resonance for her, but that she had no role in determining their distribution in the text (Asibong and Jordan 195–96). Such randomness leaves us entirely free to construct what narratives we will, and NDiaye has deliberately created a "self-portrait" that puts any idea of an autobiographical pact to the test. This singular foray into autobiographical terrain insists on the tensions inherent in any attempt to read visual evidence, and *Autoportrait en vert* reduplicates instances of defective vision. It speaks to us of missing, of nonrecognition, of intuiting but failing to see, of the visually unintelligible. The photographs' blurred focus, their emphasis on acts of scrutiny (subjects within several of them peer at horizons or at what is near to hand), their disorientating duplication, and a degree of trickery (the detail from *Eco e Narciso* referred to earlier is reproduced upside down) all call the reliability of visual evidence into question.

To conclude, *Autoportrait en vert* does not permit us to "see" the writer or to piece together her allusive material into something unequivocally autobiographical. NDiaye acknowledges, but does not collude with, the popular trend in self-revelation, and if there is a degree of identification between the author and the "women in green" pictured in these photographs, this is limited to the way in which their interestingly disorientating quality constitutes, as the writer/narrator puts it, "my own originality" (77). Her emphatic blurring is consistent with Tisseron's statement: "Blurred photographs [. . .] are not so much trying melancholically and painfully to eternalize the ephemeral as to make permanent the uncertainty which is inherent in all symbolic enterprises" (159). As Catherine Poisson remarks with reference to the use of photography by both NDiaye and Laurens, each author eschews illustration, providing instead a productive but troublesome "interference" or "friction" between text and image.

My next two focuses are more direct explorations of the photograph as autobiographical evidence (evidence of being, of having been, of having been somewhere). Here we return to the status of the photograph as documentary source—although not, as we shall see, in any simple way.

TRAJET D'UNE AMOUREUSE ÉCONDUITE: DOUBLE TRACES

The distinctly amateur photographs in Anne Brochet's *Trajet d'une amoureuse éconduite* piece together the fragmented narrative of a failed love relationship and work intensively, like the texts already analyzed in this chapter, with photography's presence/absence dichotomy. Brochet's color snaps are, like her narrative, mundane and minimal in terms of both content and execution. The written component, a spare and emotionally flat account, gives snatches of conversation and notational records not so much of events as of nonevents. Although written in the present tense, it is clearly retrospective. We gather that the narrator became obsessed with an inaccessible married man who has now left her but who was in fact absent more than present from the beginning. Brochet goes on to fill her time by excessively recording absence. Her intimate chronicle accordingly displays an enormous number of photographs, all of them taken after the relationship had finished, thus replacing one obsession with another in a nervously compulsive compensatory gesture. The documentary value of photographs comes into play here but with a twist, for their taking constitutes an attempt to access a past that has already passed, and Brochet's account is doubly belated since both image and text are constructed after the event. On the trail of traces, these photographs (re)capture nothing and confirm nothingness.

A curious idiom develops in Brochet's chronicle. Her photographs fall into two categories: those representing the private sphere (banal features of the author's domestic interior) and those depicting public spaces (Paris streets and cafés, a station concourse, a platform, an underground car park, an airport). The feature linking them is that they are all evacuated of human presence apart from that of the photographer, which we intuit. I propose briefly to look at each category, domestic shots first, keeping in mind the overarching question: what happens to intimacy in these photographs?

The iconography of Brochet's interior shots links them to the work of well-known photographers who make intimate studies of the everyday: for instance, she shows us her empty bed, a much-used trope of the superprivate that now seems somewhat weary, overlaying as it must our invitations to other beds, from Nan Goldin's to Sophie Calle's to Tracey Emin's. Other snapshots of the author's apartment are more unusual in focus and often in angle, appearing to invite access by training the camera on a doorway, presenting to us the corner of her sofa or revealing the contents inside two of her cupboards (she accompanies these images with verbal inventories and a short narrative regarding her use of certain items at a given point). Brochet photographs her toilet, her telephone, her computer and, the image chosen for the book's cover, her ceiling. What is especially curious is that the domestic environment depicted is clinically stripped: there is little of the intimate debris that betrays human presence and gives us that excitingly edgy feeling that—as we will see with Ernaux and Marie—we are seeing something we should not. Everything appears scrubbed, tidied, voided, so that this nondescript photodiary of loss seems paradoxically almost entirely evacuated of intimacy. At most, we might detect within the angle of certain shots a poignant tension between presence and absence: the high- or low-angle shots of a staircase, for instance, or pictures that "gaze down" on empty chairs implicitly remap the physicality of past rendezvous as well as being present witnesses to emptiness and erasure.

Brochet's images of public space, equally nondescript, are also characterized by impoverished iconography. A post, a barrier, traffic lights, a street corner, and other apparently arbitrary bits of the urban environment are recorded in a puzzlingly off-center way that foregrounds its own disregard for composition. The author's intensive attentiveness to emptiness gives rise to some unusual city scenes that focus on swathes of asphalt, concrete, or paving stones, as if to confirm a loss of bearings, or that life is elsewhere and nothing is here. These snaps of the void express a sense of romantic loss, uneasily underpinned by the postmodern experience of Augé's much-discussed "non-places."

What of the "I" in this text? The *quatrième de couverture* [back cover] presents it in straight autobiographical terms: "From the first meeting up to the final separation, Anne Brochet retraces a love affair. For each stage, each episode, she has taken a photograph, a silent witness that accompanies the account." As if to confirm autobiographical centrality, an image of Brochet herself appears halfway through the chronicle, but it is a most peculiar one. Taken in a photo shoot for a magazine, it shows her thin, naked body as she lies on her back. Her face is impassive and the image is cold and stripped of emotion. What is most distinctive about it is the thick, semitransparent

4. Anne Brochet: a degree zero of photographic evidence. From *Trajet d'une amoureuse éconduite*. Photograph by Anne Brochet. Photo © Anne Brochet.

plastic sheet that partially conceals her nakedness and layers the photograph with meanings related to intimacy, exhibitionism, exposure, and boundaries. At the same time, it lends the portrait a startlingly clinical, even mortuary resonance: we are uncomfortable with the juxtaposition of this unyielding wrapping material with human skin. Significantly, Brochet's portrait is another performance of emotional voiding. Equally significantly, it raises the whole question of performativity that nags at any interpretation of this phototext. The reader is aware from the outset that there is no guarantee of "truth" in the document: it may be entirely or partially fictitious and Brochet, as her bizarrely staged yet withdrawn portrait suggests, may scarcely be revealing herself at all.

To conclude, perhaps the whole point of this listless phototext is to present a sort of degree zero of photographic evidence, an attempt not to remember through photographs but to photograph memory itself or to photograph melancholy by showing again and again that there is no residue in settings where emotion was experienced. If, as Marguerite Duras and Roland Barthes suggest, the most resonant photograph is the photograph that was never taken (the young Duras crossing the Mekong) or that is not shown (Barthes's mother as a child in the Winter Garden), the saturation of this chronicle in "evidence" of nothing diminishes photography's resonance—and perhaps that is precisely the point: there is no narrative left; the story is over. The throwaway aesthetic of these amateur photographs, their largely random focus on the infraordinary, and their neutrality of style simply go on reflecting the implied emotional paralysis of their taker. We shall see that Ernaux and Marie's emphasis on the everyday in photography, which also uses the ordinary as a means of reflecting on love and loss, is very different indeed.

L'USAGE DE LA PHOTO: PHOTOGRAPHING TRACES

In *L'Usage de la photo* Annie Ernaux and Marc Marie, even more than Brochet, are involved in creating organized breaches into their intimate life. Ernaux, an idiosyncratic autobiographer/ autoethnographer, frequently brings us to consider our relationship to photography and uses her own family photographs as springboards in her writing. Here she adopts a less familiar tactic, not describing photographs from her past but making photographic records of her present through a disturbingly unclassifiable category of image around which *L'Usage de la photo* is constructed. There are fourteen photographs in all, reproduced in black-and-white, with captions recording the place, date, and sometimes the time of day of their taking: from 6 March 2003 to 7 January 2004. Each image is followed by short written narratives, first from Ernaux, then from Marie, which describe and interrogate it. Photographs are used as memory markers to chronicle the course of a relationship and are puzzled over in their own right as documents with troubling phenomenological and ontological status, whose ultimate meaning and value are unclear. To greater or lesser degrees, they are uncomfortably private. They show a domestic interior (that of Ernaux), usually from a high angle, focusing on the floor and featuring small heaps of tangled clothes that are turned inside out and abandoned by the couple prior to lovemaking. These images "speak to" a range of other works that highlight the eloquence of empty clothes (works by Sophie Calle, Annette Messager, Christian Boltanski, and others) but are nonetheless distinctive in their unmistakably forensic quality. Marc Marie correctly notes that they resemble images taken in deserted houses by crime-scene investigators (30, 93), a metaphor that activates the complex debates around photography as evidence.

This unconventional album is a departure for Ernaux, not least due to its status as a "project" (Gratton and Sheringham). It obeys a self-imposed regulatory framework of rituals and rules that are "almost fetishist" (Fayet 309) and of which the most notable involve not tampering with the "evidence" and maintaining secrecy about the emerging written responses until the project is complete. Critically, photography not only provides a visual narrative related to the couple's relationship but becomes a key part *of* that relationship. Equally critically, this phototext also chronicles Ernaux's treatment for breast cancer, which she was undergoing at the time. If, as Susan Sontag suggests, merely possessing a camera is likely to "inspire something akin to lust" (179), this suddenly voracious image making, linked to voracious lovemaking, is clearly also connected to a newly stark fear of death, of really becoming no more than a trace. Ernaux, like Brochet, marvels through these insistent and obsessive photographs at absence and its implications. Not only can it be said that these photographs *are* traces (in the sense that all photographs are), they are also photographs *of* traces, becoming for that reason metaphotographic documents. There is much to be said about this text (for an extended analysis, see Jordan), but I shall limit myself in what follows to a restricted number of comments on its photographic logic.

First, this is explicitly a narrative about photographic acts as well as a place for displaying and analyzing images. Ernaux scrupulously records every aspect of the photographic cycle, from her initial fascination with the traces that she and her lover have left to the ritual of image taking, the pleasures of waiting for the photographs to be developed, and the curious distancing that takes place when they are viewed. Already strange a few days after the event, photographs that were "intended to give more reality to our love" serve only to "derealize it" (146). Ernaux also raises the paradox of intimacy with a new twist: not only is the reality of the lovemaking that gave rise to the image unavailable to other gazes, it has also become unavailable to her: "I am no longer in the reality that gave rise to my emotion and then to that morning's shot. It is my imagination that deciphers the photo, not my memory" (24). Photography, unlike writing, places her at two steps removed from the intimate act of lovemaking it is intended to record.

Ultimately Ernaux senses that the ways in which photography has begun to inflect her life include a blurring of motivation, which means that it is not always clear whether the couple is making love in a "naturally occurring" way or in order to generate more photographs. This period of heightened alertness to love and death that she and Marie choose to experience in part, at least, through photography, arguably provides an unusually clear instance of the ways in which, more broadly, we live events in symbiosis with photography. Increasingly a way of composing our days and conferring meaning upon them, photography constructs stories not only analeptically but also proleptically: "[T]he life that you live in order to photograph it," writes Italo Calvino, "is already, at the outset, a commemoration of itself" (225). We are reminded here of the comment made by Marie about the interfolding of Ernaux's life with writing: "You only got cancer so you could write about it" (56)—evidently not true but an important observation nevertheless, and one that suggestively links Ernaux's work in the current project to the position of French art's game player in chief, Sophie Calle. Ernaux and Marie's experiment also recalls Sontag's comment that taking photographs constitutes a distorting of experience "by limiting [it] to a search for the photogenic" (9). The authors of *L'Usage de la photo*, beginning to feel cornered by a photographic imperative of their own devising, become disenchanted with its contrivance and ultimately abandon the strategy. They draw their phototext to a conclusion by confirming that the device has exhausted itself, and at a moment when Ernaux's relationship to time has subtly shifted so that she situates herself somewhere between the statements "I've got cancer" and "I had cancer" (149).

A further point is that this work is especially revealing for what it tells us about photography and public/private boundaries. As Tisseron states, "[T]he practice of photography forces constant decisions as to what can and cannot be shown" (136). Photography is thus operative in terms of helping to create and to keep in place symbolic categories. Ernaux's writing has been a lengthy process of pushing at these categories, especially where they apply to the connection between women and intimacy and the social proscriptions and taboos that have traditionally regulated women's association with the private sphere. Here, through photography, she interrogates norms and renegotiates boundaries. Some things are not to be shown: the photograph taken of Marie's erection, which is described at the start of the text (15); the photograph imagined at the text's end that would have captured Marie nestling with his head between Ernaux's legs as if he were being born from her (151). To show her ailing body would also be a step too far for Ernaux. Her baldness, blackening gums, and loss of body hair as well as the chemotherapy apparatus are described, but they are not shown. Ernaux fantasizes about women who have undergone a mastectomy feeling able to offer their bodies to the camera, but no such body is shown. What is broken instead is a taboo related to domestic disorder. This new exhibitionism of the banal has its own obscenity: in fact, Ernaux observes that the images of what are intrinsically inoffensive items (clothes, pens and pencils strewn on her study floor, the paraphernalia of an ordinary kitchen) have a quality of intimacy that is more shocking than the graphic photo of Marie's arousal. Tisseron's observations on the tensions embodied in photography's tactile appeal may be of relevance here: these images, like pornography, create a contact space that invites us not just to look at but to touch the minutiae of the author's life, and this unconventional overture constitutes a radically new device in Ernaux's ongoing self-revelations.

To conclude, Ernaux's and Marie's relationship with photography seems, like that of Brochet and Laurens, to owe much to Barthes's fundamentally melancholic attachment to the medium as linked to death, desire, and repeated wounding. One could, however, see this phototext as differently nourished by Tisseron's account of photography and psychic separation management that I discussed at the start of this chapter. Tisseron makes a deliberate shift away from photography as wounding in favor of a more curative emphasis on photography as healing or scarring: "The photographic image is called upon to bear witness to two things: that a close union really did exist between the subject and the world; and that that union came to an end in a way that marked both parties with an indelible scar, but not an open wound" (164). Perhaps it is in such a perspective that the heuristic, compensatory work that I have been exploring in this chapter might be interpreted. It remains to be seen whether the procedure will be repeated by these authors or whether, in each case, recourse to photography will turn out to have been a "healing" solution, scarring over a particular situation of loss.

CONCLUDING THOUGHTS

What do these four texts tell us? That photography, concurrently with the rise of interest in autofiction and the problematization of the writer/reader "pact," is being used intensively and heuristically in ways that further destabilize conventional understandings of autobiography. That the promise of proximity to autobiographical subjects, characterized in recent years by an escalating trend for ever more intimate revelations, is paradoxically both met and challenged by photographs: even as they draw us in (as spectators, witnesses, intruders, "crime-scene investigators"), they also hold us at a distance and foreground uncertainty about the positioning between "fact" and fabrication of the texts they punctuate. That photography encourages episodic or fragmentary structures based around albums and diaries that are porous and elliptical, that induce new rhythms and methods of reading, and that, since they are woven around photography's temporal dynamic, highlight time in new ways. Finally, these recent intimate chronicles represent a concentrated stage in photobiographical thinking: one that remains poised between technologies and theories of photography past, and a rapidly evolving digital present. Remarkable in all these writers is a very Barthesean tethering of the photograph to loss and a fixation—nostalgic, ludic, or both—on traces. Their phototexts belong to the current environment of photographic excess and bring us some way toward considering how newly ubiquitous practices of taking, storing, circulating, and manipulating photographs are inflecting our sense of what photography can tell us about ourselves. What they take no account of is the power of invention that digital technology is conferring upon us and that lends photography a still more fluid relationship with our imagination. It will be interesting to see, then, whether a quite different emphasis—no longer elegiac and concerned not with traces but with the subtle modalities of photographic self-invention—will be an important aspect of photobiographical expression in the near future.

NOTES

1. See Barthes's thoughts on the "punctum" in *La Chambre claire*, and also the exploration of photography's affective power for Barthes in Cadava and Cortés-Rocca.

2. NDiaye may well have been attracted by the fact that authors contributing to this series are invited to select images that will not so much illustrate their text as enter allusively into dialogue with it.

3. NDiaye's partner is writer Jean-Yves Cendrey; she is a mother; she lived at the time of writing beside the Garonne; her parents are separated; her father is from Senegal.

WORKS CITED

Andrews, Margaret. "Camille Laurens." *Contemporary Women's Writing in French*. (21 Feb. 2009.)

Asibong, Andrew, and Shirley Jordan. "Rencontre avec Marie NDiaye." *Marie NDiaye: L'Etrangeté à l'œuvre*. Villeneuve d'Ascq: Presses Universitaires du Septentrion, 2009. 187–99.

Augé, Marc. *Non-lieux: Introduction à une anthropologie de la surmodernité*. Paris: Seuil, 1992.

Baqué, Dominique. "Paradoxes et apories de l'intime." *Photographie plasticienne, l'extrême contemporain*. Ed. Dominique Baqué. Paris: Regard, 2004. 73–87.

Barthes, Roland. *La Chambre claire: Note sur la photographie*. Paris: Gallimard Seuil, Cahiers du Cinéma, 1980.

Brochet, Anne. *Trajet d'une amoureuse éconduite*. Paris: Seuil, 2005.

Cadava, Eduardo, and Paola Cortés-Rocca. "Notes on Love and Photography." *October* 116 (Spring 2006): 3–34.

Calvino, Italo. "The Adventure of a Photographer." Trans. William Weaver. *Difficult Loves*. New York: Harcourt Brace, 1984. 220–35.

Duras, Marguerite. *L'Amant*. Paris: Minuit, 1984.

Ernaux, Annie, and Marc Marie. *L'Usage de la photo*. Paris: Gallimard, 2005.

Fayet, Agnès. "Les Images fantômes du texte: Usage romanesque de la photographie dans trois textes contemporains (Guibert, Ernaux, Toussaint)." *Études romanesques* 10 (2006): 305–14.

Garat, Anne-Marie. *Photos de familles*. Paris: Seuil, 1994.

Gratton, Johnnie, and Michael Sheringham. *The Art of the Project: Projects and Experiments in Modern French Culture.* Oxford: Berghahn, 2005.

Guibert, Hervé. *L'Image fantôme.* Paris: Minuit, 1981.

Hirsch, Marianne. *Family Frames: Photography, Narrative and Post-memory.* Cambridge MA: Harvard University Press, 1997.

Jordan, Shirley. "Improper Exposure: *L'Usage de la photo* by Annie Ernaux and Marc Marie." *Journal of Romance Studies* 7.2 (2007): 123–41.

Juarroz, Roberto. *Quinzième poésie verticale.* Paris: José Corti, 2002.

Kuhn, Annette. *Family Secrets: Acts of Memory and Imagination.* London: Verso, 2002.

Laurens, Camille. *Cet absent-là.* Paris: Léo Scheer, 2004.

———. *Dans ces bras-là.* Paris: POL, 2000.

———. *Philippe.* Paris: POL, 1995.

Lebovici, Elisabeth. "L'Intime et ses représentations." *L'Intime.* Ed. Elisabeth Lebovici. Paris: Ecole Nationale Supérieure des Beaux-Arts, 2004. 11–21.

Méaux, Danièle, and Jean-Bernard Vray, eds. *Traces photographiques, traces autobiographiques.* Saint-Etienne: L'Université de Saint-Etienne, 2004.

NDiaye, Marie. *Autoportrait en vert.* Paris: Mercure de France, 2005.

Poisson, Catherine. "Frictions: Mot et image chez Marie NDiaye et Camille Laurens." *Contemporary French and Francophone Studies* 11.4 (2007): 489–96.

Rabaté, Dominique. *Marie NDiaye.* Paris: Textuel, 2008.

Sontag, Susan. *On Photography.* London: Penguin, 1971.

Tisseron, Serge. *Le Mystère de la chambre claire: Photographie et inconscient.* Paris: Flammarion, 1996.

3

THE ABSENT BODY

PHOTOGRAPHY AND AUTOBIOGRAPHY IN HÉLÈNE
CIXOUS'S *PHOTOS DE RACINES* AND ANNIE ERNAUX AND
MARC MARIE'S *L'USAGE DE LA PHOTO*

Natalie Edwards

Autobiography, and its inflections with biography, fiction, and historiography, has long been a primary point of interrogation in Annie Ernaux's writing, as her works explore her memories of childhood and adolescence in a provincial working-class environment. In works such as *Une femme* [*A Woman's Story*], *La Place* [*The Square*], and *L'Evénément* [*The Event*], this author concentrates upon her developing selfhood and her discomfort as an adult looking back upon how her progress has distanced her from her roots. Hélène Cixous, who has been labeled a "French feminist" due to her theoretical texts of the 1970s, has written over fifty novels and plays and has recently authored a series of semiautobiographical texts. None of these texts are described or labeled as autobiographies, but their interrogation of the narrator's childhood in Algeria constitutes a *récit de soi* [self-narrative] of this author, who regularly explores the genre of autobiography in her ever-popular Collège de France lectures.[1] In texts such as *Les Rêveries de la femme sauvage* [*Reveries of the Wild Woman*], *Osnabrück*, and *OR: Les lettres de mon père* [*OR: The Letters from My Father*], Cixous remembers her formative years in the colony and the trauma of belonging to neither the colonialist nor the colonized societies there. Both authors have pushed the boundaries of what it means to approach the construction of a self in narrative: blending different genres into their writing, developing multiple narrators, pointing to the gaps in their memories and refusing the coherent, complete self of the autobiographical pact.[2] In recent texts, they have both widened their experimentation to write autobiographical narrative that includes photographs.

The inclusion of photographs in autobiographical narrative is a recent phenomenon in French literature. Many writers have written autobiography on the basis of photographs that they choose not to reprint in their texts: Assia Djebar, Patrick Modiano, Hervé Guibert, Marguerite Duras, and Marcel Proust, for example.[3] In the last two decades, however, perhaps following the example of André Breton's 1928 *Nadja* or of Roland Barthes's 1975 self-narrative *Roland Barthes par Roland Barthes*, many writers have printed photographs amid their first-person narratives: Marie NDiaye, Leïla Sebbar, Camille Laurens, and Raymond Depardon, among others. Incorporating photographs into an autobiography would appear to be an appeal to the real, providing evidence of the author's lived reality beyond the way that she or he may manipulate it in words; photographs constitute a physical trace of a reality and seem therefore more referential than language. As Susan Sontag remarked, the photograph represents "something directly stenciled off the real, like a footprint or a death mask" (350). The photograph may be an illustration or verification, it may provide another version of a self, it may provide links between elements of the text and forge a more intimate relationship between autobiographer and reader. And the photograph is associated with immediacy, with capturing the past and preserving it for posterity, just as autobiography might seem to be. As Linda Haverty Rugg comments, "[P]hotographs in an autobiographical context also insist on something material, the *embodied* subject, the unification (to recall the autobiographical pact) of author, name, *and* body" (13). Although a photograph may not necessarily make explicit the identity of a subject, Rugg points out that the photograph incorporates the *body* of the autobiographer into the self-narrative, thus creating a physical reminder that the body is the origin of language; as Janet Varner Gunn has written, "[T]he autobiographical self always comes *from* somewhere" (16). Sidonie Smith writes that the inclusion of the physical presence of the autobiographer in works of self-narrative that combine different media is a "body of evidence" that may be used tactically by women to subvert the patriarchal forces of objectification. She notes that "making-bodies-visible is a weighty enterprise" (134) given that the female autobiographer can take her body and control the mechanisms of its representation and contribution to her identity, as opposed to being objectified by the collusion of the male artist and onlooker.

In the cases of Ernaux and Cixous, however, the body is conspicuously absent. In their recent autobiographies that intertwine text and photographs, the photographs that they select are of somebody, or something, else. Cixous's *Photos de racines* [*Rootprints*] appeared in 1994 and is comprised of several different texts by Mireille Calle-Gruber and Cixous, including interviews, essays, a text by Jacques Derrida, and an autobiographical piece by Cixous herself. This piece concentrates upon what Cixous describes as her "so strange/foreign roots" (181): she grew up in colonial Algeria, the daughter of a German mother and a Sephardic Jewish father of Spanish descent. In the section "Albums et légendes" ["Albums and Legends"] Cixous intertwines narrative and image as she writes of photos in her family album that depict elements of her in-between roots. Very few of the thirty-eight photographs and images around which the text is based even contain the writer, and only two show her in adulthood. Instead, this photographic graveyard begins with Cixous's great-grandparents, followed by her grandparents and then by her parents as she tells the story of their successive migrations. *Photos de racines* even opens with a description of an old, damaged family album that Cixous compares to a cemetery, thus hinting that she views photographs, the content of the album, as tombs, the content of the cemetery.

Ernaux, ironically for an avid writer of autobiographical texts, opens *L'Usage de la photo* [The Use of the Photo] with, "I searched for a literary form that would contain all of my life. It did not yet exist" (27). Well known for her subversion of conventional literary genres, Ernaux thus claims to be in search of a new literary form that would contain all of her life, rather than the autobiographical fragments of which her work to date is comprised.[4] In *L'Usage de la photo* she also makes photographs the focus of the volume and comments upon these images in narrative. Ernaux was diagnosed with breast cancer in her early sixties and uses this text in part as the written record of her illness. Having embarked upon a love affair with a man in his twenties, she prints photographs of clothes belonging to her and her lover, Marc Marie, strewn across the floor before they make love. The fourteen photographs contain nothing beyond clothes, furniture, and papers, and Ernaux describes them as a "nature morte" [still life], literally "dead nature" (71). As Martine Delvaux writes, "These are the traces of a crime, the chalk outline of absent bodies, as if they had been murdered. At the heart of these photos are shells, clothes emptied of their bodies like the pajamas of a dismembered rabbit" (144). So why incorporate images of "dead nature" into an autobiography, the story of a life?

On one level, the technique of incorporating photos of something or somebody else refuses the objectification to which the female body has traditionally been subjected in art. As Smith writes, "[R]emembering her [the female model] and dismembering her, the artist in his studio, or, in the latter half of the nineteenth century, the artist in *plein air*, projected through his figuration of the female nude a phantasm of sensuality and desirable femininity" (132). The choice to include images that remove the female body may therefore represent a feminist agenda that intends to subvert a double patriarchal bind: that of art and that of autobiography, since this has traditionally been a male-dominated genre. The expansion in female autobiographical writing that has occurred since the 1970s reminds us that many women—and indeed minorities—have long been excluded from this genre; rather than writing tomes that testify to their public exploits and achievement like their male counterparts, many women who have attempted life writing have frequently done so within private genres, such as diaries, journals, and letters.[5] By experimenting with the autobiographical "I" and simultaneously experimenting with the traditionally patriarchal gaze of the spectator, these texts thus perform a double feminist move. What interests me in this chapter is the effects of this double feminist move on the construction of the self in narrative. How does the absent body impact upon the story of self? How do these texts articulate a self while simultaneously hinting at but removing the image of that self? What is at stake in the inclusion of photographs of others in first-person narrative, and what does this technique signify in terms of the limits and possibilities of autobiography?

WEAVING TEXT AND IMAGE

The place accorded to the photograph in each text is very different. In Cixous's work, the text that runs between the images could exist by itself, as Cixous very rarely makes any reference to them in her writing. The photographs of her dead ancestors hang amid the narrative as though they were suspended. The work appears to be a photograph album, with images and captions, but the captions do not describe the images as one would expect. The narrative is rather a written record of stories that Cixous had heard about her ancestors, some factual information that had been handed down to her about them, and some details gleaned from her personal research. Just as is the case with the photographs, she is almost absent from her narrative as well, since she recounts the stories of her ancestors as opposed to her own story, thus leaving the reader to deduce the impact of these strange roots upon her present self. The photographs are frozen remnants of the distant past, not linked to the present self of the writer in any attempt to create a coherent self in narrative, contrary to a traditional autobiography. From the outset of her project, Cixous thus questions the referentiality of autobiography, hinting that it refers to a specter, a phantom presence that is unseeable and unknowable.

In *L'Usage de la photo*, by contrast, the bodiless photograph is the focus of each piece of writing. Each chapter begins with a photograph and is followed by Ernaux's description of it, including the thoughts and memories that arise as she looks at it. She states that she first conceived of the project when seeing her clothes one morning and feeling dismayed at how they were "destined to disappear" (9). It thus appears that for Ernaux, photographs are a way of preserving the present, preventing its disappearance and maintaining its part in her reality. She claims, "I try to describe the photo with a double gaze, one past and the other current. What I see now is not what I saw that morning" (24). In this way, Ernaux conceives of her project of writing about photographs as a means of obtaining a double vision; as she writes of a photograph, she views it with the gaze of the past time of the scene and the gaze of the present time of writing. Ernaux thus dramatizes the difference between the narrated "I" and the narrating "I" of the autobiographer and draws attention to the way in which image is her link between them. Images are thus her springboard for moving from the recent past (the time of the photograph, that of the narrated "I") into the immediate present (the time of writing, that of the narrating "I"), and the writer consequently gains a new perspective on her present self. Yet Ernaux's text goes even further than moving from the recent past into the present time of writing. Ernaux often writes about her illness and the way in which it transforms her body into an "extraterrestrial creature" (83) and about other memories of her illness that resurface as she gazes at the photograph. In one telling example, Ernaux describes visiting the house of Marc Marie's mother after this woman's death and viewing the inanimate objects that survived her. Ernaux gazes upon the "the living, multiple images of a woman whom I had not met" and feels some connection with her; listing the cookery books and knitting that this woman left behind, Ernaux feels that "without ever having met her, I knew her all the same. And [. . .] what was more troubling, she knew me as well" (73). She thus feels a reciprocal relationship with this woman due to the traces of lived reality that she glimpses. Presumably, Ernaux's choice to remove her physical self from this autobiography paints a different version of herself, the elements of herself that will survive her and create connections with other women when she ceases to exist. Ernaux's implicit aim in using photographs is a movement toward the future, a means of creating posterity beyond her physical disappearance. The way in which Ernaux incorporates photographs into her work thus performs the opposite movement to that of Cixous's text. Ernaux's photographs move time forward, imagining a future time and a future self, whereas Cixous's photographs move in the opposite direction, imagining a past representation of a self, rather than a teleological exploration of present subjectivity.

WEAVING VOICES

In addition to doubling her text in terms of medium, incorporating both image and words, each writer also doubles the narrative voice. Although Cixous's text stands apart from the images she selects, there is one section of the text in which image and text coalesce, and the writer plays in this instance with narrative voice. She includes a photograph of her grandfather Michael Klein, a photograph of his tomb, and a copy of the telegraph announcing his death amid text that gives details of his life. Copying the telegraph, Cixous writes, "[J]e recopie et je pleure. Pourquoi ce pleur? Parce que je suis mort. Je suis si mort" [I copy and I cry. Why do I cry? Because I am dead. I am so dead] (188). Cixous thus changes narrative voice, writing in a masculine voice (*mort* rather than the feminine *morte*) that she subsequently identifies as belonging to Michael Klein, and from the perspective of his gravestone as he looks around him and notices who is buried adjacent to him. Mairéad Hanrahan identifies this technique as prosopopoeia (284): this short section of text is still narrated in the first person, but the "I" has obviously changed from the voice of the autobiographer to the imagined voice of the ancestor. As we read on, there is no announcement of the narrative voice returning to that of the autobiographer, but we suddenly read, "Do I come from this man who is leaving?" (189), thus conveying that Cixous has at some point returned to the narration. Cixous thus links herself to the self of her ancestor, imagining his voice and his perspective, yet moves quickly from this section to recounting the story of her grandmother. Cixous is here one persona and another persona, one self and another self simultaneously; as Claire Boyle suggests, the most crucial aspect of this text is "the ethic of fusion between self and other" (142). Furthermore, this autobiographical section is framed by a number of other texts that all write about Cixous from a different perspective: interviews and texts written about her and her work by different commentators. Taken together, these multiple voices and multiple images create a plural, multifaceted self and insist upon a self-perpetuating, evolving, and irreducible identity. Thus the absence of photographs of bodily evidence serves to multiply the autobiographical self that the text creates, rather than obliterating or effacing it.

Ernaux and Marc Marie's text also doubles the narrative voice, since each chapter consists of the photograph followed by a text written by Ernaux in response to it followed by a text written by her lover in response to the same image. The ritual that the two established was to both look at the scene together in the morning, take the photograph, and proceed to write about it separately, without showing their text to one another. Marie's texts are based upon his descriptions of Ernaux and memories of experiences that the two had shared. He even mentions that he had stopped writing his diary to write this narrative in its place. It is striking that several pieces written by Marie mirror those of Ernaux, but he recounts other scenes with different memories, describing the "facts" of the scene and describing her, objectifying her, in a different light. Ernaux is thus rendered both subject and object of her autobiography. It is important to note, however, that she controls its mise-en-scène. She writes the preface and the postface, and the text that she writes in response to each photograph comes first. The photographs are all taken on her territory, in her apartment, apart from one in a hotel room. Ernaux also writes about other photographs taken by the pair that they had chosen specifically not to include. She even compares the camera to a penis and claims to feel in possession of a phallus when she aims her lens at a subject. Elizabeth Richardson Viti points out that Ernaux writes of Marie's penis, objectifying and fragmenting his body and placing him in the role of the sex object, in a reversal of the way in which women have traditionally been objectified in images. Marie, even though he does not have the same control over the text as Ernaux, does nevertheless play a major role in the self-narrative that the text orchestrates. He does not write of Ernaux's body nor of her desire and sexuality. Instead, he writes his version of their shared experiences and he thus creates a different persona for her; she is one self and another self, and yet more selves as a result of all the photographs. The doubling of narrative voice that both Ernaux and Cixous use therefore moves the autobiographer further from her autobiography and serves to multiply the selves that she represents. The bodiless photographs therefore result in more selves rather than an absent self. In addition to testing the boundaries of the genre of autobiography and subverting the norms of self-representation, these writers simultaneously move the narrative into a different temporality. Just as Cixous's photographs move her text into the past, so does her technique of doubling the narrative voice with that of an ancestor, since it temporarily removes herself and her present reality from the text and concentrates upon past time. Likewise, just as Ernaux uses photographs as a springboard to the future, the way in which she includes another voice also moves the text into future time; she may succumb to the cancer, but Marie will survive her and his memories of her, now recorded in writing, imagine a version of her in a different temporality.

The refusal to incorporate the physical trace of the self within their autobiographies (or partial refusal, in the case of Cixous) is thus a mechanism for subverting the way in which a photograph freezes the body within a frame. The photograph of a person imposes the walls of the photograph's limits on the body and freezes it into one scene, static and unmoving. The language of photography is predicated upon this; we talk of "capturing" a scene or a person and, as Rugg has pointed out, "taking" a picture (3). The act of capturing somebody on film is tantamount to trapping her or him into one image of embodiment. By contrast, these literary texts show that a self is not the single, immutable image of unchanging identity that we necessarily see in a photograph; the essence of the identity that Cixous and Ernaux construct lies in its fluidity and movement. By refusing to limit themselves in any frame, and by rejecting a series of images of their bodies that would insist upon stasis, these authors use photographs as a way of pointing to the unstable, plural, and evolving nature of their autobiographical selves. Since their texts, predicated upon the doubling of medium and the doubling of narrative voice, point to the multiplicity of self in narrative, it is therefore fitting that they avoid static and unmoving images of their bodies in their accompanying photographs.

Furthermore, the way in which these two autobiographers use photographs to erase their bodies and interrogate themselves in a different time frame is also a way of writing beyond the self, beyond fixity and, ultimately, beyond death. Cixous describes the successive deaths of her ancestors, and her text moves chronologically through them until she arrives at herself. At this point the texts ends abruptly, as she leaves Algeria for France and adopts what she refers to as "literary nationality" (207). No physical nation is appropriate to her; none offers her hospitality, belonging, or identity, so she takes refuge in an imagined nationality. Rather than deal with her own life and eventual death, as she had for the other bodies of this text, the writer imagines a fictive, universal, and timeless identity for herself. Ernaux's text is also self-consciously written against death as she removes her diseased body and imagines a future time for it. One image, which is described in the text rather than photographed, stands out in this regard. Ernaux recounts a day she spent with Marie in the Montparnasse cemetery. Marie's grandparents are buried there and the couple goes to view their grave, only to find that it is buried in snow. Ernaux describes in detail the gravestone as it is slowly unearthed by the two sweeping away the snow and chipping away at the ice with a key ring. As a name appears, she writes, "I imagined my name in its place, on the stone. I could see it very well but it was not real" (111). Just as was the case with Cixous, Ernaux ponders the gravestone as an image of death, but Ernaux links her own mortality to that image. For Cixous, the physical graveyard in which Michael Klein is interred and the metaphorical graveyard formed by the photograph album belong to the distant past and form part of her quest for an understanding of her roots. For Ernaux, the image of the gravestone is part of her will to imagine her future and preview the images that will remain of her beyond death. Her body, however, does not form part of this; what will remain, we infer, is her clothes, her furniture, her texts, and her gravestone. She even states, "When I look at our photos, it is the disappearance of my body that I see. Yet it is not that my hands and my face are no longer there that bothers me, nor is it that I can no longer walk, eat, screw. It's the disappearance of thought. I have said to myself several times that if my thoughts could continue elsewhere, dying would be indifferent to me" (111). The body is thus unimportant since it is merely a vehicle that she uses in order to think, create, and write. While Cixous's body was absent from her photographs because she was more interested in the bodies of others, Ernaux's body is absent from hers since her body is merely a vehicle that permits her to do something worthwhile, and her ability to use the body for pleasure with a twenty-year-old man while it is riddled with cancer becomes the perfect metaphor for this.

Moreover, the removal of the photographed body also forces us to narrativize the selves at which these writers are hinting, because we as readers/spectators have some information about their identities and about their bodies, but they leave us guessing about the rest. In the case of Cixous, we wonder what relationship she had to the ancestors whom she met, how the stories that she heard about them affected her, and how her present identity results from their influence on her. The fact that she includes photographs but does not elucidate her relationship to the people they depict in her writing adds a further level of intrigue to the text. In the case of Ernaux, her words describe her body in great detail, which renders the fact that the body is missing from the photographs even more stark. Indeed, the absence of the body amid the pictures of the hastily discarded clothing renders the text supremely titillating since the reader cannot help but imagine what the bodies look like! For both writers, therefore, the photographs represent parts of a jigsaw puzzle that is knowingly incomplete, and it is up to us as readers to connect the pieces. Their removal of the body thus forces us to tell yet another story, to create another version—or other versions—of the self that they are portraying. Therefore, the absent bodies further the fragmented, incomplete, and evolving nature of the self that these authors are establishing.

The absent body thus both foregrounds and distances the self of the autobiographer from her text. On one level, these two writers reveal important parts of their identities through their photographs: their living space, their ancestors, their intimate relationships, for example. Yet simultaneously, the fact that their bodies are absent from their photographs hides a significant portion of their identities. Their works thus become a push-and-pull between showing and hiding, and they conceal at least as much of their identities as they reveal. But ultimately, this is what the genre of autobiography is predicated upon. When one writes autobiography, one is obliged to choose what to incorporate, which memories to include and which to repress or discard. Jacques Derrida argued in *Mal d'archive* [*Archive Fever*] that the process of creating an archive is based upon the attempt to preserve something to be remembered and simultaneously to leave out something to be forgotten. In Cixous's and Ernaux's textual and photographical archives, they highlight how knowledge of an autobiographer from her or his autobiography is just as illusory as knowledge of a society from its archive; both are based upon the category of the absent, the part of it that is consigned to be forgotten. Cixous's and Ernaux's technique of removing their bodies thus pushes autobiography to its logical conclusion; this genre of writing is all about the interplay between showing and hiding and the illusion of "knowing" or "establishing" a self in narrative. By absenting themselves, they highlight the control that the autobiographer has over the autobiographical narrative, reminding the reader that we are not reading the self but a partial construction of a version of a self that is tightly controlled, implicitly or explicitly, by the writer. While it is certainly true that texts escape their author's control, these texts push us as readers/viewers to question the limits, the possibilities, and the politics of the genre of autobiography, which is based more upon concealing than it is upon revealing.

CONCLUSION

Thus the "usage of the photograph" is very different for these two autobiographers, neither of whom feels that narrative alone is a sufficient means of rendering the self in text. The faceless, bodiless photographs take on a ghostly image, settled uncannily within narrative that uses them as a springboard to other meditations upon subjectivity and to other temporalities. Text and image are juxtaposed in both of these texts but do not intermingle; both rely upon the other for the portrayal of the self in narrative, but both exist as separate records of selfhood. Placed together upon a page, they point up the incompleteness of the self in text rather than its coherence. Taken together, these two autobiographies, based upon the doubling of medium and upon the doubling of narrative voice, are testament to the artists' attempt to mitigate trauma through art, in Cixous's case by using photography to interrogate her origins and in Ernaux's to interrogate her future. Both escape the trauma that results from their present bodies (the cancer for Ernaux, the problematic identity due to her multiple points of origin for Cixous) through removing their bodies and using images of something or somebody else to interrogate the self—or the selves—in another, less painful reality. It is all the more ironic, therefore, that Ernaux chooses *not* to publish the photographs that form the basis of her subsequent work, *Les Années* [The Years], a text that begins with the line "All images will disappear" (11). Moreover, the narrator of Cixous's recent work *Si près* [So Close] has this to say about photographs: "I am haunted by a mental camera, I who in all my life have not taken a photo. Photography, I have always thought, is the enemy, mine precisely, the adversary: one cannot take photos and write" (11). Ultimately, *Photos de racines* and *L'Usage de la photo* present the push-and-pull between revealing and concealing and thus function on a generic level to question the conditions and the possibility of autobiography itself. Both works play with us as readers/ spectators, forcing us to recognize the absence as well as the presence of the self and reminding us that when we as readers approach autobiography, we are merely the voyeur in somebody else's tightly orchestrated game.

NOTES

1. Christa Stevens, for example, has written of the autobiographical elements in Cixous's recent work. Her works of autobiography include *OR: Les Lettres de mon père*, "Les Pieds nus," "Stigmata; or, Job the Dog," "Mon Algériance," and *Osnabrück*. In her regular lecture series on Saturdays at the Collège de France, Cixous analyzes a variety of autobiographical writers, including Saint Augustine, Jean-Jacques Rousseau, Jean Genet, Marcel Proust, and Colette.

2. The "autobiographical pact" is Philippe Lejeune's definition of the condition of autobiography: "un récit rétrospectif en prose que quelqu'un fait sur sa propre existence quand il met l'accent principal sur une vie individuelle, en particulier sur l'histoire de sa person- nalité" (14) ["retrospective prose narrative written by a real person concerning his own existence, where the focus is his individual life, in

particular the story of his personality" (3)]. For a work to be considered autobiographical, Lejeune states, the names of the author, narrator, and character must be identical (15).

3. I use the term "autobiography" very loosely here, since not all of these self-reflexive texts correspond to any prescribed definition of the genre. Examples include Assia Djebar's *L'Amour, la fantasia*, Patrick Modiano's *Dora Bruder*, Hervé Guibert's *A l'ami qui ne m'a pas sauvé la vie*, Marguerite Duras's *L'Amant*, and Marcel Proust's *A la recherche du temps perdu*.

4. As Sylvie Romanowski has written in relation to Ernaux's 1991 *Passion simple*, Ernaux's texts defy the codification of a variety of genres, including the pornographic novel, the sentimental novel, autobiography, testimonial, and the novel itself.

5. This is not to say that men have always written of their public exploits in autobiography; several writers, such as Jean-Paul Sartre and Michel Leiris, have written texts that (at least partially) efface these. Likewise, many female writers, such as George Sand or Colette, have written of their exploits in autobiographical texts. I point rather to the relatively small number of female-authored autobiographical texts, as demonstrated by Bella Brodzki and Celeste Schenck, for example.

WORKS CITED

Barthes, Roland. *Roland Barthes par Roland Barthes*. Paris: Seuil, 1975.
Boyle, Claire. *Consuming Autobiographies: Reading and Writing the Self in Post-war France*. London: Legenda, 2007.
Breton, André. *Nadja*. Paris: Gallimard, 1963.
Brodzki, Bella, and Celeste Schenck. *Life Lines: Theorizing Women's Autobiography*. Ithaca NY: Cornell University Press, 1988.
Cixous, Hélène. "Mon Algériance." *Les Inrockuptibles* 20 Aug.–2 Sept. 1997: 71–74.
———. *OR: Les Lettres de mon père*. Paris: des femmes, 1997.
———. *Osnabrück*. Paris: des femmes, 1999.
———. "Les Pieds nus." *Une Enfance algérienne*. Ed. Leïla Sebbar. Paris: Gallimard, 1997.
———. *Rêveries de la femme sauvage*. Paris: Galilée, 2000.
———. *Si près*. Paris: Galilée, 2007.

————. "Stigmata; or, Job the Dog." Trans. Eric Prenowitz. *Philosophy Today* (Spring 1997): 12–17.

Cixous, Hélène, and Mireille Calle-Gruber. *Photos de racines*. Paris: des femmes, 1994.

Delvaux, Martine. "Des images malgré tout: Annie Ernaux/Marc Marie: *L'Usage de la photo*." *French Forum* 31.3 (2006): 137–55.

Derrida, Jacques. *Mal d'archive: Une impression freudienne*. Paris: Galilée, 1995.

Djebar, Assia. *L'Amour, la fantasia*. Paris: Albin Michel, 1985.

Duras, Marguerite. *L'Amant*. Paris: Minuit, 1984.

Ernaux, Annie. *Les Années*. Paris: Gallimard, 2008.

————. *L'Evénément*. Paris: Gallimard, 2000.

————. *Une femme*. Paris: Gallimard, 1987.

————. *Passion simple*. Paris: Gallimard, 1991.

————. *La Place*. Paris: Gallimard, 1983.

Ernaux, Annie, and Marc Marie. *L'Usage de la photo*. Paris: Gallimard, 2005.

Guibert, Hervé. *A l'ami qui ne m'a pas sauvé la vie*. Paris: Gallimard, 1990.

Gunn, Janet Varner. *Autobiography*. Philadelphia: University of Pennsylvania Press, 1982.

Hanrahan, Mairéad. "Of Altobiography." *Revisiting the Scene of Writing: New Readings of Cixous*. Ed. Julia Dobson and Gill Rye. Spec. issue of *Paragraph* 27.2 (2000): 282–95.

Lejeune, Philippe. *Le Pacte autobiographique*. Paris: Seuil, 1975. (*On Autobiography*. Ed. Paul John Eakin. Trans. Katherine Leary. Minneapolis: University of Minnesota Press, 1989.)

Modiano, Patrick. *Dora Bruder*. Paris: Gallimard, 1997.

Proust, Marcel. *A la recherche du temps perdu*. Paris: Gallimard, 2009.

Romanowski, Sylvie. "*Passion simple* d'Annie Ernaux: Le trajet d'une féministe." *French Forum* 27 (2002): 99–114.

Rugg, Linda Haverty. *Picturing Ourselves: Photography and Autobiography*. Chicago: University of Chicago Press, 1997.

Smith, Sidonie. "Bodies of Evidence: Jenny Saville, Faith Ringgold, and Janine Antoni Weigh In." *Interfaces: Women, Autobiography, Image, Performance*. Ed. Sidonie Smith and Julia Watson. Ann Arbor: University of Michigan Press, 2005. 132–59.

Sontag, Susan. *On Photography*. New York: Farrar, Straus, & Giroux, 1973.

Stevens, Christa. "Hélène Cixous, auteur en 'algériance.'" *Expressions maghrébines* 1.1 (2002): 77–91.

Viti, Elizabeth Richardson. "*Passion simple*, 'Fragments autour de Philippe V' and *L'Usage de la photo*: The Many Stages of Annie Ernaux's Desire." *Women in French Studies* 14 (2006): 76–87.

4

THE PHOTOBIOGRAPHICAL TODAY

SIGNS OF AN IDENTITY CRISIS?

Floriane Place-Verghnes

> If my pictures and my stories, however commonplace, are
> not everybody's, my uses of the one and my methods of
> arriving at the other could very well be.
>
> • ANNETTE KUHN, *Family Secrets*

The photobiographic act is not strictly speaking a new phenomenon.[1] One has only to think of *Roland Barthes par Roland
Barthes* [*Roland Barthes by Roland Barthes*] in 1975, Hervé
Guibert's *Suzanne et Louise* in 1980, Anny Duperey's *Le Voile
noir* [The Black Veil] in 1992 or, outside the francophone sphere,
the work of W. G. Sebald: for example, his 1992 *Die Ausgewanderten* [The Emigrants].

It seems to me, nonetheless, that the last few years have
seen a considerable growth in this hybrid genre: Raymond
Depardon's *Errance* [Restless Wandering] (published in 2000,
this presents for my purposes the advantage of being a work

by a photographer who writes rather than a writer who takes photographs), Camille Laurens's 2004 *Cet absent-là* [That Missing One], Leïla Sebbar's *Mes Algéries en France* [My Algerias in France] and *Journal de mes Algéries en France* [Diary of My Algerias in France], published in 2004 and 2005 respectively, Annie Ernaux and Marc Marie's *L'Usage de la photo* [The Use of Photography] in 2005 or, more recently still, Claire Legendre and Jérôme Bonnetto's *Photobiographies*, published in 2007. The list could, furthermore, be extended with Marie NDiaye's *Autoportrait en vert* [Self-Portrait in Green] and the actress Anne Brochet's *Trajet d'une amoureuse éconduite* [The Journey of a Woman Dismissed by Her Lover], both published in 2005, or Emmanuel Guibert, Didier Lefèvre, and Frédéric Lemercier's three-volume series *Le Photographe* [The Photographer], published from 2003 to 2006, an interesting mixture of comic strip and photographs, and the work of other photographers, like Denis Roche and Sophie Calle, who constantly interrogate the relation of their art to autobiography, or even the numerous blogs scattered throughout the web in which hordes of anonymous writers use texts and images to recount their lives, with varying degrees of success.

From these many examples I have selected a corpus of five works as a point of departure for a consideration of certain theoretical questions. All of these texts have in common a profound reflection on being. Camille Laurens's *Cet absent-là*, for example, takes the form of an interrogation of "present absence," the elusiveness of the essence of subjectivity and filiation, the passing of identity from one generation to another (which I shall call "the braided identity"). *L'Usage de la photo*, a photojournal kept by Annie Ernaux and her partner, Marc Marie, at a period when Ernaux, suffering from breast cancer, was undergoing chemotherapy, embarks on a reflection on illness and death, which amount to an assault on identity. Unlike these works, which aim for a reappropriation of identity, Raymond Depardon's *Errances* advocates the banishment of the very idea of identity: the author tries to meld the self and the Other together in the same crucible, to reduce the distance between the two. The issue of identity in a postcolonial context is a particularly complex and fertile subject. With *Mes Algéries en France* and then *Journal de mes Algéries en France*, Leïla Sebbar tackles the thorny question of Franco-Algerian identity.[2] The author sees herself as a link between the two cultures and tries to reconstruct her own identity through the narrative of a collective history: an identity that is a collage made up of multiple encounters (a Sebbar trait) and a range of visual documents (here *Mes Algéries en France* notably departs from Sebbar's oeuvre). And so this gives rise to a reflection on what I shall call "unraveling identity"; but it should be noted that the metaphor of the storyteller who "weaves" a narrative from scattered threads is already central ("threaded," one might say), in *Mes Algéries en France* (62–63). And finally, *Photobiographies* by Claire Legendre and Jérôme Bonnetto, with its generic hybridity and its snapshots whose meaning is indeterminate, pushes the boundaries of the photobiographical and brings into play a dreamlike identity.[3] This chapter asks questions such as: is this sudden rise of photobiography simply a fashion among French publishers (and so bound inevitably to wane), or are we really witnessing a fundamental change in the way that lived experience is narrated? How is identity reconfigured in these photobiographical works? How is the tension between fragmentation and unity negotiated? How are the individual and the collective, the self and the other, articulated in the work of memory?

A reflection on photobiographical discourses can be articulated around three major axes: first, and fundamentally, identity (or rather, as we shall see, identities); second, at the two extremes of the photobiographic act, memory (which involves the author); and third, reception (of the reader/spectator). This chapter will focus on the first point—the issue of identity crises.

I will first examine how the subject, already decentered by postmodern autobiographical discourse, is further fragmented by the inclusion of images in the text. The evaporation of the subject is, then, intensified in the photobiographical narrative, and this is even more the case when it is constructed by a process of juxtaposition, assemblage, collage—whether at the level of the text or the image. The questions of collage and archive creation will be considered in the second section. Finally, given that most of these texts were written by women, I will briefly discuss at the end of the chapter the feminine experience that comes through in photobiographical work.

FRAGMENTING THE SUBJECT

In the postmodern era the subject has lost its reference points, particularly given that the "grand narratives" that previously underpinned the world (religions, theories, philosophies) have crumbled and have undergone a crisis of legitimacy and authority—this is, indeed, the definition of postmodernity, according to Lyotard.[4] The major contribution of postmodern thought is to have called into question all forms of totalizing knowledge, or univocal truth.[5] Postmodernity means, admittedly, the advent of relativism and of contradictions but also of new ways of thinking about things. In art and literature, postmodernity is characterized by rupture, fragmentation, the refusal of coherence, narrative or other, the search for a plurality of ways of attaining truths in the absence of a single truth, and the representation of identities, in the plural, once the concept of a stable identity has become outdated. As Christopher Butler comments, "The work of postmodernists was deliberately less unified, less obviously 'masterful,' more playful or anarchic, more concerned with the processes of our understanding than with the pleasures of artistic finish or unity, less inclined to hold a narrative together, and certainly more resistant to a certain interpretation" (5). Significantly, this major change in the representation of the self is concomitant with the increasing prevalence of photography: as the self splits and finds expression through ramification into a multitude of small narratives, photography plays an ever greater role in the representation of this plurality.

Although there is little original in noting the simultaneity of photography's accession to the status of major art and the death of the "grand narrative" in favor of the "small narrative" of everyday life and the autobiographical turn in contemporary art and fiction, I am nonetheless struck by André Rouillé's interpretation of this phenomenon. For him, this simultaneity cannot be accounted for by the fact that photography is the *medium* of the everyday par excellence (a thesis frequently upheld), but "because it has been selected *and* worked by artists in such a way as to destroy any sense of the universal in art" (478; emphasis in the original). All autobiographies work toward this destruction of the universal by putting forward an experience that is very personal. Nonetheless, destroying the universal does not only mean concentrating on the particular: the particular is by no means the sworn enemy of the universal. Indeed, the latter trades in the former, given that all individual experience can have a wider, collective applicability (see, for example, the notion of the "transpersonal I" beloved of Annie Ernaux). This argument is further corroborated by Jérôme Bonnetto, who notes with a certain irony that "it takes a dreadful effort to achieve the objective neutrality of the technician" and thereby to obtain an image that is "*perfectly* impersonal" (Legendre and Bonnetto 109;

my emphasis). Impersonal, undoubtedly, but not in an arbitrary way—for to capture intimacy accurately, talent must be deployed in the display of impersonality: "a photograph is never more intimate than when it affects the strict and deceptive uniform of impersonality" (110).

Given that the destruction of the universal means attributing importance to what seems unimportant to others and concentrating on the negligible, *the* meaning is sabotaged so as to allow multiple meanings to rise to the surface. This is a sabotage that operates both at the level of the text, through *écriture blanche* [plain writing], and the images: the "artlessness" of the snapshots in *L'Usage de la photo* or *Trajet d'une amoureuse éconduite* (the former depicting the lovers' clothes on the floors of various venues, the latter commonplace sights on the narrator's "journey"—various streets and shop fronts, the interiors of bars and restaurants, different rooms and objects in her apartment, and so on), the juxtaposition and the leveling in *Journal de mes Algéries en France*, or the "low points" in Depardon's work, which contrast with the "decisive moments" in Cartier-Bresson's work, when photographs had a single meaning.[6]

This may be true, but the arrival of the postmodern is hardly recent news. How can we explain why the photobiographical genre is developing at such speed only now, rather than thirty years ago? The phenomenon can perhaps be partly explained by the policies of a number of French publishers and also, perhaps, by technological advances that have reduced the cost of reproducing images. However, if the hypothesis is valid for certain publications (for example, the "Folio" edition of *Autoportrait en vert*, which reproduces the images in black-and-white on fairly poor-quality paper), it does not explain others (like *Errance* or *Mes Algéries en France*, with black-and-white and color plates respectively, both on glossy paper).[7]

Moreover, all the authors chosen for this study already enjoyed well-established popularity before embarking on their photobiography—and one could wager that the first photobiography by an unknown would stand little chance of being published, given the financial imperatives of the publishing industry. The publishing context does not explain everything, however. It seems to me that, however slowly (reality is resilient), our faith in the capacity of photography to offer a transcription of the real has become eroded, and that this is just what has allowed photography to show something different—since it is no longer the guarantee of an external referent, it can move inward. Thus, according to Fredric Jameson, photography is "renouncing reference as such in order to elaborate an autonomous vision which has no external equivalent. Internal differentiation now stands as the mark and moment of a decisive displacement in which *the older relationship of image to reference is superseded by an inner or interiorized one*" (179; my emphasis). And it is essentially this fading of the referent in favor of a refocusing on the author's self that has made photography a key component of autobiography. In *L'Usage de la photo*, for example, an almost mystical transformation of lived experience is made possible by photography: "the act of making love [. . .] was both materialized and transfigured, [. . .] it now existed *elsewhere*, in a mysterious space" (11). In *Cet absent-là*, a good photograph is the product of the wholly internal feeling of the photographer: "For me there is a kind of intimate relationship between this technique and the art of love-making. You need love to capture a face, *love is what makes things visible*" (15; my emphasis). Because, as Arlette Farge writes, "photographs offer the unheard-of possibility of simultaneously presenting what is registered on the film, what exists, and what does not appear" (40), it allows almost unlimited possibilities to the autobiographer.

COLLAGE, COLLECTION, ARCHIVE

A second point that is linked to the theme of fragmentation is the idea of collection. According to Susan Sontag, photographers—and one could add autobiographers—"suggest the vanity of even trying to understand the world and instead propose that we collect it" (82). One can argue that collection is a first step toward understanding (this, in any case, is the project of *Mes Algéries en France*, for example). But, crucially, collection appears as both the cause and the effect of fragmentation: any attempt to apprehend a dis-located subject or world necessarily gives rise to a fragmented representation; at the same time, the collection and archiving of these scattered documents restore a kind of cohesion that enables them to take on a testimonial function.

Cet absent-là, a work that draws a great deal from Barthes's *La Chambre claire* [*Camera Lucida*], brings a fragmented form of writing into play, through its chapters (brief snapshots) and within sentences (where the lack of punctuation reflects the flux of thought). In this case, again, photography continues the process of evaporation of the subject. In her search for the deep selfhood of the beloved person, Camille Laurens hypothesizes that isolating one element of a photograph and blowing it up could bring this selfhood to the surface. The result is, as one might imagine, disappointing: "However, in spite of all my efforts, I never know everything, I never see everything; something always eludes me, all memories are myopic. Either I can call your face completely to mind, my love, I can kiss it all over, but it is blurred—I can't say that I recognize you, let's say instead: I know that it's you—, or I can isolate a detail, but this fragment doesn't deliver up your face. Too far, too near, heat haze that casts a veil or iciness that freezes it, the form escapes, and meaning goes with it" (24). This problem of distance and meaning acts as an indisputable echo to Barthes's words about the photographs of his mother: "I never recognized her except in fragments, which is to say that I missed her *being*, and that therefore I missed her altogether. [. . .] I recognized her differentially, not essentially. Photography thereby compelled me to perform a painful labor; straining towards the essence of her identity, I was struggling among images partially true, and therefore totally false" (65–66). The meaning is not, however, necessarily attenuated (and still less lost) by fragmentation—or, to take the opposite viewpoint from Barthes, an accumulation of partially true images or documents does not necessarily produce a totally false image.

L'Usage de la photo, to move on to a different case, is presented as a dialogue with built-in constraints, like the surrealists' game of *cadavre exquis* [exquisite corpse]: the chapters alternate the voices of the two authors presenting the same photograph, with no knowledge of what the other has said of it. Each section or chapter begins with a minute description of the photograph that introduces it, itself preceded by a caption giving the place and time of the photograph. *L'Usage de la photo*, based on the appropriation and exhibition of intimate photographs, is a knowing Oulipian game played against death, the rules of which are clearly set out at the beginning of the book (10–13). It functions by a process of collection, collage (of text and image), and archiving intended—precisely—to bring meaning to the surface. However, it has to be said that the project ends in partial failure (due to the ever-present possibility that the photographs have been contrived and staged), and, ultimately, this was only a brief incursion into the world of photography for Annie Ernaux: her most recent book, *Les Années* [The Years] (published in February 2008), takes as its point of departure the recounting of photographs, described, again, with great precision, but this time evacuated from the book.

From the auto-socio-biographical enterprise of Annie Ernaux to the (auto)-ethno-biographical project of Leïla Sebbar, the phototexts under discussion here all reveal the obsession of their authors with the recovery of documents and the establishment of an archive. *Mes Algéries en France*, "a meticulous ethnographic work, concerned for a society which will soon no longer exist" (42), establishes a number of points of contact between documents and individuals. Documents both recount individual experiences and reproduce them. Like the members of a family, documents can undergo hybridization (the text becomes image, the image becomes text). Documents, like people, can be forced into a diaspora, widely scattered. In fact, the richness of the narrative is the result of the fertilization of a document (of a culture) by another. We thereby witness a quadruple cross-fertilization of the document: not only of the text and the image but also of the images among themselves (photographs as well as various other kinds of documents and objects—which can even enter into relationships of mise en abyme), of the texts among themselves (with ever-ambiguous generic categories) and, within the texts, different narrative instances.

If the representation of identity cannot be stable in a fragmented world, neither can the boundaries between genres be easily maintained: *Errance*, by the most celebrated of French photojournalists, is not strictly speaking to be categorized as a work of photojournalism—a fact upon which Depardon insists: "I think this is the first time that I have been so clear on any subject. I make no claims: quite the opposite, since all I am doing is photographing my own obsession. I want to affirm this distinction. For once, I am not doing journalism, and nor is this some kind of pseudo-poetic photography. I am doing something else, I have entered a realm where responsibilities are clearly defined" (72).

Similarly, *Mes Algéries en France* and *Photobiographies* fuse different genres (like fairy tales, poetry, interview), blur the boundary between fiction and reality and, in the case of *Mes Algéries en France*, introduce a range of visual elements (photographs, maps, postcards, drawings, comic strips). As the historian Pierre Nora has indicated, in a world that has split apart, devoid of reference points or obvious links between people, there are no longer any clear pathways to understanding, and any object whatsoever can be invested with historical significance: "The loss of a single explanatory principle has plunged us into an exploded world, at the same time as it has enabled any object, however humble, probable or inaccessible, to attain the dignity of historical mystery. The point is that we used to know whose children we were, and that we are now the children of no one and of anyone" (xxxii).

If the confusion of genres and the proliferation of documents can obscure the narrative and make its interpretation harder, it is just as possible, as Georges Didi-Huberman maintains in *Images malgré tout* [Images in Spite of Everything], that the production of meaning benefits from fragmentation, which provides a magnified context (that is to say that the decoding of each fragment by the spectator/reader takes place in relation to other fragments). Or, as Camille Laurens notes in another of her novels: "Everything counts, every detail has its importance: a dream, a memory, an intuition, a fragment of a sentence [. . .], anything can be the missing piece which will make the incomplete mosaic of facts comprehensible and allow them to be reconstructed" (*Ni toi ni moi* 60).

THE (FEMININE) OTHER

A final point, by way of conclusion: the majority of the texts in my corpus having been written by women, it is worth considering the issue of sexual identity as it is raised by these works. In *What Does a Woman Want?* Shoshana Felman declares that women have no autobiography of their own: "[N]one of us, as women, has as yet, precisely, an autobiography" (14). If one admits that female readers are steeped in a masculine ideology from which they are excluded, then it would seem that they cannot do other than reproduce dominant ideology when they set about writing. However, Felman puts forward the hypothesis that "we might be able to engender, or access, our story only indirectly" (14). This hypothesis certainly finds an echo in the photobiographic genre, which is in effect a way of indirectly representing the gendered nature of the experience. Nonetheless, "indirectly" for Felman means "by way of the Other": one becomes a woman by writing, but equally (and perhaps chiefly) by being read by others. And so women's story "cannot *become* a story except through the *bond of reading*, that is, through the *story of the Other* (the story read by other women, the story of other women, the story of women told by others), insofar as this story of the Other, as *our own* autobiography, *has as yet precisely to be owned*" (14; emphasis in the original).

Through its recourse to fragments of a life (the writer's own but also that of others), it is highly possible that photography could ultimately be the only possible way of representing women's experience. The most convincing illustration of this hypothesis can be found in *Mes Algéries en France*. For Sebbar, indeed, autobiography is a collective matter (if we do not have our own, at least we can acquire one by making a detour via the Other), and the writer makes frequent reference to her

Algerian "sisters" (a product of multi- and transculturalism, the author does not identify as fully Algerian; yet she relates to what one may term the great Family of Women).[8] Similarly, Camille Laurens considers photography as an essentially palimpsestic medium, able to convey not only traditional filiation but also, at a more comprehensive level, humanity. In a photograph, she writes, one can sense "the father in the lover, the child in the man, and the man in the child, and the one who is missing in the one who is there, so many faces in every single face, ghosts haunting them, or else the opposite, one single face in every face" (37). As in the work of Pierre Nora, for whom the accumulation of insignificant objects on which it is attempted to confer historical significance results from the lack of cohesion between people ("We are now the children of no one and of anyone"), in the work of these authors collection and collage are an attempt to respond to problems of filiation and transmission between generations. It is an analogous quest that animates Annie Ernaux in *L'Usage de la photo*: "In all the photos and postcards that include an ad, a book cover, a newspaper, anything made up of writing, I always try to crack the code. Like a sign of the times that's more real than anything else" (64). When the written word of the book fails to act as a clear signifier, one must turn to less traditional places in order to grasp one's relationship with time (and by extension, one's relationship with the Other). Any written and/or visual object is thus potentially endowed with meaning, and the act of making sense of these textual/visual clues is for the decipherer (whether intratextual, in the case of the narrator, or extratextual, in the case of the reader) a way of regaining a sense of identity through a collective enterprise. Comparing her work to that of the novelist Assia Djebar, Sebbar writes: "Assia and myself are *our fathers' daughters*, memory-tellers. As women writers, will we be able to transmit a new kind of filiation?" (32; my emphasis). Through this rag-and-bone collection, this desire to safeguard collective memory, there can, then, be discerned the possibility of writing women's stories indirectly, in such a way that they may now become, precisely, the daughters of someone.

NOTES

1. I term photobiography any autobiography or autofiction illustrated by photography; this particular phrase is modeled on Philippe Dubois's "photographic act."

2. I will discuss only *Mes Algéries en France* here.

3. The ideas presented in this chapter are further developed in a larger work that is currently in progress: *Bioptique 2000: Le Discours photobiographique au XXIe siècle* (Bern: Peter Lang, forthcoming).

4. "Scepticism about metanarratives is taken to be a characteristic of modernity" (Lyotard 7).

5. "The basic attitude of postmodernists was a scepticism about the claims of any kind of overall, totalizing explanation" (Butler 15).

6. Cartier-Bresson famously opened his 1952 book *Images à la sauvette* (subsequently translated in English as *The Decisive Moment*) with an epigraph by Cardinal de Retz: "There is nothing in this world that does not have a decisive moment."

7. I am grateful to Antoine Compagnon for drawing these points to my attention.

8. This feeling of connectedness with members of a "sisterhood" finds an echo in the writings of Nancy Chodorow, for whom "growing girls come to define and experience themselves as continuous with others; their experience of self contains more flexible and permeable ego boundaries [whereas] boys come to define themselves as more separate and distinct, with a greater sense of rigid ego boundaries and differentiation. The basic feminine sense of self is connected to the world, the basic masculine sense of self is separate" (169).

WORKS CITED

Barthes, Roland. *La Chambre claire: Note sur la photographie*. Paris: Gallimard Seuil, Cahiers du Cinéma, 1980. (*Camera Lucida*. Trans. Richard Howard. London: Flamingo, 1984.)

———. *Roland Barthes par Roland Barthes*. Paris: Seuil, 1975. (*Roland Barthes by Roland Barthes*. Trans. Richard Howard. London: Macmillan, 1977.)

Brochet, Anne. *Trajet d'une amoureuse éconduite*. Paris: Seuil, 2005.

Butler, Christopher. *Postmodernism: A Very Short Introduction*. Oxford: Oxford University Press, 2002.

Cartier-Bresson, Henri. *Images à la sauvette*. Paris: Verve, 1952.

Chodorow, Nancy J. *The Reproduction of Mothering: Psychoanalysis and the Sociology of Gender*. Berkeley: University of California Press, 1999.

Depardon, Raymond. *Errance*. Paris: Seuil, 2000.

Didi-Huberman, Georges. *Images malgré tout*. Paris: Minuit, 2004.

Dubois, Philippe. *L'Acte photographique*. Paris: Nathan, 1983.

Duperey, Anny. *Le Voile noir*. Paris: Seuil, 1992.

Ernaux, Annie. *Les Années*. Paris: Gallimard, 2008.

Ernaux, Annie, and Marc Marie. *L'Usage de la photo*. Paris: Gallimard, 2005.

Farge, Arlette. "La Photographie et le battement du temps." *Traces photographiques, traces autobiographiques*. Ed. Danièle Méaux and Jean-Bernard Vray. Saint-Etienne: L'Université de Saint-Étienne Jean Monnet, 2004. 39–45.

Felman, Shoshana. *What Does a Woman Want? Reading and Sexual Difference*. Baltimore: Johns Hopkins University Press, 1993.

Guibert, Emmanuel, Didier Lefèvre, and Frédéric Lemercier. *Le Photographe*. 3 vols. Charleroi: Dupuis, 2003–06.

Guibert, Hervé. *Suzanne et Louise*. Paris: Hallier, 1980.

Jameson, Fredric. *Postmodernism; or, The Cultural Logic of Late Capitalism*. London: Verso, 1991.

Laurens, Camille. *Cet absent-là*. Paris: Léo Scheer, 2004.

———. *Ni toi ni moi*. Paris: POL, 2000.

Legendre, Claire, and Jérôme Bonnetto. *Photobiographies*. Paris: Hors Commerce, 2007.

Lyotard, Jean-François. *La Condition postmoderne*. Paris: Minuit, 1979.

NDiaye, Marie. *Autoportrait en vert*. Paris: Mercure de France, 2005.

Nora, Pierre. "Entre mémoire et histoire." *Les Lieux de mémoire*. Vol. 1. Paris: Gallimard, 1984. xvii–xlii.

Rouillé, André. *La Photographie: Entre document et art contemporain*. Paris: Gallimard, 2005.

Sebald, W. G. *Die Ausgewanderten*. Frankfurt: Vito von Eichborn, 1992.

Sebbar, Leïla. *Journal de mes Algéries en France*. Saint Pourçain-sur-Sioule: Bleu Autour, 2005.

———. *Mes Algéries en France*. Saint Pourçain-sur-Sioule: Bleu Autour, 2004.

Sontag, Susan. *On Photography*. London: Penguin, 1977.

5

RECLAIMING THE VOID

THE CINEMATOGRAPHIC AESTHETIC OF
MARGUERITE DURAS'S AUTOBIOGRAPHICAL NOVELS

Erica L. Johnson

Both a filmmaker and writer, Marguerite Duras imbues her literary works with a notably cinematographic aesthetic. *L'Amant* [*The Lover*], the second and most celebrated of Duras's trio of autobiographical novels about her childhood in French colonial Indochina, is a vividly visual text in its voyeurism, its examination of the colonial gaze, and its presentation of the autobiographical subject through a series of photographs—the most important of which was never actually taken. Duras uses descriptions of ekphrastic photographs and cinematic scenes to decenter, mask, and absent the autobiographical subject insofar as she makes a clean break between image and referent in both cases.[1] That is, photographic and cinematic images appear as complex, fabricated visual texts that Duras revises, reinterprets, and alters at will, thereby changing the semiotic content of the image. Thus, when Jean-Jacques Annaud attempted to suture this break in his film version of *L'Amant*, for which he adopted the English title *The Lover* (1991), Duras felt compelled to articulate her aesthetic in even stronger visual terms by rewriting her story in the form of her cinematic novel, *L'Amant de la Chine du Nord* (1991) [*The North China Lover*]. While Duras's final novel is often read as a rewriting of her earlier novel, *L'Amant*, this essay shows how the later work is, more accurately, a corrective rewriting of Annaud's *The Lover*. In her use of photographic images and through her response to Annaud's film, Duras demonstrates a characteristic of French life writing by displacing the autobiographical referent and locating her subjectivity in multiple, contradictory, unfixed, and even inaccessible sites.

PHOTOGRAPHY AND SELF-PORTRAITURE

The visual aesthetic of Duras's writing can be traced back to the genesis of *L'Amant* as well as *L'Amant de la Chine du Nord*: the first was literally inspired by a series of photographs and the second sparked by Annaud's film. *L'Amant* began when Duras started writing captions to a series of photos her son wanted to publish; as the captions began to take the shape of a novel she used the working titles "La Photographie absolue" [The Absolute Photograph] (Hirsch 201) and "L'Image absolue" [The Absolute Image] (Sheringham 316). *L'Amant de la Chine du Nord* also builds upon visual text insofar as it was Duras's direct response to Annaud's film, by which she felt deeply betrayed. As Gérard Brach, Annaud's screenwriter, recalls of the well-publicized falling-out between Duras and Annaud, "the only scenario that could have seemed acceptable to her would have been the one that she would have written herself" (qtd. in Marrier 88), and indeed Duras set out to undo the film's images by rewriting it to her satisfaction in the form of her final novel.[2] Concerned as they are with visual images, though, neither novel includes photos; they are purely written texts. Whereas her engagement with photographs and cinema is foundational to these two autobiographical novels, then, her literary inscriptions of photographic and cinematic images work to thoroughly unsettle, rather than reinforce, the autobiographical referent. In so doing, she participates in what Michael Sheringham calls a "hallmark of French autobiography" in that she exhibits an author's "awareness of the problems and contradictions which beset his or her undertaking, manifesting [. . .] critical insight and self-conscious lucidity" (ix) in the ways she performs and simultaneously reflects upon the nature of self-representation.

Duras's use of visual media to do this adds a critical dimension to our understanding of the politics and poetics of self-representation. As Timothy Dow Adams points out in his comprehensive review of autobiographical theory in *Light Writing and Life Writing*, photography in autobiography brings to the fore the primary issue of both genres: referentiality. Adams sums up, "In short, autobiography and photography are commonly read as though operating in some stronger ontological world than their counterparts, fiction and painting, despite both logic and a history of scholarly attempts that seem to have proven otherwise" (15); he continues, "[L]ife writing and photography, both by definition and common perception, have a strong felt relationship to the world, a relationship which upon examination seems to disappear" (483). He goes on to chronicle the ways in which both referential systems have been thoroughly deconstructed and reconstructed in a nearly cyclical pattern. The critically contested referential gaps that pervade the genres of autobiography and photography are precisely what work for Duras who, through the interplay of written and visual texts, explores ekphrastic representational technologies to establish a semantic system in which the autobiographical referent cannot be fixed.

This gesture would appear to run counter to the semiotics of photography, in light of Roland Barthes's observation that the photograph is "connatural with its referent" (119). Barthes draws on the physics of the photograph in his observation that "[t]he photograph is literally an emanation of the referent. From a real body, which was there, proceed radiations" (80). The photographic referent would appear to be fixed in a technical sense, but Barthes goes on to point out that photo portraits compel the viewer to "strain toward the essence" (66) of the referent's identity and, taking the example of his search for his mother's essence after her death, he demonstrates the ways in which the "connatural" referent of the photograph can also be unfixed. Gazing at many photos of his mother, he finds that her essence eludes him until he comes across a photo taken of her as a child in the Winter Garden. Barthes makes two critical points about this photo: first, he asserts that the photo and its referent *can* indeed be connatural in the eyes of the beholder and, second, he chooses to publish another, entirely unrelated picture of the photographer Nadar's "[m]other (or wife)" (109) in the midst of his discussion of the Winter Garden photo. This subtle act of substitution—along with the fact that the referent in the printed photo is indeterminate—privileges ekphrastic description over the visual image itself, as does Duras. Through language, Barthes can convey truths revealed to him in the photo, whereas the photo itself "cannot establish an objectivity, in the positive sense of the term; at most it would interest your *studium*: period, clothes, photogeny; but in it, for you, no wound" (3). It is the dynamic between the visual and written text that produces the photo's meaning.

THE PHANTOM PHOTO

Duras uses photographs in *L'Amant* in a similar fashion, in that they are sources of linguistic meaning. It is essential to her representational strategy that she contradicts specific accounts in one text with those in another and that she presents visual images that elude the voyeuristic gaze. The net effect of these strategies is that she destabilizes the objective status of the photographic image, rendering it instead a site of subjectivity. In a version of Barthes's Winter Garden photo, the first photograph Duras offers to the reader is wholly inaccessible—and not simply because the text lacks photos but because the photo was never taken in the first place. This nonexistent photo has received a tremendous amount of critical attention, but to sum up: Duras spends the first third of *L'Amant* describing a nonexistent photograph of herself as a "child" in her infamous thin silk dress, gold lamé heels, and masculine hat. When this now-iconic figure of the young girl on the Mekong ferryboat demands, through the retrospective narrating voice, "[O]n the ferry, look" (16), she renders the gaze a fully articulated element of the scene by assuming the contradictory position of subject status even as she offers herself as an object of the gaze. As Sheringham points out, "It is the girl's capacity to apprehend herself as an object of desire that makes her a subject of desire and *jouissance*. Thus, the experience of *jouissance* which will follow is already virtual on the ferry" (318). This apt reading keeps all of the elements of Duras's self-portraiture in play: her pluralizing of the subject, the artistic end of the desire she portrays, and the postmodern chronotope of the narrative, which enables the mobile, unfixed, and sometimes even absent autobiographical referent of the text. Moreover, this is all in keeping with her assertion that "[t]he story of my life doesn't exist. Does not exist. There's never any center to it. No path, no line. There are great spaces where you pretend there used to be someone, but it's not true, there was no one" (8).

Duras weaves these nonexistent referents and the nonexistent photo in and out of meditations on her family, and in so doing she frames the image with two other "real" photographs, one of her twenty-year-old son taken many years later in California, and the other a childhood family portrait that throws into relief their destitution and the mother's desperation. What remains of the image is the writer's description of it, and by shifting from visual to written imagery Duras creates parity between the real and the nonexistent photos.[3] She privileges ekphrastic writing over the visual texts such writing represents. That it takes her forty-four pages to describe one "photo" of the young girl speaks to the complexity of the image and points out the extent to which it signifies not just a single subject but draws its meaning from the child's familial relationships, the colonial relations in which she is embedded, the mature authorial voice that describes her to the reader and, among these many referents, the gaze of the wealthy Chinese man ensconced in his luxurious car on the ferry. The image can signify this much material precisely because it is absent:

> I think it was during this journey that the image became detached, removed from all the rest. It might have existed, a photograph might have been taken, just like any other, somewhere else, in other circumstances. But it wasn't. The subject was too slight. [. . .] And that's why—it couldn't have been otherwise—the image doesn't exist. It was omitted.

Forgotten. It never was detached or removed from all the rest. *And it's to this, this failure to have been created, that the image owes its virtue: the virtue of representing, of being the creator of, an absolute.* (10; my emphasis)

This "photograph . . . never taken of the girl on the ferry" (13) was never frozen by the apparatus of a camera, nor was it developed in photographic ink and paper, and therefore it lingers on the verge of textuality as a site of multiple meanings. For example, the narrator recalls the moment in which the child's costume coheres when she dons the hat for the first time. Glancing at herself in the shop's mirror, she experiences a Lacanian moment: "Suddenly I see myself as another, as another would be seen, outside myself, available to all, available to all eyes, in city traffic, journeys, desire" (13). Dovetailing her self-perception with the regard of others, the narrator reveals the machinations of subject construction as a projection of multiple perspectives of which the subject's is but one.

Furthermore, this dynamic, reflexive, and intersubjective subject construction is one that Duras contrasts with a particular tradition of photography that clearly influenced her understanding of the medium, and this is the use of photos in the animist tradition of Vietnam. The narrator recalls her mother's participation in this tradition, in which photo portraits of the deceased appear on tombs or in shrines to enhance ancestor worship. Near the end of her life, the narrator's mother has a photo portrait done of herself, and the narrator explains how "the better-off natives used to go to the photographer's too, just once in their lives, when they saw death was near. [. . .] All these photographs of different people, and I've seen many of them, gave practically identical results, the resemblance was stunning" (96). The narrator goes on to describe how the photos are touched up to permanently inscribe a venerable image of the ancestor, and how "[m]y mother's expression in the photograph with the red dress was the same. Noble, some would say. Others would call it *withdrawn*" (97; my emphasis). The attempt to essentialize and thus memorialize an individual in a photograph, she implies, results in an eradication of the subject of the photo because the photo comes to replace, rather than refer to, its subject. Duras points out in *La Vie matérielle* that photography serves forgetting rather than memory — "it helps forgetting" (113) — and she takes a circumspect approach to the play of visual images and their referents in her description of photos in her writing as well as in her construction of visual images in her own filmmaking.

Autobiographical truth, as Aliette Armel explains in *Duras et l'autobiographie* [Duras and Autobiography], is generically constructed upon "extratextual references" whereas "[i]n *The Lover* there seems to be an explicit will to render this verification impossible" (17). Indeed, Duras provides geographical, familial, and episodic referents that can be verified, but she puts them into play against one another in order to advance a shifting, thematized identity in place of the transparent, chronological narrative that Annaud's film presents. With regard to the photos, Duras inverts extratextual referents by incorporating them into the text as written rather than visual images. She could have published some of the photos of which she speaks in *L'Amant*, and they are easily accessible in biographies of Duras. In her novel, however, Duras converts her memories of her family, of which photos are mere markers, into "cursive writing" (29); as she says of her mother: "It's over, I don't remember. That's why I can write about her so easily now, so long, so fully. She's become something you write without difficulty, cursive writing" (28–29).

Although *L'Amant* is rife with visual cues and photographic points of reference, the privilege granted to writing along with its thoroughly decentered narrative structure would seem to make it untranslatable to the visual medium of film. The gap between Duras's novel and Annaud's film adaptation of it are evident in the different narrative and aesthetic dimensions of the two works as well as in the fact that the conflict between the author's and the director's visions rose to the level of public spectacle. An issue of *Avant scène cinéma* dedicated to Annaud features their feud as well as the contradictory critical responses his film sparked. Originally, Duras gave Annaud her blessing and intended to write much of the screenplay herself, but then Annaud asked his longtime collaborator Gérard Brach to draft the screenplay, which Duras found to be traitorous of her novel. Brach and Annaud contend that their adaptation is true to the novel—but Annaud clarifies that "I claim to have been faithful to the way that I received it" (qtd. in Alion 82). In effect, Annaud's fidelity to the text takes the form of *authenticity*: he delves into the historical setting, architecture, and landscape that Duras describes in the portions of her novel that take place in Indochina. Ironically, this gesture toward authenticity truncates Duras's text in the sense that her novel is concerned not simply with the *narrative* of the love affair that took place within the thin walls of an apartment in 1920s Cholen but rather with the ways in which this affair serves as a means of erotic and artistic self-discovery on the part of the writer. Indeed, Evy Varsamopoulou has convincingly identified *L'Amant* as a *Kunstlerinroman*, or a feminist portrait of the artist, whereas Annaud interprets the novel as a simple story of forbidden love. In Duras's text,

123   *Erica L. Johnson*

everything that happens in her childhood, from her first love affair to her harsh family life, happens so that the author can one day write about it. She describes her family thus: "It's in its aridity, its terrible harshness, its malignance, that I'm most deeply sure of myself, at the heart of my essential certainty, the certainty that later on I'll be a writer" (75). In contrast, the people and places upon which Duras draws as backdrop to her self-portrait as a writer appear in the foreground of Annaud's film and form the substance of his narrative.

This conflict over Annaud's version of authenticity is thrown into relief by Duras's and Annaud's diametrically opposed views of how the film should be set, for Duras felt that the film could be made in France and she strongly opposed Annaud's extravagant plan to film on location in Vietnam. In an interview, Brach explains, "I believe that Duras saw a film she could have made on Jatte Island, and Annaud saw something to film in Vietnam! They couldn't understand each other. Maybe she would have made a film that [. . .] would have taken place in Paris, with the narrator in Paris, with mental images of a toned-down, far-away and imperceptible Vietnam, I don't know" (Marrier 89).[4]

This decision made by Annaud is consequential indeed, for by setting the entire film in Vietnam—with the exception of a concluding one-minute scene in Paris—he creates a problematically nostalgic vision of colonial Indochina and also condenses Duras's postmodern chronotope and double-voiced narrative into a linear plot with a singular autobiographical subject. While he does preserve the narrator's retrospective voice in the form of Jeanne Moreau's voice-over, which delivers passages taken verbatim from the novel, the voice-over serves only the story of the young girl growing up in Vietnam—the older narrator has no presence of her own as she does in the novel. In the film, her narration is confined to the passages that describe the affair. This interpretation of Duras's auto-biographical endeavor alters her story considerably in that she is able, in her novel, to possess her own story precisely through the art of splintering subjectivity and suspending such figures as the young girl in Vietnam, the young woman living in occupied Paris, and the accomplished older writer between different points of reference. The multiplicity and indeterminacy of the autobiographical subject in the novel, allegorized in Duras's construction of a nonexistent photo as a central point of reference, defy Annaud's notion of authenticity or of being "true" to a narrative.

The film's attempt to secure authenticity is also problematic in that it embraces a colonial view and aesthetic that Duras eschews in her novel. Duras observes the perversity of the race-class colonial hierarchy as it is manifest in such figures as "children like little old men because of chronic hunger" (6) and the beggar woman, *la mendiante*, whose tortured and tragic figure haunts many of her novels. All such markers of suffering and colonial violence are absent from Annaud's film, a scenario that brings out the irony of his artful, expensive construction of authenticity on location. He espouses a broadly colonial attitude in his explanation that he felt qualified to work in Vietnam because he had filmed in Africa before and was "sufficiently familiar with 'tropical' feelings" (qtd. in Alion 81). He recounts his disappointment upon arriving in Vietnam and finding socialist squalor layered thickly over the remnants of colonial splendor that he sought and ultimately re-created through the power of studio funds. In his excellent critique of the film's colonial nostalgia, Panivong Norindr observes the colonizing gesture of Annaud's portrayal of French Indochina. Quoting André Bazin, Norindr explains that this process "creates 'coherent and transparent texts and subjects,' and 'participates—across a range of discourses—in the *fixing* of colonized cultures, making them static and unchanging rather than historically constructed'"; in effect, "these filmic texts 'fix' and mediate historical memory, and participate in the construction and re-configuration of a collective memory of Indochina" (122). Norindr's postcolonial reading of the film speaks to the same issues at stake in Annaud's condensation of Duras's autobiographical subjectivity to one character and his concretization of that character in the waiflike figure of the model and actress Jane March set against the backdrop of a reconstructed colonial Indochina. In other words, Annaud's film not only simplifies Duras's narrative, it colonizes the novel. This creates an acute contradiction, given that Duras's novel participates in the work of decolonization, as Gillian Whitlock defines such work in her analysis of postcolonial autobiography: "If binaries, thinking in terms of origins and authenticity, centre and periphery, and the separation into consistent and homogenous identities are fundamental to colonizing discourses, then the work of decolonization is to return ambivalence and duplicity, and to look to intersubjectivity in cultural formations and texts" (6). The strategies of containment, simplification, and *fixing* give the director leverage on Duras's complex, elusive subject and enable him to create an easily digestible, simple narrative about the sexual awakening of a teenager in the exotic locale of the colonies whereas, as Laure Adler explains, even this central plot of the film distorts the novel's portrayal of sex as but a mode of self-discovery central to the girl's development as a writer (91–92).

THE GIRL, THE DRESS, AND THE PURLOINED PHOTO

Annaud's *The Lover*—and his decision to make an English-language film can be read as a betrayal of Duras's text as well—was not well received by literary scholars like Adler, but it gleaned much critical acclaim within the film community. For those critics who accept Annaud's version of authenticity, one of the most impressive elements of his film is certainly the success with which he transforms Duras's nonexistent photo taken on the Mekong ferry to a concrete image, although his use of the nonphoto also provides the clearest evidence of the divergence between Duras's self-portrait and Annaud's portrait. As Barthes explains, cinema may build on the raw material of photographs, but "it is a different phenomenology, and therefore a different art which begins here, though derived from [photography]" (78). Whereas a past, lost moment is pressed into the present through a photograph, the pastness and concomitant melancholy of the photo is destroyed by film: "[T]he [photographic] pose is swept away and denied by the continuous series of images" (78). There can be little question that Jane March resembles existing photos of Duras as a teenager, and the costume of the silk dress, gold lamé shoes, and man's hat is exquisitely evocative of Duras's nonphoto. However, by fleshing out and fixing the photo, Annaud violates its entire premise in the novel, in which the image serves as an absent point of reference for the author's articulation of loss, lack, and desire. Alex Hughes argues that the nonphoto of the child on the ferry is fetishized in *L'Amant*, but this argument would apply even more readily to Annaud's film than to Duras's text. While Hughes is apt in her assessment of the photo as an expression of lack, her assertion that the photo represents lack in the Freudian idiom—the child's identification as the missing maternal phallus—construes the "phantom photo" as a pathological figment. In contrast, feminist readings of self-portraiture recognize such strategies of deferral as a means by which women autobiographers refuse to establish a whole, unified, and verifiable autobiographical subject in their texts.[5] Annaud, though, does fetishize the image in that he uses it in place of the novel's subject. Rather than attempting to represent the interwoven image of the girl, her older alter egos, her contradictory roles as daughter, lover, writer, voyeur, and object of the gaze, he substitutes the powerful image he is able to conjure and condense from the novel's extended labyrinthine description. Unlike Duras's complex representation of the haunting figure of the child on the ferry, the film voyeuristically pans from the girl's shoes up her legs, her dress, her face, and her hat and then repeats this image in scene after scene, leading up to the final scene in which, clad in the same costume, she again leans against the railing of a boat (this time it is the steamboat that will "repatriate" her to France).

5. This image of the girl leaning on the railing of the steamship near the end of the film duplicates her pose on the Mekong ferry earlier in the film. Her dress, hat, shoes, and stance are identical in the two scenes. Still from Jean-Jacques Annaud's *L'Amant*.

The unchanging fixity of this image is relentless. She wears the same flimsy silk dress in nearly every scene with her lover: she wears it in the opening shot on the ferry where they meet, upon her first encounter with him afterward, upon her first derobing by him, at their dinners together, at the dinner with her family and her lover, and so on. Given Duras's assertion that the significance of the phantom photo rests upon its absence, Annaud inverts the image to make it omnipresent in the film, thereby fixing Duras's moving referent.

Furthermore, the repetition of the dress works to hammer home the nymphet quality of the girl whereas, ironically, Duras identifies not the dress but the shoes and the hat as the permanent fixtures of the child's couture. In contrast to

6. Here is the original view in the film of the girl leaning on the ferry railing moments before she meets her lover for the first time. This is the image that becomes fixed and essentialized over the course of the film through the frequent reappearance of the girl's costume and the later repetition of the image as a whole. Still from Jean-Jacques Annaud's *L'Amant*.

the dress, whose function is to reveal the girl's thin, undeveloped body beneath it, the shoes and the hat are acts of self-expression and choice; the dress is subject to the voyeuristic gaze but the hat in particular signifies the girl's reflexive view of herself in a mirror. In the novel, she tries on the hat and looks into the shopkeeper's mirror to see herself transformed: "Suddenly I see myself as another" (13). In observing her own transformation in the mirror, the girl gains an appreciation for her status as a complex signifying form.

REWRITING ANNAUD: *L'AMANT DE LA CHINE DU NORD*

Given Annaud's appropriation and condensation of Duras's autobiographical subjectivity, it is understandable that she resisted his project. Even Annaud admits, writing about their relationship five years after her death, that "she had the impression that I was entering into intimacy with her without having been invited. It's true that it was troubling" (98). He recognizes his colonizing gesture as an invasion of privacy. He also pleads the difficulties of gaining access to the life story of someone possessed of powerful emotions and means of expressing them in a short essay whose title translates as "Marguerite Duras and I were in a space of emotional violence." Here, he explains, "I knew Marguerite's work well enough to know the love/hate relationship that she had with the outside world, and her fascination with destruction" (95). It is not enough, though, to view Duras's negative response to his film as characteristically mercurial behavior in light of the way that she ultimately processed her rejection of Annaud by rewriting his film in the form of *L'Amant de la Chine du Nord*. Annaud recognizes this novel as her attempt at "a sort of authentic text" (97), again expressing the value that he sets on the concept of authenticity. Duras's cinematic rewriting of Annaud's film in the final novel of her life shatters Annaud's film and presents a thorough look at the role of visual self-representation.

L'Amant de la Chine du Nord is a novel cum screenplay, so overt is its address to the genre of film. Whereas there is not a single line of dialogue in *L'Amant*, which is told in vignettes of interior monologue, *L'Amant de la Chine du Nord* is nearly solid dialogue accompanied by directorial notes and set descriptions. In addition to rewriting several scenes from her earlier novel, Duras incorporates a few of the scenes that Annaud created for his film into her cinematic novel, thus including his film among her many autobiographical points of reference, which range from her own life to her earlier texts to others' texts. For example, she recoups sexuality as a shared terrain through which the girl and the man explore themselves as well as each other. Whereas Annaud depicts their sexuality as strictly object-oriented desire, Duras insists that it functions on many levels, including erotic desire, self-expression, and material for literary artistry. Annaud's narrativization of the novel's sexuality is apparent in a scene of his own creation in which the man rapes the girl as an act of retribution when they return from a family dinner at which her mother and brothers humiliate him. The rape scene is designed to explain the impropriety of the sexual relations Duras describes in *L'Amant*, in which the lovers engage in both gentle lovemaking and violent recriminations in a single passage of text. The novel, though, does not offer a narrative explanation of these paradoxical expressions of desire and contempt, whereas Annaud fabricates the explanation that the lover's violence is a reaction to humiliation. In *L'Amant*, the complexities of the couple's sexual relations overlap without narrative intervention when Duras writes, "He calls me a whore, a slut, he says I'm his only love [. . .] all is swept away in the torrent, in the force of desire" (42–43). Therefore, Duras corrects Annaud's inaccurate simplification of the sexual relationship in *L'Amant de la Chine du Nord* by imitating his narrative of having the lovers return to his room after the humiliating dinner, but rather than reacting in anger, the lover falls into a state of lassitude and the girl cares for him with infinite gentleness: "She soaps him. She bathes him. He lets her. Their roles are reversed" (124). In other words, there is continuity in their sexual relations that cannot be ascribed to cause and effect. Their sexuality is deterritorialized and a means of self-exploration through which the narrator routes self-representation.

There are many such cases of Duras rewriting Annaud in her novel. Interestingly, for all of her corrective scene reconstructions, she also borrows several scenes directly from the film, including that of the girl kissing the window of the man's car early in their acquaintance—"[She] puts her mouth on the glass, kisses there, lets her mouth settle there. Her eyes are closed like in the movies" (52)—and that of the girl dancing barefooted with Hélène Lagonelle. But more comprehensively, Duras rewrites Annaud by imitating the reduced narrative scope of the film and simulating its depiction of the affair in Indochina to the exclusion of its subject's later experiences—in such a way that she defies his voyeuristic gaze. No longer does the narrative encompass the mature writer, whose existence is merely implied in the footnotes of *L'Amant de la Chine du Nord*. In further imitation of Annaud, Duras eliminates the sections from *L'Amant* set in Paris during the war and she does not follow up on her mother's death in France, to cite two examples. The novel runs parallel to the film to the extent that its status as a contrapuntal reconstruction of Annaud's *The Lover* is clear.

Perhaps the most important rewritten image is that of the film's opening scene on the ferry, which Duras no longer presents as a photograph in *L'Amant de la Chine du Nord*, given that the visual trope of the text is already in place. Duras describes the Chinese man just as the actor Tony Leung plays him in Annaud's film, pointing out that he is "other than the one in the book. [. . .] He is more 'cinematic' than the one in the book," whereas "she, she has stayed the way she was in the book, small, skinny, tough, hard to get a sense of, hard to label, less pretty than she looks" (26). Duras explains in a later footnote the most important quality of the girl: "If this book is made into a film, the child can't just have a pretty face. [. . .] Beauty doesn't act. It doesn't look. It is looked at" (61n). In a clear swipe at Annaud's casting of a model in the role of *la petite*, Duras points out how the film misses the self-reflexive nature of the regard in *L'Amant*, in which the girl on the ferry is indeed the object of the gaze but the gaze is also her own. In the film, the girl is dispossessed of the gaze; never does the camera catch her in the act of *looking* as it does her lover. In *Chine du Nord*, "He looks at her. They look at each other" (26) in their first encounter. The girl is imbued with a gaze described as "unabashed" and "fresh" (27). By rendering the nonphoto from the first novel as a cinematic scene in this rewriting, Duras grants her subject agency from her stance as a filmmaker, thus throwing into relief the extent to which Annaud's character remains an object of his directorial gaze.

Duras presents another pronounced decentering technique, designed to mediate the power of the viewer and the object of the gaze, in her repeated suggestion in her directorial notes that images of characters should be separated from their voices. Instead, she directs the camera to a listener, or to an object, while someone is speaking. For example, in a scene in *Chine du Nord* in which the children watch the younger brother dance, Duras provides a footnote stating that the children watching should be filmed, rather than the child dancing. "In the film, all the action would occur this way, through the gaze. [. . .] Those who watch are watched, in turn, by others. The camera bars exchange" (158n). The point of this note is, once again, to dismantle the voyeuristic gaze of the camera. In another example, when the mother recounts her tragedy to her children, Duras footnotes the scene with the suggestion that "[f]or a movie [. . .] we can see the table and children as the mother *talks about them*" (18n). Marianne Hirsch, writing about *L'Amant*, explicates Duras's strategy in these and other scenes as "creat[ing] an image in the space-off that then absorbs the focus as though it were centrally located within the frame" (203). Whereas Annaud's camera focuses on the lush plenitude of all that he can capture within the frame, Duras's cinematic vision incorporates those points of reference beyond the photographed image. By decentering the camera's gaze, Duras broadens the scope and complexity of *la petite*, whose story is told by different voices within and beyond the visual field of the film Duras writes.

In addition to shaping her cinematic aesthetic through directorial footnotes, Duras appends a log of images to be interspersed in the film. She explains, "[The images] would be scattered through the film as the director chooses, and would in no way determine the story" (227). In contrast to Annaud's shots of Vietnam as a means of authenticating his exoticized love story, Duras suggests that such material merely "punctuate" (243) the film. What is more, she reintroduces the elements of life in colonial Indochina that Annaud's nostalgic view so carefully eliminates, including barefooted peasants toiling at the side of the road, beggar children, and the pointed contrast provided by "the millionaires' American cars slowing down in these villages because of the children [. . .] looking on without understanding" (230). Pointing out the deliberate, selective nature of Annaud's "authenticity," Duras is insistent in *L'Amant de la Chine du Nord* on depicting what she describes elsewhere as "the vampire of colonialism," and this gesture also brings the story back to the material of her own childhood, which was very much defined not only by love and desire but by poverty and human suffering.[6]

Finally, Duras's concluding passage in *L'Amant de la Chine du Nord* establishes *L'Amant* as an originary text and thus privileges her own self-portrait over Annaud's portrait of her text. Here, Duras reprints the final passage of *L'Amant* verbatim and then adds a final paragraph in which "[s]he was no longer there. She had become invisible, unreachable" (226). Her defining move, in the culminating lines of multiple texts and of her career, is to absent herself from her own story. She confirms her authorial status, her ability to traverse those vast swathes of her life where, as she asserts in *L'Amant*, there is "[n]o path, no line" (8), where no reader or viewer can follow. Constructing her autobiographical subjectivity in the space-off of photos and films, Duras sets her life into play through a rich and constantly shifting set of intertextual resonances and, more important, absences.

NOTES

1. By "ekphrasis," I refer to a written description of a work of visual art.

2. Translations of *L'Amant*, *L'Amant de la Chine du Nord*, and *La Chambre claire* are taken from the published translations. All other translations are by Natalie Edwards.

3. This is a point that I work out in more detail in my book *Home, Maison, Casa*.

4. When the interviewer, Marie Marrier, observes that Brach cut out all of the novel's scenes set in Paris, he responds that he had quite frankly forgotten there were any such scenes, so focused was he on one aspect of Duras's complex postmodern narrative.

5. Sidonie Smith and Julia Watson identify in male autobiography the "bourgeois" or "sovereign" self and contrast the linear narratives of such autobiographical subjects with those of women writers, whose

work is more decentered and whose subjectivity is comparatively elusive and complex. They demonstrate the complex processes and politics involved in women's autobiographical representation most forcefully in *De/Colonizing the Subject: The Politics of Gender in Women's Autobiography*.

6. Duras makes this observation in *Un Barrage contre le Pacifique*, the first of her autobiographical "Indochine" novels.

WORKS CITED

Adams, Timothy Dow. *Light Writing and Life Writing: Photography in Autobiography*. Chapel Hill: University of North Carolina Press, 2000.

Adler, Laure. "Il est évident que *L'Amant* de Marguerite Duras n'est pas le même que celui de Jean-Jacques Annaud." *Avant-scène cinéma* 500 (March 2001): 91–92.

Alion, Yves. "Entretien avec Jean-Jacques Annaud." *Avant-scène cinéma* 500 (March 2001): 81–82.

Annaud, Jean-Jacques. "Avec Marguerite Duras nous étions dans un espace de violence émotionelle." *Avant-scène cinéma* 500 (March 2001): 95–98.

Armel, Aliette. *Marguerite Duras et l'autobiographie*. Paris: Le Castor Astral, 1990.

Barthes, Roland. *La Chambre claire: Note sur la photographie*. Paris: Gallimard Seuil, Cahiers du Cinéma, 1980. (*Camera Lucida*. Trans. Richard Howard. London: Flamingo, 1984.)

Duras, Marguerite. *L'Amant*. Paris: Minuit, 1984. (*The Lover*. Trans. Barbara Bray. New York: Pantheon, 1997.)

———. *L'Amant de la Chine du Nord*. Paris: Gallimard, 1991. (*The North Chinese Lover*. Trans. Leigh Hafrey. New York: New Press, 1992.)

———. *Un Barrage contre le Pacifique*. Paris: Gallimard, 1950.

———. *La Vie matérielle*. Paris: Gallimard, 1987.

Hirsch, Marianne. *Family Frames: Photography, Narrative, and Post-memory*. Cambridge MA: Harvard University Press, 1997.

Hughes, Alex. *Heterographies: Sexual Difference in French Autobiography*. Oxford: Berg, 1999.

Johnson, Erica L. *Home, Maison, Casa: The Politics of Location in Works by Jean Rhys, Marguerite Duras, and Erminia Dell'Oro*. Madison NJ: Fairleigh Dickinson University Press, 2003.

Marrier, Marie. "Entretien avec Gérard Brach." *Avant-scène cinéma* 500 (March 2001): 87–89.

Norindr, Panivong. "Filmic Memorial and Colonial Blues." *Cinema, Colonialism, Postcolonialism.* Ed. Dina Sherzer. Austin: University of Texas Press, 1996. 120–46.

Sheringham, Michael. *French Autobiography: Devices and Desires; Rousseau to Perec.* Oxford: Clarendon, 1993.

Smith, Sidonie, and Julia Watson. *De/Colonizing the Subject: The Politics of Gender in Women's Autobiography.* Minneapolis: University of Minnesota Press, 1992.

Varsamopoulou, Evy. *The Politics of the Künstlerinroman and the Aesthetics of the Sublime.* Aldershot UK: Ashgate, 2002.

Whitlock, Gillian. *The Intimate Empire: Reading Women's Autobiography.* New York: Cassell, 2000.

6

ILLUSTRATION REVISITED

PHOTOTEXTUAL EXCHANGE AND RESISTANCE IN
SOPHIE CALLE'S *SUITE VÉNITIENNE*

Johnnie Gratton

I imagine that many if not most of the contributors to this
volume would readily endorse the critique of the notion of
illustration offered by W. J. T. Mitchell in his influential work
Picture Theory. It would be fair to say that contemporary theorizing of text-image relations has fostered a habit of frowning
on illustration as the product of what Mitchell calls a "stereo-
typed division of labor" between writer and visual artist (313).
Mitchell basically dismisses illustration for two main reasons:
not only does it bring about an undesirable "suturing" of the
visual to the verbal (94), it also subordinates the visual to the
verbal. The notion of illustration is therefore bound to end up a

conceptual casualty in a work that seeks to promote strategies for achieving "the independence or co-equality [of text and image] that permits collaboration in a truly composite form" (302). All I shall say in my own defense at this stage is that, in revisiting the notion of illustration, I have no wish to argue against this promotion of the "co-equality" of text and image. Rather, I shall seek to show how a revised notion—and practice—of illustration bears out a more complex understanding of this "co-equality," one embraced by Mitchell himself when he commends the "dialectic of exchange and resistance" (289) to be found operating between photography and language in examples of the photo-essay genre at full stretch. Here, while "exchange" echoes intermedial "collaboration," "resistance" refers to the mutual capacity of the textual and the visual to withstand one another's solicitations: image and text can work apart as much as they can work together.

Mitchell echoes a number of preceding semiotic contributions to illustration theory that have been partial, firstly in the sense of being undeveloped, and secondly in the sense of being negatively slanted. What follows is a modest attempt at illustration theory that seeks to avoid both of these pitfalls. The stage of theoretical reconsideration and revision prepares the way for an analysis of illustrative disruption of "straight" documentarism in the work of Sophie Calle.

ILLUSTRATION: THE PROTOTYPE

The loosest sense in which we might label something an "illustration" is what I shall call the editorial sense of the term, which covers any kind of visual image, from a pie chart to a Picasso, inserted alongside text on the pages of a book, magazine, newspaper, doctoral thesis, and so on. Like numerous terms that are semantically ill defined as categories, this one tends in practice, and over time, to become simultaneously understood in terms of a prototypal meaning that is more strongly delineated yet nevertheless widely accepted and invoked.[1] Reading the relevant definition of the word offered by the *Trésor de la langue française* [Treasure of the French Language] dictionary, one notes that, while it aims to be very broad, it actually introduces a stipulation: "représentation graphique (dessin, figure, image, photographie) généralement exécutée pour être intercalée dans un texte imprimé" [graphic representation (drawing, figure, image, photograph), generally executed to be inserted in a printed text].[2] Here, the phrase "executed to be inserted"—or, more fully, "in order to be inserted"—already begins to tighten up the editorial sense of the term: an "illustration" is not just a visual item slotted into a text but one made for that purpose, and therefore presupposing a prior act of commission, whether formal or informal, whether initiated by an author or an editor. While this specific feature is admitted to apply "generally" (rather than universally), it is deemed characteristic enough of the way we think about illustration for the definition of the prototype to be made to hinge on the practice of *custom-made* illustration. Mitchell's "stereotype" of illustration in essence merely offers a negative take on this established, more or less generic "prototype" of illustration.

The attribute of being custom-made presupposes another defining attribute of this prototype, that of belatedness. Illustration postdates text. Despite the element of logical necessity here (how can you illustrate something before it exists?), this quality of belatedness has inspired a spate of critical discourse about how illustration plays second fiddle, how it is expressly produced to *serve* text. We think again of Mitchell, wringing the stereotype out of the prototype. To be fair, the idea of servility almost certainly originates in the prototype of custom-made illustration and, as a charge, has been variously leveled against the illustrator, his or her art, and, as with Mitchell, the whole paradigm of illustration. Servility is registered in the entrenched notion that the illustrator's task is to "respect" the text or be visually "faithful" to it, a notion parried by the argument that illustrations can often actively "interpret" a text, in various ways "counterpoint" it, or even deliberately "betray" it. In fact, much recent work on illustration has set aside its prototypal features and focused instead on the reader-viewer's perspective, thereby opening up a field in which text and image are copresent and interact on more or less equal terms. However, unless there has been some collaboration between artist and writer (or editor), or unless the artist is also the writer, the critic must ultimately acknowledge that, at the level of production, the text and its illustrations stand in a fundamentally asymmetric relation to one another. While the making of the illustrations is inspired and formatively guided by the text, the writing of the text, though it may encourage future illustration, cannot be reciprocally inspired by illustrations that do not yet exist. Illustration's place in the chronology of production renders it extraneous, in potentially interesting ways, to writing. A good illustration is probably one in which "respect" for the text has been shadowed by a recognition and creative affirmation of this extraneity. I shall return later to this condition of extraneity, which lies latent, as it were, in the prototype of custom-made illustration.

If this established prototype still has currency, it is probably because as children we all read children's illustrated books and because, as mature academics working in the arts, the first base we are likely to touch when we tune in to this prototype is the acknowledged "golden age" of the illustrated book, the nineteenth century, and in particular the nineteenth-century illustrated novel. Indeed, the prototype of custom-made illustration came into its own during this period. To the extent that these two instances still operate as exemplars of the prototype, we can plausibly infer that two further properties have regularly been assigned to it. For good reason, we still tend to think of illustration as a characteristically figurative mode of visualization, that is, as depiction of a scene, event, or character detailed in an adjacent text. There is no better proof of this, perhaps, than Picasso's famous dismissal of all figurative art as mere "illustration." The property of being figurative or depictive, of course, extends to—and, historically speaking, ushers in—so-called photographic illustration. At odds with this absorption of photography, however, is the second property evidenced in my two proposed exemplars of the prototype of custom-made illustration: namely, that such illustration is primarily handmade or, to invoke a term used by Jonathan Friday, "manugraphic," as distinct from "photographic" (39). Even today, when we come across the words "Illustrated by . . ." or "Illustrations by . . ." on a book cover, we do not expect to find photos in the book.

PHOTOGRAPHY: FROM DOCUMENT TO
NEO-PROTOTYPE OF ILLUSTRATION

Photography, then, does not slot easily into this prototype—a problem highlighted and exacerbated by the fact that there are numerous generic environments—including, more notably, biography and autobiography—in which inserted photographs overwhelmingly *pre*date the writing of the text. Indeed, rather than being made to order by an artist, such photos tend to be either taken, owned, or acquired by the writer, who *uses* them as "illustrations." Except that, by now, if one persists in referring to such photos as illustrations, it can only be in a very loose sense of the word. And it is perhaps this question of the way photography has been used, so much used and so variously used, often at the expense of prototypal illustration, that has occasioned the emergence of a more recent prototype, geared specifically toward photography, which assigns a new meaning to "illustration" by testing it against the protocols, functions, and values of the photograph as "document." Still overshadowed by the established prototype, this new meaning remains unrecognized by lexicographers. I shall now briefly trace its emergence as a related but alternative prototype, a "neo-prototype," in order to show how it redefines the idea of illustration along a new binary axis.

The neo-prototype of illustration almost certainly originated in the discursive field of journalism, and more specifically of photojournalism, where, in an age of digital manipulation that threatens the bedrock credibility of the photograph, the need to distinguish between "documentary" and "illustrative" uses of photography has become a key plank in the visual ethics policies of newspapers, magazines, and press associations. Hard news requires use of the camera as a hands-off, nonintervening witness to events. However, as Gunther Kress and Theo van Leeuwen indicate in their book *Reading Images*, the late twentieth century saw a "semiotic shift" in news magazine covers from "documentary photographs—photographs recording events or portraying newsworthy people" to photos that are "contrived and posed, using conventional symbols to *illustrate* the essence of an issue" (30; my emphasis). Whether staged in advance or digitally altered after an assignment, such illustrative photos convey "conceptual images" rather than indexical traces connecting with the real and aligned to firsthand seeing. As the authors observe, "[T]hese are still photographic images, but they might as well be drawings" (30). Inasmuch as images composed from two or more photos point along a slippery slope to the capacity of new imaging technologies to generate totally simulated images, they might be said, like manugraphic art (including traditional illustration), to begin with a blank canvas.

The distinction between document and illustration is regularly invoked in discussions of misleading news visuals. *Newsweek* magazine was reprimanded by the National Press Photographers Association when its 7 March 2005 issue featured a cover image of Martha Stewart that looked real but was in fact a composite image of Stewart's head superimposed on the clothed body of a younger, slimmer female model. Only in the magazine's table of contents was it mentioned that this was an "illustration." The NPPA's concern was to protect the visual integrity of photojournalistic practice through clear flagging, either within or beside the image, of any deviance from documentary norms. The magazine's editor was forced to apologize for causing confusion but continued to defend the magazine—and, with it, the notion of illustration as "conceptual image"—by explaining that the image had been intended as "playful visual commentary, not a real picture of Stewart or an attempt to simulate one" (National Press Photographers Association). To apply a useful distinction advanced by Patrick Maynard, the illustration is a photograph "about" the American celebrity, not "of" her (121–23). Thus envisaged, "illustration" lies at a meaningful and justifiable remove from "document."

Rooted in the discursive field of journalism, the neo-prototype of illustration has already begun to spread into other discourses, such as that of commercial photography, where the difference between the "documentary" and "illustrative" approaches is one between relatively simple taking and more elaborate making, between "straight" photography and a strongly directorial mode of photography producing images based on a previsualization of how a scene should ideally look. At one level, as in photojournalistic illustration, the visible world is treated as a blank canvas. At another level, again as found in photojournalistic illustration, the "custom-made" element of the older prototype of illustration persists, except that what gets illustrated in the new prototype is less an autonomous text than a conceptual and aesthetic blueprint for the photograph.

Another discursive field in which the neo-prototype has begun to appear is that of art criticism. This brings me to the example that first jolted me into rethinking illustration beyond its status as a denigrated stereotype. On engaging with this passage, I immediately felt that the author was indeed using the right word to counterpoint the notion of photograph as document, yet also remained confused as to why this should be the case. Only then did I start inquiring into the terminological history that I have been trying to trace in the first part of this essay. Published in 2005, Martha Buskirk's book *The Contingent Object of Contemporary Art* is a lively set of essays on contemporary, broadly conceptual art practices. In a chapter on practices situated at the interface of conceptual and performance art in the 1960s and '70s, she analyzes the role played by photography and video in the recording of so-called ephemeral projects, actions often played out in the street. Such performances, Buskirk contends, partake of both immediacy and delay: "The immediacy is in the unscripted interactions between the artist and an unsuspecting public. The delay is in the dissemination of knowledge about the work to an audience that has access to the activity only through the accounts and documentation the artist decides to provide" (217).

Two initial points emerge here. Firstly, it would seem that, in the case of such projects, the notion of text and photo assemblages as documents cannot fail to be considered. The reader-viewer may not finally endorse their status as complementary documents, but initial consideration of the texts as disseminators of knowledge about the project, and of the photos as indexically guaranteed and iconically rich evidence that the project took place, will always come into play. The premise that the phototext has been produced *as* documentation is the very condition of our gaining access now to the project then. Secondly, although Buskirk is referring here specifically to work by the artists Adrian Piper and Vito Acconci, she might almost be addressing the work of Sophie Calle, about whom she will indeed have something to say later in the same chapter.

Where does the notion of illustration come into all this? As it happens, only through a passing comment, but one that gave me pause. It arises in the context of a discussion of Vito Acconci's *Following Piece*, subtitled "Activity, 23 days, varying locations. New York City." Acconci's own summary of his self-imposed program of activities, as carried out between 3 and 25 October 1969, reads as follows: "Choosing a person at random, in the street, any location, each day. Following him wherever he goes, however long or far he travels. (The activity ends when he enters a private place—his home, office, etc.)" (Lippard 117). The record of the project consists of twenty-three index cards presenting brief handwritten logs of the artist's activities, one for each day of the project's duration, and four photographs, all of Acconci following a man in a white short-sleeved shirt and dark trousers, two of them taken from behind Acconci and his quarry and two showing the men advancing along a pavement toward the camera, yet "seemingly unaware," as Buskirk puts it, of the photographer's presence. The latter pair of photos in particular leads Buskirk to surmise that there are "strong internal indications that this particular instance has been staged." Indeed, she now proceeds to point out some intermedial indications of staging:

"In fact none of the hand-written lists for the different days, eventually assembled in an array that also includes two of the photographs, describe this man. The lack of correspondence between described action and photographs suggests that these particular images are better understood as illustrations rather than evidence of these activities" (221).

The general import of this analysis is clear enough. By classifying the photos as "illustrations," Buskirk assigns them a certain efficacy as visual data—we are shown depictions of an act of following—but this is an efficacy that falls short of authenticating the actions described in the adjacent text. Just as close inspection of the photos suggests that they have been staged, so close reading of the text reveals that not one of the eleven followed men described by Acconci was dressed like his male quarry in the four photos.[3] The photos tally with the text only insofar as they show *an* act of following, not any of *the* acts of following logged on the artist's index cards. We read "something" but see something only similar, something that, in its very similarity, is thereby something "else," other, extraneous to the text. The kind of extraneity found here marks the transition from the old to the new variety of illustration, for this outsideness is now far more clearly a site (and, for the reader as viewer, a sight) of "resistance." These photos are illustrations insofar as we register that they do not function as visual documents supporting, or even on a par with, the adjacent written document.[4]

This is illustration returning with a vengeance. Contemporary artists appear to have recognized that the "mereness" so frequently attributed to the art of illustration can be transformed into an unsettling virtue. Thus what in other contexts might be thought of as a shortfall, a failure to achieve documentary status, now serves as a niggling discrepancy with the capacity to *subvert* documentarism from within. In the context of project and performance art, I ask that documentarism be understood quite broadly as the production of a truth or transparency assured by the smooth alignment of text and image, such that they can be held to be mutually validating components of a nonfictional work. In the case of projects featuring the artist as primary agent and first-person narrator, any undermining of documentarism will inevitably destabilize the autobiographical dimension of the work, as Buskirk herself implies when she suggests that part of the power of Acconci's and others' photos as discordant illustrations will lie in "the challenge they pose about whether to believe the artists' claims to have done what they describe" (221). Thus the longer we ponder over these phototextual records of projects, the more they appear to prompt us to engage in the hermeneutics of suspicion and to envisage them as dubious documents, teetering dangerously on the edge of fiction.[5]

Buskirk, then, follows my previous examples in bringing out the stagy, contrived, uncandid nature of the neo-prototype of illustration, but diverges from them in the way she plays it off against document, because, for her, illustration is the upshot of a *décalage*, a lack of fit between image and text, which in turn endows the image with a power of *in*subordination, a capacity to resist recruitment into the role of visual documentary support. Mitchell's much-echoed complaint about the servile allegiance and adherence of illustration to text has effectively been turned on its head.

As I mentioned earlier, Buskirk does go on briefly to discuss Sophie Calle as a later project artist who, like Acconci, produced a number of "following works" (221), such as *Suite vénitienne* (no change of title in the English translation), *Le Carnet d'adresses* [The Address Book], and *La Filature* [The Detective]. Her take on Calle differs slightly, however, from her take on Acconci, for Calle's work, she suggests, contains photographs that, though entirely "plausible" as visual documentation, "could still be read as an inversion of the proof they posit" (221–23). Unfortunately, Buskirk does not develop her suggestion. So, what makes Calle's project photos so suspect despite their plausibility? I want now to turn specifically to *Suite vénitienne* in order to show how Buskirk's argument can indeed be applied to this work.

SUITE VÉNITIENNE AS BELATED ILLUSTRATION

Briefly, *Suite vénitienne* is the record of a project spawned in Paris in late 1979, by which time Calle had started following people around Paris, mainly as a way of rediscovering the city after a long period of absence. On one occasion, having followed a man around the city streets, Calle then coincidentally met him the same night at a private viewing in a Parisian art gallery, where she learned he would soon be taking a trip to Venice. So she decided to travel to Venice ahead of him, track down his hotel, and then follow him—and his female partner—around the city, taking notes and photos in the course of her pursuit. The project lasted for thirteen days, only two of which were taken up with the physical pursuit of her quarry. Eventually the man recognized her through her disguise, confronted her, and tried to prevent her from taking a close-up of him. From that point on, the game was up. In her interview with Christine Macel, published as an integral part of the book *Sophie Calle M'as-tu vue* [Sophie Calle Have You Seen Me] (2003),[6] Calle sets the record straight on the place of *Suite vénitienne* in the chronology of her works:

> Ma toute première activité a donc consisté à suivre des gens dans les rues de Paris. Et mon premier projet a été *Suite vénitienne*. Si on observe attentivement ma biographie, on

peut penser que je mens. Que mon premier projet a été *Les Dormeurs*. Mais en fait la *Suite vénitienne*, qui est datée "1980" se déroule en 1979. Parce que, quand on a voulu publier le livre, un avocat a pensé que l'homme que j'avais suivi pouvait porter plainte. On a donc gardé les dates exactes, les jours, le mois, mais on a changé l'année. (78)

[So my very first activity involved following people round the streets of Paris. And my very first project was the *Suite vénitienne*. If you take a close look at my biography, you might think I'm being misleading. That my first project was *The Sleepers*. But the *Suite vénitienne*, which is dated 1980, actually took place in 1979. Because when we wanted to publish the book, a lawyer thought that the man I'd followed might lodge a complaint. So we kept the exact dates, days and months, but we changed the year.]

Calle cues us in here to the whole issue of delay, as raised by Buskirk. I should point out in this regard that *Suite vénitienne*, Calle's first book, was not finally published until 1983.

Not only does *Sophie Calle M'as-tu vue* contain a limited sampling of the phototextual documentation making up *Suite vénitienne*, it also reproduces two grouped selections of pages from Calle's *journaux intimes*, which are actually more like notebooks or scrapbooks than private diaries. The second group of pages contains handwritten texts and adjacent photos recording Calle's various following activities in the late 1970s, including the Venice project. These selected pages construct a patchy narrative corroborating the fact that Calle's trip to Venice did indeed take place in 1979, beginning with her departure from the Gare de Lyon on Monday, 19 February and ending with her return to the Gare de Lyon, once more ahead of her quarry, on Sunday, 4 March (she wanted to be at the station to take one last photo of him arriving in Paris).

The end date of the project appears on a double-page spread containing photos of Calle's furtive following activities in Venice as well as the last two paragraphs of her written report (probably an already written-up version of original notes). Beyond this instance of corroboration, however, these two diary pages open up a veritable can of worms. If we first compare them with Calle's interview assertions, we find that they fail to bear out her statement that, despite moving the year from 1979 to 1980, she otherwise stuck to the dating of the original project. For, in her published text, the project runs from Monday, 11 February to Sunday, 24 February (same days, different dates). If we now compare the diary pages directly with the published text, we see that, while both cover the same final stage of the project, they also differ considerably. The diary version is shorter than the published version and less detailed in its timing of events. And we are taken by surprise upon learning that the diary version named Calle's subject as "D.H.," where the published version has him down as "Henri B." (so we move from a Lawrentian to a Stendhalian figure). Let's concede for the moment that the diary version is no more than a first draft; that the change of day and month was forced on Calle because 1980, unlike 1979, was a leap year; and that the change of name is associated with the need to reduce the chances of D.H., if those were the man's real initials, lodging a legal complaint.[7] That still leaves us with the problem of a mismatch between the photos shown on this page and one photo in particular, reproduced in *Sophie Calle M'as-tu vue* in relatively large format as part of the sampling of the book version of *Suite vénitienne*. This is supposedly a surreptitious snapshot of the followed man holding his own camera and peering down at a Venetian canal through the railings of a bridge. The photo offers us a clear glimpse of the left side of his face. We see the railings, the wall behind them, and a large white notice board on the wall. If we now return to the three photos stuck onto the diary page beneath Calle's handwritten text, we note at once that two of them feature this very same setting. However, despite the poor quality of the reproduction and the merely contact-print size of the photos, we can discern that the crouching subject is here wearing either a darker colored or a less brightly lit coat than in the published version. And his hair and hairstyle are different: this man's hair seems to be receding. There is, moreover, something we no longer see, the white notice board, either because this photo was taken from a different position or because, when the photo was taken in 1979, there was as yet no notice board fixed to the wall . . .

How, then, to explain this discrepancy between the photos in the private and published versions of the project? Calle has clearly not told the full story in her interview with Macel. Yet the missing element has been in the public domain for some years. Jean Baudrillard collaborated with Calle on the 1983 edition of *Suite vénitienne* as author of the book's afterword, an essay titled "Please Follow Me." A short fragment from Baudrillard's *Cool Memories*, published in 1987, mentions the "hero" of *Suite vénitienne* as having "slipped away," with the result that "il a fallu refaire toutes les photos sans lui" (83) [all the photos had to be retaken without him]. In a later work, cowritten with Marc Guillaume, Baudrillard proves more expansive. Here, he reminds us that in Venice the followed man did eventually rumble Calle's game, and with it her identity. This meant that he was both alerted and opposed to any published form of Calle's project. Thus, as Baudrillard explains, "pour publier le livre, elle a éte forcée de retourner à Venise avec un couple d'amis qu'elle connaissait, et de reprendre toutes les photos dans les mêmes décors avec quelqu'un d'autre" (145) [in order to publish the book, she was forced to return to Venice with a couple of friends she knew, and to retake all the photos in the same settings with someone else]. Further details that have come my way include the information that the lawyer mentioned in Calle's interview was her publisher's legal representative; that the two friends who accompanied her to Venice in 1980 were actors; and that it was not a question of reshooting all the photos but only those featuring her quarry, alone or with his partner. We are dealing, then, with a set of images that postdate the 1979 project and that were probably taken between the dates given in the published book, 11–24 February 1980, so that Calle's stay could overlap once more with the Venice Carnival. The later photos are therefore staged photos, revealing that Calle's purpose was to replace the real Frederick Henry Bohen with a stand-in; then, with his help, to duplicate some of the original photos; and finally to use these photos as substitutes for the originals: something similar, something else. By this point, with the erasure of the original photographed subject, Calle's task has been accomplished and her lawyer satisfied.

To summarize, the later photos are not visual documents, not evidence of the project described in Calle's adjacent written report, but belated and extraneous illustrations of it. We recognize here certain features of both the established and the emergent prototypes of illustration. The problem with these replacements, however, is that they slot so plausibly and seamlessly into the published version of the project, alongside the remaining original photos, that the reader-viewer can gain no sense of their separate status and therefore has no way of divining that they result from a set of subsequent actions performed by Calle. Thus, what some readers find to be a disturbingly frank account of an act of stalking turns out to conceal an untold story. This was to remain the case with the republication of *Suite vénitienne* in book 4 of *Doubles-jeux*

[Double Game] (1998),[8] despite the fact that, on this occasion, Calle produced a "Préambule" [Preamble] displaying for the first time twelve double-page spreads from her private diaries recording the buildup to her departure for Venice. Only with the publication of *Sophie Calle M'as-tu vue* in 2003, as I have tried to show, are we finally able to compare samples of the initial and final phototextual drafts of *Suite vénitienne*, and to infer from this cross-checking that the published version is an amalgam of a following project and a follow-up project, of documents and illustrations, of fact and fiction. As an amalgam, it is close to what I have elsewhere dubbed a case of "documontage" (Gratton).

Are we to take it, then, that Calle in 2003 still wishes to keep her follow-up project a secret, as suggested by the lack of candor shown in her interview, or that she has deliberately offered us some new clues betraying her lack of candor? She arguably invites such wondering herself in asking us the very question "M'as-tu vue?" not least when she superimposes it as a title over the teasing self-portrait featured on the front cover of her book. Posing with her left hand placed vertically over the left side of her face, Calle is narrativizing herself from the outset as a player of a game of autofictional hide-and-seek, as the cunning practitioner of a dialectic of self-exhibition and self-concealment. That she may indeed be offering us certain clues within the frame of this dialectic is further suggested by at least two editorial facts about the book *Sophie Calle M'as-tu vue*. Firstly, the text of Calle's interview with Christine Macel has been inserted between the reproduced double pages of her diaries and the samples of text and photos representing *Suite vénitienne*. Secondly, the two-page spread that is causing all the trouble (to both the interview and to our understanding of *Suite vénitienne*) is the only one of the eight spreads in *Sophie Calle M'as-tu vue* not to have previously featured among the twelve spreads making up the "Préambule" to the 1998 edition of the Venice book. It is therefore improbable that the sole newly declassified two-page spread was chosen casually.

The strange thing about Calle's caginess in her interview is that she could easily have justified her recourse to the follow-up project in the very same terms she uses to explain the switch of date from 1979 to 1980. Was it not, after all, a necessary salvage operation carried out solely to circumvent the legal obstacles put in the way of her eagerness to see her first book published? For this was an eagerness fired by earlier frustration, due to the fact that, as her first editor Alain Bergala explains, "[A]ucun éditeur n'avait voulu de *Suite vénitienne*, tous jugeant que les photos étaient amateur et que le texte n'avait aucune valeur littéraire" (Bergala and Depardon 10) [No publisher was interested in *Suite vénitienne*, because they all thought the photos were amateurish and the text had no literary value]. Equally, could Calle not have pointed back to the whole history of documentary photography, where countless photographs of the apparently unrehearsed real have turned out, once researched, to be the results of careful directorial staging? Reluctant to play the role of historian, Calle has never played the conceptualist card, either. It is not in her makeup to accredit her work as a planned or principled subversion of documentarism, or indeed of the aesthetic and institutional foundations of Art. As an interviewee, she prefers to account for her work narratively, pointing up the contingent and the circumstantial. She often adopts a faux-naïf persona, insisting on how little she knows about conceptualist or situationist artworks that seem to anticipate her own. As she quips in a 2002 interview with Fabian Stech: "Disons que je suis une midinette conceptuelle, ou une conceptuelle midinette" (101) [Let's say that I'm a romantic schoolgirl who's also a conceptualist, or a conceptualist who's a romantic schoolgirl]. The chances are, then, that, if Calle were ever to openly acknowledge the existence of her follow-up project, she would probably admit that it does subvert the documentary status of the finished work, but only inadvertently, that the subversive effect is but a by-product of what was otherwise a concerted effort to save her autodocumentary from nonpublication.

FOLLOWING SUIT, FOLLOWING UP, FOLLOWING ON

Given that Calle's actions in both projects are always carried out with a future audience in mind, I shall now develop the question of illustration as subversion from the perspective of the reader-viewer. Once alerted to the inscription of the staged photos into the work that could not be completed without them, the reader-viewer is clearly in a position to reassess that work. How irremediably do the staged photos, and the altered dates and names, subvert the work's overall value as an exercise in documentary *art*?

Moving now beyond the analysis offered by Buskirk, I wish to argue that Calle's follow-up project can be seen to be prefigured by the original project, thus making it continuous with, and not just subversive of, the original's more credible documentation: a realignment hinted at in the work's very title, where *suite* as "pursuit" is shadowed by *suite* as "continuation." An initial point worth considering in this respect is that both components of the project have in common that they are surreptitious in nature, the first with regard to Calle's quarry, the second with regard to her reader-viewer. In neither case, moreover, does she seek to justify or apologize for her covert activities. This leads me to my first example of prefiguration as such.

When finalizing her book, Calle presumably had the option of adding a note of apology or explanation to the effect that she had taken certain liberties—as in contemporary TV news and documentary programs, where resorting to old footage is signaled as archival or where switches to docudrama are flagged as reconstructions, precisely in order to clarify the journalistic difference between "document" and "illustration." That she declined this option is figured in the published text and photos by a similar reluctance to justify her furtive activities. For example, in the very first entry of her log, she openly represents herself as a covert operator en route for Venice, equipped with items of disguise and tools of detection:

> Dans ma valise: un nécessaire de maquillage qui m'aidera à modifier ma physionomie, une perruque blonde coupée au carré, des chapeaux, voilettes, gants, lunettes noires, un Leica et un Squintar (cet accessoire qui se visse sur l'objectif est muni d'un jeu de miroirs permettant de prendre des photos de côté, sans viser le sujet. Je photographie les occupants des autres couchettes et je m'endors. (*Suite vénitienne* 43)[9]

> [In my suitcase: a make-up kit so I can disguise myself; a blonde bobbed wig; hats; veils; gloves; a Leica and a Squintar (a lens attachment equipped with a set of mirrors so I can take photos without aiming at the subject). I photograph the occupants of the other berths and then go to sleep. (*Double Game* 81)]

A number of images shot with the aid of this periscopic lens attachment are shown early in the book, though none of the photos of her quarry are attributed to its use. Here, Calle could easily have tried to legitimize her furtiveness by appealing to historical precedents within the photodocumentary tradition. In 1914 the American photographer Paul Strand built what was possibly the first periscopic-lens camera in order to catch his subjects unawares on the streets of New York. Later, Helen Levitt did much the same thing. Between 1938 and 1941, Walker Evans, perhaps the greatest documentary photographer of the twentieth century, sat regularly in trains on the New York subway taking close-ups of unsuspecting passengers sitting opposite him "with a camera under his coat, its lens invisibly exposed between buttons and a cable release running down his sleeve to a bulb in his hand" (Sante 13). Evans sought encounters that were strictly photographic, engineered solely by "the gaze of a machine" (Lugon 155). Calle, of course, wanted—and experienced—more than a mere machine-made encounter, becoming at times as much her subject's suitor as his follower. But if she fails to invoke previous instances of photodocumentary subterfuge, it is probably less because they might not legitimize her own subterfuge sufficiently than because she felt no need for any aesthetic or moral alibi. Both the text and the photos narrate this heedless, disinhibited self, which is equally a self taken over by the project, a self subjected to her own project. As Calle writes, on arriving in Venice: "Je me vois aux portes d'un labyrinthe, prête à me perdre dans la ville et dans cette histoire. Soumise" (*Suite vénitienne* 44) ["I see myself at the labyrinth's gate, ready to get lost in the city and in this story. Submissive" (*Double Game* 83)]; or, several days later, now shadowing her quarry: "Je me sens déterminée" (80) ["I feel determined" (101)]. The more "determined" she is *to* keep following, the more "determined" she is *by* the one she follows, and/or by the rule she follows—which is, precisely, to follow.

On now to a very different kind of prefiguration of follow-up project by project of following. Calle learns during her stay in Venice that D.H./Henri B. is there to find settings for a film he intends to make, and also that he is taking photos of Venice for an English writer, identified only by the initial "C."—hence the fact that she regularly sees her quarry carrying and using his camera. One photographer following another. One photographer taking photos of another photographer taking photos. This recursive structure, which Calle must certainly have enjoyed creating by her own photographic act, opens in turn onto an iterative structure when she decides, on four separate reported occasions, not just to follow and photograph her quarry but to follow his example by shooting the same scenes he has just photographed: the follower-suitor *follows suit*. Each of these photos is incorporated into the book, and each is among the few captioned photos to be found in it. In both the 1998 edition of the book and its English translation, the captioned photos are grouped into two pairs and set alongside one another on facing pages, thereby acquiring strong visual prominence. The captions too are iterative, quotations from Calle's own text. On the first double page, from left to right:

Campo San Polo—il désigne une église, prend une photo de la place. Je fais de même. (68)

[Campo San Polo—he points to a church, takes a picture of the piazza. I imitate him. (94)]

Ponte de la Madonnetta—il s'accroupit pour photographier le canal, ou bien ce bateau qui passe? Avec quelques secondes de retard, je l'imite. (69)

[Ponte de la Madonnetta—he crouches to snap a shot of the canal, or perhaps of that passing boat? After several seconds, I imitate him. (95)]

The second pair is presented in the same layout, above the following captions:

Campo San Angelo, je le vois. Il me tourne le dos et photographie un groupe d'enfants qui jouent. Vite je l'imite. (88)

[Campo San Angelo, I see him. He turns his back to me and photographs a group of children playing. Quickly, I do the same. (104)]

Ponte del Teatro. [. . .] Il photographie le canal ou bien la maison de Marco Polo. À mon tour, je photographie ces lieux qu'il fixait. (89)

[Ponte del Teatro. (. . .) He photographs the canal or perhaps Marco Polo's house. In turn, I photograph these places he was staring at. (104–05)][10]

(The second caption here, in both French and English, involves minor rewording of the text.) The writer-photographer is very insistent here in the way she courts our attention. Her imitative performances are visually confirmed by the documentary inclusion of the photos she "in turn" took, while the captions attached to them are textual reiterations of the acts of iteration reported in Calle's log—captions that, moreover, are internally repetitive in their verbal renderings of her acts of copying.

As readers "in the know," so to speak, what we may be alerted to by this spate of iterative activity is the way Calle's acts of imitation assume once more a recursive function, but now with regard to the imitations of her own photos that she set out to produce during her follow-up project. I return to Calle's second caption, adding the participial clause that follows it in its source text: "Ponte de la Madonnetta—il s'accroupit pour photographier le canal, ou bien ce bateau qui passe? Avec quelques secondes de retard je l'imite, m'efforçant de faire la même photo" (70) ["Ponte de la Madonnetta—he crouches to snap a shot of the canal, or perhaps of that passing boat? After several seconds, I imitate him, trying my best to take the same pictures" (95)]. As we saw when comparing the photos from the follow-up project with those from the following project, one can only strive to take or make the "same" photo. In the photo taken by Calle from the Ponte de la Madonnetta, the motorboat has presumably chugged its way further along the canal from where her quarry snapped it, attesting to the inevitable afterness and secondness of imitation, whether the delay be of a few seconds or one year. Like the traditional illustrator, another latecomer, the photographic imitator is doomed to produce no more than a kind of "artist's impression," an approximation: not the "same" photo, but at best an *illustration* of it.[11]

The passage I have just quoted thus offers a recursive prefiguration of the follow-up project. It is a mise en abyme, in what one takes to be the text of the 1979 project, of the actions carried out by Calle in the 1980 project. Just in case we have missed the point, Calle continues in the very same sentence to record how her quarry and his partner move on, only to pause once more, as something catches *their* attention: "Avec quelques secondes de retard je l'imite, m'efforçant de faire la même photo, — campiello dei Meloni — ils s'intéressent à une publicité murale pour photocopieuses" (70) ["After several seconds, I imitate him, trying my best to take the same pictures — Campiello dei Meloni — they seem interested by a poster advertising photocopiers" (93)]. How appropriate (too much so?) that circumstances should have thrown up an object of interest that in turn throws up a word that, right down to its gender, so resonantly encapsulates the photographer's role as rephotographer, not just in the very same sentence but globally, in both of her projects: Sophie Calle, *photocopieuse*.

This second type of prefiguration consists of actions, perceptions, and textualizations in which Calle must have taken pleasure. As such, these prefigurations can also be considered to ordain her recourse to the follow-up project, and indeed to realign it as a follow-*on* project. In other words, we are encouraged to consider the later project to be the logical extension—or conceptual illustration—of certain behaviors recorded as belonging to the original project. As I have moved through this analysis, it has proved more and more difficult to separate the projects-then from the documents-now, to distinguish documentary material from illustrative material, and even to divide the two projects from each other. If I have referred repeatedly to Calle's "quarry," it is because of my increasing uncertainty as to whether I should call him "D.H." or "Henri B." Thus I have reached a point whose crux is nicely articulated by Philip Auslander in an essay on documented performance pieces: "It may well be that our sense of the presence, power, and authenticity of these pieces derives not from treating the document as an indexical access point to a past event but from perceiving the document itself *as a performance* that directly reflects an artist's aesthetic project or sensibility and for which we are the present audience" (9).

I concur with the gist and spirit of this proposal, and would add only one rider to bring it into line with my own concluding perspective on *Suite vénitienne*. My sense of this work is not at all one of its "authenticity," but rather that of its dubious yet admirable integrity as a manifoldly composite work.

NOTES

1. In this essay, my use of the term "prototype" alludes, rather than adheres, to work done in cognitive linguistics on the "prototype theory" of categorization.

2. This definition is endorsed by the art historian Ségolène Le Men as offering a fair summary of "le sens visuel, aujourd'hui le plus courant du mot *illustration*" [the visual sense, today the most common usage of the word *illustration*].

3. The photographed man, as Buskirk points out, is wearing a white short-sleeved shirt. For confirmation that no man so dressed is mentioned in Acconci's written report, see Acconci.

4. It is important to note that this resistance works both ways. Thus Acconci's laconic notes prove inhospitable to the accompanying images, neither mentioning them nor even acknowledging that any photos were taken.

5. On the prevalence and variety of "dubious documents" in contemporary art, see Drucker 174–87.

6. The literal English translation fails to render the ambiguity of the title, which is also used adjectivally to refer to a vain, pretentious person. Thus *M'as-tu vue* was retained as the title of the English translation of the book.

7. In an essay published since I wrote the first draft of this chapter, Cécile Camart has reported Calle's revelation to her that the real name of the followed man was Frederick Henry Bohen (377). Curiously, "Henri B." turns out to be closer to the real name than the original abbreviation.

8. The English translation fails to render the play on words of the original, which is a homophone for "Double I's."

9. I use the 1998 version of the book as the first version (Paris: L'Étoile, 1983) is out of print.

10. In fact, the caption beneath what is one and the same photograph (except for minor changes in the way each is cropped) has been changed in *Double Game*, suggesting that someone may have alerted Calle during production of the translation of *Doubles-jeux* to the fact that she may have been mixing up her Venetian bridges: "Ponte della Cortesia—he points toward the canal as if to show something to the woman. I take a picture in the same direction" (*Double Game* 105; corresponding to *Suite vénitienne* 85).

11. For more on illustration as approximation, see Mark Haddon's wonderful novel *The Curious Incident of the Dog in the Night-time*, where, almost systematically, the illustrations, attributed to the first-person narrator, are preceded by the words "like this," meaning that the ensuing image is something similar or hypothetical or approximate in relation to whatever was textually marked as "actual."

Acconci, Vito. *designboom*. (27 Aug. 2008.)

Auslander, Philip. "The Performativity of Performace Documentation." *PAJ: A Journal of Performance Art* 84 (2006): 1–10.

Baudrillard, Jean. *Cool Memories*. 2 vols. Paris: Livre de Poche, 1993.

Baudrillard, Jean, and Marc Guillaume. *Figures de l'altérité*. Paris: Descartes & Cie, 1994.

Bergala, Alain, and Raymond Depardon. *New York*. Paris: Cahiers du Cinéma, 2006.

Buskirk, Martha. *The Contingent Object of Contemporary Art*. Cambridge MA: MIT Press, 2005.

Calle, Sophie. Interview. *J'ai parlé avec* . . . By Fabian Stech. Paris: Les Presses du Réel, 2007. 91–103.

———. *Sophie Calle M'as-tu vue*. Paris: Centre Pompidou / Xavier Barral, 2003.

———. *Suite vénitienne. A suivre* . . . Vol. 4 of *Doubles-jeux*. Arles: Actes Sud, 1998. 37–109. (*Suite vénitienne*. Trans. Dany Barash and Danny Hatfield. *Double Game*. London: Violette, 1999.)

Camart, Cécile. "Les Stratégies éditoriales de Sophie Calle: Livres de photographies, photo-roman, livres d'artiste." *Littérature et photographie*. Ed. Jean-Pierre Montier, Liliane Louvel, Danièle Méaux, and Philippe Ortel. Rennes: Presses Universitaires de Rennes, 2008. 373–89.

Drucker, Johanna. *Sweet Dreams: Contemporary Art and Complicity*. Chicago: University of Chicago Press, 2005.

Friday, Jonathan. *Aesthetics and Photography*. Aldershot UK: Ashgate, 2002.

Gratton, Johnnie. "Du documentaire au documontage: *Vingt ans après* de Sophie Calle." *Intermédialités* 7 (2006): 167–79.

Haddon, Mark. *The Curious Incident of the Dog in the Night-time*. London: Jonathan Cape, 2003.

Kress, Gunther, and Theo van Leeuwen. *Reading Images*. 2nd ed. London: Routledge, 2006.

Le Men, Ségolène. "Histoire de l'art et histoire du livre—Illustration." *Encyclopédie Universalis*. (15 Aug. 2008.)

Lippard, Lucy. *Six Years: The Dematerialization of the Art Object*. Berkeley: University of California Press, 1997.

Lugon, Oliver. *Le Style documentaire: D'August Sander à Walker Evans, 1920–45*. Paris: Macula, 2001.

Maynard, Patrick. "Drawing and Shooting: Causality in Depiction." *Journal of Aesthetics and Art Criticism* 44 (Winter 1985): 115–29.

Mitchell, W. J. T. *Picture Theory*. Chicago: University of Chicago Press, 1994.

National Press Photographers Association. "NPPA Calls *Newsweek*'s Martha Stewart Cover 'A Major Ethical Breach.'" *nppa.org*. (27 Aug. 2008.)

Sante, Luc. Foreword. *Many Are Called*. By Walker Evans. New Haven CT: Yale University Press / Museum of Modern Art, New York, 2004. 11–14.

Trésor de la langue française. Analyse et traitement informatique de la langue française. (20 Dec. 2010.)

7

VIEWING THE PAST THROUGH
A "NOSTALGERIC" LENS

PIED-NOIR PHOTODOCUMENTARIES

Amy L. Hubbell

Since their departure from their homeland in 1962, the Pieds-Noirs, or former French citizens of Algeria, have published numerous coffee-table photodocumentary books filled with images of their past in Algeria. Although in recent years the images have migrated to the Internet, the importance of these icons of their life stories has not wavered. The overt goal of Pied-Noir image-based texts has been to preserve the communal memory of the homeland and to share the beauty and history of Algeria with a wider French public, yet major visual contributions by prominent scholars such as Jacques Derrida and Benjamin Stora call our attention to the motives that underlie these works. Through an investigation of the repeated and overlapped images of the Pieds-Noirs' Algerian past in collective photodocumentary works, films, and websites, this essay demonstrates how nostalgia functions in visual memoirs to draw the exiles together and to create a sense of unity with a country that is no longer their home. It then explores how the multiplicity and displacement of images, especially as seen in Pied-Noir Internet communities and films, simultaneously deconstruct the past they attempt to unify.

THE PIEDS-NOIRS

For the most part, the Pieds-Noirs who left Algeria did so unwillingly, and their departure during and after the Algerian War (1954–62) was traumatic. Nearly a million French citizens of Algeria fled their homeland in violent and uncertain conditions to become permanently exiled in France. Upon their arrival in a country most of them had never even visited, they were confronted with poor and cramped living conditions with no clear system of integration in place.[1] Because of the stigma surrounding the war and colonialism in general, in addition to specific stereotypes of the community as rich colonialists, the Pieds-Noirs faced a cold welcome in France. Consequently, the Pieds-Noirs began creating communities in which they could speak freely and abundantly of Algeria, and from which they would receive needed material and psychological support. This once diverse population quickly became a close-knit community, with ties rooted in suffering, separation, and loss of homeland. While the psychological and physical wounds of the Pieds-Noirs' departure did not easily heal, scars began to form as they banded together.

As early as 1962 the Pieds-Noirs began publishing both fictional and autobiographical accounts of their past in Algeria, and these stories were almost immediately nostalgic.[2] Today, nearly fifty years after exile, the community still thrives on memories of the past. Numerous individuals have taken up preserving personal and collective autobiographies of the Pied-Noir people in publications, films, and websites. The earliest works documenting the Pied-Noir community were primarily photo-laden coffee-table books, of which one of the most prominent was Marie Cardinal's *Les Pieds-Noirs* in 1988. Cardinal, perhaps the most prolific Pied-Noir author, wrote at least nine of her thirteen major works based on the Pieds-Noirs. Although *Les Pieds-Noirs* is a collaboration with other prominent authors such as Albert Bensoussan, Janine de la Hogue, and Francine Dessaigne, only Cardinal is credited on the cover and the first eighty pages of the work recount the author's childhood in Algeria.[3] As one of her few purely autobiographical works, the book includes images and stories that invite a rereading of material previously presented as fictional.

Whereas Anselm Haverkamp in "The Memory of Pictures" writes, "There is no better 'souvenir,' it seems, than the self-made photographic picture, which is meant to preserve individual memories from individual moments of an individual life" (258), Cardinal uses her own photos alongside those from news sources to represent all Pieds-Noirs. Her accompanying autobiography in this photodocumentary text attempts to represent the diverse experiences of her community.[4] Cardinal expresses this diversity, which is a source of communal pride: "We were different from one another, but we lived together in one reality that shared several religions, several languages, several laws" (*Pieds-Noirs* 9). Cardinal was born in 1929, a year before the Algerian centenary. The majority of her account in *Les Pieds-Noirs* focuses on her memories of World War II. This period was greatly significant to the Français d'Algérie because, as the author claims, it was World War II that legitimized Algeria as a part of France: "From 1943 on, because it was on our ground that modern France had begun to legitimately, if not legally, exist, we believed that we were truly French, that we had rights over France, over the direction of its politics" (72). Although Algeria may have redeemed France, the colony quickly learned it would not be accorded the power and respect it had expected.

In addition to displaying and recounting highly important historical events for the community, Cardinal also reproduces the city of Algiers using iconic images and personal memories of the most significant neighborhoods (Bab el-oued and the Port d'Alger), streets (la rue Michelet), and specifically European activities, represented by pictures of well-known cafés and beaches as well as a photo of young men ogling young women on the street. She elaborates the importance of the Pied-Noir culture (dress, attitudes, activities) and differentiates them from their Arab counterparts in both words and images (31). At the same time, Cardinal ties herself to the indigenous Algerians by describing her familial attachment to the farmhands on the family's colonial estate (12–15, 19) and by using pastoral images of Arab men, women, and children working in the fields and smiling.[5]

She ends her story with an image of the iconic Cemetery of Saint-Eugène (81)—a location frequently reproduced in the memoirs of other Algerian-born French citizens. Without elaborating her departure, or that of her community, she simply concludes with, "I haven't forgotten the fratricidal war," and "I do not deny my people, I love them. But I judge them and it is this judgment that I do not want to write. Family problems should be dealt with in the family" (80). This self-proclaimed uncritical approach to history is essential to nostalgia writing. As Svetlana Boym explains in her seminal work *The Future of Nostalgia*, unlike melancholia, "nostalgia is about the relationship between individual biography and the biography of groups or nations, between personal and collective memory" (xvi). As the community's past exists now only in shared memories, writings, and photos, any dissent or internal criticism would potentially endanger the Pieds-Noirs' fragile identity. *Les Pieds-Noirs*, like the majority of visual texts from the Pied-Noir community, practices "restorative nostalgia," attempting a "transhistorical reconstruction of the lost home" and believing itself to be "truth and tradition" rather than nostalgia (xviii). Because of her duty to her community within the text, Cardinal similarly refuses to directly address the trauma of her exile, further underscoring the nostalgic function of the text. While she hints at what is left behind (the graves, for example), she cannot afford to draw attention to the pain or shame of loss. Rather, as Boym explains of restorative nostalgia, Cardinal's work "ends up reconstructing emblems and rituals of home and homeland in an attempt to conquer and spatialize time" (49).

What is exceptional about Cardinal's work is that it does not end with her autobiographical take on the community. Where her personal story ends, the second, collaboratively written part begins with a broad history of the Pied-Noir people, including the sections "Terre et hommes" [Land and Men], "Le Temps de la modernisation" [The Time of Modernization], "Histoire et politique" [History and Politics], and "Le Temps de vivre" [Time to Live]. A quote from Algerian-born Albert Camus introduces the nostalgic value of this community portrait: "We arrive through the village that is already opening onto the bay. We enter a yellow and blue world where the odorous and acrid sigh of the summer earth in Algeria welcomes us" (qtd. in *Les Pieds-Noirs* 85). Then, in words and images placed side by side, the book dissects each city and community. The book highlights the architectural marvels constructed by the French and underscores the industrious nature of the Pieds-Noirs.

In this photodocumentary book created for the Pied-Noir community, important matters such as integration and the welfare of all Algerians are prominently represented with images of colonial hospitals and schools, but the text offers sparse commentary on problematic issues such as the push for the Algerian right to vote in 1937 (206) and the Algerian nationalist uprising in 1945, which ended with approximately fifteen thousand dead (227).[6] Under images of rows of Algerians with their hands in the air, the captions read, "Submission of the communes of Oued Marsa and Djidjelli" and "Some dissident *douars* submit" (226). After concluding, "In Algeria, May 1945 in the Constantine region is a crucial date. Nothing will ever be like it was before" (227), the next few pages of text briefly discuss Algerian representation in the colonial administration and then move abruptly back to unifying and stable images of European-style cathedrals and other important monuments in the next section. It is as though nothing dramatic, violent, or revolutionary had ever happened.

Les Pieds-Noirs ends abruptly with the departure, hidden under allusions to vacationing in the Métropole (292). The last two pages of the book depict people arriving in France from an Air France flight and an enormous steamer leaving the Port d'Alger. In the accompanying text, La Hogue likens the end of colonial Algeria to a sudden nightfall. The violence of revolt gives way to exile in her poetic "Ballade triste pour une ville perdue" [Sad Ballad for a Lost Town]:

> We could more deeply feel how much these men, these women had put all of their wealth, all of their love in it, and that they were defenseless against death. They had lived intensely, physically, and then the violence of their life, of the sun, the wind, the waves, became a mental violence.

My childhood town. [. . .] It was ready for revolt, it will be astonished by defeat. And for us, its distraught children, Destiny had already traced the paths of exile. (293)

These heartfelt closing words to *Les Pieds-Noirs* are the only ones in the text relating the exile of the Français d'Algérie, and yet, the very term "Pieds-Noirs," as Cardinal explains, was not given to the community until they arrived in France (80).

CONTINUALLY NOSTALGIC PHOTODOCUMENTARIES

The uncritical approach to the colonial past in visual terms was not entirely surprising in the 1980s because of the lack of a scholarly counterbalance. For years after the war, the French maintained a willful and public silence regarding the Algerian War.[7] But from the 1990s historical texts written by Algerians and French citizens alike began appearing en masse and what was previously known as the "Algerian conflict" is now frequently discussed candidly in academic forums, in documentary films, and in the media.[8] Even though France's colonial past is now being openly analyzed by all parties, nostalgic photodocumentaries have not been slowed. The same unified vision of Algeria continues to be recounted in books such as Elisabeth Fechner's series, Souvenirs de là-bas [Memories from Over There]: *Alger et les Algérois* [Algiers and the Algérois], *Constantine et les Constantinois* [Constantine and the Constantinois], *La Gloire de l'Algérie: Ecrivains et photographes de Flaubert à Camus* [The Glory of Algeria: Writers and Photographers from Flaubert to Camus], and *Le Pays d'où je viens* [The Country I Come From], all written between 1999 and 2002. Fechner, like Cardinal, seeks to represent the story of her people, providing a deeply personal and individual experience for her readers. Her only commentary appears in her introduction, which outlines the history of the French presence in the region in nostalgic terms. She openly evokes the technique called "nostalgérie," re-creating the colony with the sights, smells, sounds, and tastes of Algiers. Fechner writes, "Forty years have passed, the time to make a man an elder and to yellow those old photos of white cities that everyone collects today. The Algérois will not escape the general rule of *nostalgérie*" (*Alger* 9).[9]

Using evocative phrases such as "la valise ou le cercueil" [the suitcase or the coffin] along with the common sites (such as the rue d'Isly, the rue Michelet, Bab el-oued, and the beach in Algiers), Fechner calls the Pieds-Noirs together, inviting those who have begun to forget the details to compare their dreams with the reality captured by the photograph. "The photo, then, the real deal. Blurry? Overexposed? Poorly framed? Too far away? Too close? This evening dream, who knows how it remained fixed on film" (*Alger* 9). Even though the picture may be distorted, for Fechner it remains, and thus still protects those fantastic moments of the past. Pictures stand as proof of what was lived *là-bas* [over there] and the distortions, reminding us today that these are ruins of the past, are often overlooked by the aging exiles.

Fechner's volume *Constantine et les Constantinois* begins almost identically to *Alger et les Algérois* and this repetition emphasizes the lack of importance placed on analysis. Fechner's photodocumentary presents a straightforward effort to re-create a past that is fading with time. She underscores the notion that photos will refresh and unify memory for this aging people that so heavily relies upon this common past. The repetition of images from one text to the next reinforces the shared reference points and again unifies memory. Nostalgia is sustained by re-creating the homeland piece by piece as it was, or as it is remembered, or as it needs to be seen today.

In the same vein, former military officer and former mayor

of Mostaganem Lucien Laugier begins the preface to *Souvenirs d'Oranie* [Memories of Oranie] with a personal account of his own history commingled with the community's past.[10] Laugier writes, "I have no state secret to reveal to you; you will only hear a French Algerian, born and raised and having made his career in one of these departments in which seeing the tricolor flag was the most natural thing in the world, shell out his memories like a friend shows you his slides upon returning from a vacation to a faraway land" (5). This photo album, like the others of this genre, has no academic ambitions. It continues with mostly color images and short captions, re-creating every part of Oranie with scenes that will provoke immediate nostalgia for the Pieds-Noirs d'Oranie, such as the famous view from the mountain looking down at Oran and the view looking up toward the Notre Dame de Santa Cruz church. This church, the destination for annual pilgrimages during colonial rule, remains an icon of the Pieds-Noirs' past. Groups of Pieds-Noirs continue to return there during their excursions to Algeria, and the original statue of Notre Dame de Santa Cruz has been transported to Nîmes-Courbessac, France, which is now the site of annual pilgrimages during the religious celebration of Ascension.

VISIONS OF CEMETERIES

Although French monuments are central in Pied-Noir visual texts, the cemeteries left behind in Algeria serve as the ultimate reminder of the need to return for the Pieds-Noirs. Visions of the cemetery, for example, figure heavily in Cardinal's literary works. In *Les Mots pour le dire* [*The Words to Say It*] the narrator recounts dreaded visits to her older sister Odette's grave. Unlike Marie Cardinal, Odette was a wanted child; she died of tuberculosis before Cardinal was born (299). In Cardinal's personal return to Algeria, recounted in *Au pays de mes racines* [In the Country of My Roots], however, her visit to her father's grave in the same cemetery seems to be the focus of her voyage. She asks, "Is that the reason for my trip to Algeria? To visit my father?" (126). The cemetery is then pictured in *Les Pieds-Noirs* opposite a short description of this return on the last page of her account (80).

Cardinal is not alone in her compulsion to visit her father's grave. Algerian-born philosopher Jacques Derrida asks his filmographer Safaa Fathy to find his dead brother Norbert's grave in the Jewish part of the Saint-Eugène Cemetery near Algiers for the documentary film *D'ailleurs, Derrida* [Moreover, Derrida or Elsewhere, Derrida]. The tomb is then pictured in the subsequent coauthored work *Tourner les mots* [Turning Words] along with a photo of the cemetery's registry opened to the page bearing Paul Derrida's name. Another Algerian-born Jewish author, Hélène Cixous, searches for her father's grave in her documented return to Algeria, *Si près* [So Close], published in 2007. During her voyage, Cixous uses Derrida's published visual works as a sort of guide, and she even passes in front of one of the Derrida family graves while she is searching for her own father's burial site (201).[11] Likewise, historian Benjamin Stora photographs the Jewish cemetery in Constantine to include in his return narrative, *Impressions de voyage* [Travel Impressions]. This image is accompanied by the caption "The Jewish cemetery of Constantine, above the city, immense, deserted, where two thousand years of Jewish history 'sleep'" (72).

In *Souvenirs d'Oranie*, Laugier evokes the ancestors whom he is abandoning as he flees Algeria: "June 11, 1961: At La Sénia, I take the plane for Marseille. The plane flies over Oran; before me, the mountain of Santa Cruz and the sanctuary of Notre-Dame. [. . .] Now it is over and my view is collecting the last memories. There in the countryside, in a little cemetery shadowed by cypress trees [. . .] I was leaving witnesses to this passage: Claude Laugier, father of Victor, Victor Laugier, father of Louis, Louis Laugier, father of Ulysse, Ulysse Laugier, my father" (16). Cemeteries represent what was essentially lost in Algeria. They hold the ghosts of the unsalvageable past and they are key pilgrimage sites during the return voyages of the Pied-Noir community. During the showing of the documentary film *Saïda . . . On revient!* [Saïda, We're Coming Back!] at the biannual gathering of the Pieds-Noirs of Saïda in 2007, several of the spectators broke down in tears upon viewing the dilapidated condition of the graveyards today. As the graves are destroyed by time and neglect, the permanence of this loss devastates what the photo attempts to preserve. The Internet is now perhaps the most logical home to these otherwise unvisited graveyards. The Pieds-Noirs can virtually return to the remains as numerous organizations attempt to preserve their cemeteries, if not physically, at least visually in websites and uploaded films.[12]

NOSTALGIC AND UNIFYING VISIONS

These visual texts (both virtual and print), along with the many nonvisual autobiographies that have appeared since 1962, participate in a communal autobiography. The same sorts of images are stacked and layered upon each other, creating a protective wall around the community. Because the community members mostly sought to preserve their history and to speak out against what they felt was political abandonment on the part of the French, the Pied-Noir vision of the past has been primarily filled with monuments, icons, and happy memories of their homes in Algeria. The few new images of a changed present in Algeria that are now being brought back by individuals who have recently traveled to Algeria may destabilize that nostalgically created vision of the past. These new images are sometimes rejected or simply not seen for what they are. For example, at the showing of *Saïda . . . On revient!* my viewing companion, Alphonse San Miguel, had made the trip back "home" with the group of eighty Pieds-Noirs from Saïda who contributed to the film. During the film showing, he repeatedly said to me that the film shouldn't have shown the houses and other buildings in ruins. He insisted that Saïda really wasn't like that—it really wasn't that bad.[13]

While nostalgic re-creation of the past is quite common in autobiography on the whole, it is perhaps surprising that prominent scholars like historian Benjamin Stora participate in a similar reproduction of the homeland. Stora, who, like Derrida, is an Algerian Jew, has made his academic studies of Algeria so prominent that even the Algerian people today turn to his books for their history.[14] In *Algérie: Formation d'une nation* [Algeria: The Building of a Nation], which Stora markets as a brief history of Algeria's construction of a national identity, he tacks on the visual travelogue from his return in 1998, *Impressions de voyage*. Although the first photo accompanying his account depicts Stora in the doorway of his childhood home, his vision of Algeria varies from that of the Pieds-Noirs in that he photographs Algeria "today." He explains the context of his voyage: "I haven't returned to Algeria for five years. Five long years with images of blood in my head. Fear of death for my close friends. Testimonials of daily horror" (59). Stora, like many Algerian-born French, had been exiled from his homeland by the Algerian civil war, although not permanently, as some of his compatriots were. His return, made as an invited scholar, does not aim to protect the colonial past or to evoke nostalgia. Yet the author visually underscores that he has returned to his homeland and that he is authorized to do so because he has made it his life's work. As in the works by Cardinal and others, Stora's work also uses memories to accompany his return. His vision of Algeria includes images of French monuments with Algerian youth and, as mentioned above, he recalls the cemeteries that are now abandoned. In a text aimed primarily at recounting the birth of independent Algeria, Stora inserts himself back into the country by including photos in which he poses with former Algerian militants and scholars. In this case a history commingled with personal photos of highly recognizable icons of a colonial past becomes, literally, *his story*—a clear justification of his right to be in Algeria.

In 2004 Gérard Guicheteau and Marc Combier published *L'Algérie oubliée: Images d'Algérie (1910–1954)* [The Forgotten Algeria: Images of Algeria (1910–1954)], based on Algerian postcards from Combier's collection. The authors attempt to problematize the Algeria constructed by the nostalgic attachment of the French.[15] Guicheteau reminds his readers that before the colonial conquest, "We didn't know much about Algeria, and we continue not wanting to know anything (or at least very little) of what existed 'before France'" (13). Images, without substantive knowledge behind them, remain without depth on the page. But these same images of a so-called forgotten Algeria provoke a slew of memories and always represent more than they depict for the exile. Stora, who wrote the preface to this work, puts the problem of such memory books into question.

> The more we move away from the long history of French presence in Algeria, the more the past paradoxically comes back and climbs back up to the surface of memories. Is it [. . .] a desire for stories to offer reassurance in the face of present uncertainties? The need for identity markers? [. . .] This return functions as a symptom of our societies, of an era not so long ago of the domination of the "Other," the

strange indigenous person, the dematerialization of what is real due to folklorization, or the dissolution of what is "true." Photography can play a great role in this return of memory. (7)

The primary authors of *L'Algérie oubliée* are not Pieds-Noirs and, rather than desiring to re-create the French colony, as we have seen in the works of Cardinal, Laugier, and Fechner, this work plays with the understanding that the attachment to the image is falsely made sacred by the exile the Pieds-Noirs endured and by their need to sustain their roots. Unlike Fechner, who takes the photo as a factual remnant, Stora recognizes the possible transformations of a country through the images that attempt to embody it: "Photographers have transformed the landscapes [. . .] in patterns, malleable forms, patches of a black-and-white color. All of these images construct Algeria as a décor for a tourism that never really existed [. . .], where the analogy of the visible with reality slowly moves away, all while not becoming too distant" (9). This approach is what Boym categorizes as reflective nostalgia, cherishing the "shattered fragments of memory" and temporalizing spaces (49). The authors here are fully aware that the image is distortable and capable of portraying a country other than how it was lived or perceived. The line between visual and real is blurred even in the sharpest of images.

DECONSTRUCTED IMAGES

Whether intentionally nostalgic or not, the images put together in books, Internet sites, and now increasingly available films serve to transport the exile back home and to reestablish loose roots in the past. As soon as the visual returns are undertaken, however, they are almost as quickly undone. When making *D'ailleurs, Derrida*, Egyptian director Safaa Fathy documented

Derrida's most significant "lieux de mémoire" [locations of memory] including his home, his schools and, as discussed above, his brother's grave. Upon watching the filmed return, however, Derrida found the scenes unrecognizable. He was suddenly doubly displaced from his home and became, like a tile in the entryway to his Algerian house, placed upside down, disjointing the pattern on the floor and calling attention to himself.[16]

Although not as overtly deconstructionist in their thinking, some Pieds-Noirs had a similar experience at the showing of *Saïda . . . On revient!* in Toulouse. While many felt transported back to Saïda while watching this film composed of multiple voyagers' viewpoints, others, especially those who had recently returned, felt disjointed by this version of the past.[17] Algeria seen through someone else's eyes can never match up to what

7. The mistake in the tile in Jacques Derrida's house in El Biar, Algeria. Still from Safaa Fathy's *D'ailleurs, Derrida*.

the mind has retained for the past forty-six years of exile. As Marie-Claude San Juan writes in a recent reflection on her own past in the review *Mémoire plurielle: Les Cahiers d'Afrique du Nord* [Plural Memory: The Journals of North Africa], "A town is never reduced to a town. Even in Paris, I sometimes live in Souk-Ahras, Algiers, Oran, Oujda, or Constantine, now, through the game of visual superimpositions, echoes, and faces, too. Only the odors, the sea, and the starry sky are missing."[18] This so-called game of superimposed images is perhaps more effective than those assembled and repeated in nostalgic photo books. Hélène Cixous expresses her imagined pasts in a similar manner in *Si près*: "In mixing letters of the names of towns I found myself everywhere all at once, very quickly, I witnessed unpublished transplantations, nothing is lost, nothing is created, everything is transformed" (56–57). Although the eye needs a focal point on which to found its story, the mind can live fractured and multiplied within its pasts.

While the Pieds-Noirs are quickly becoming extinct, they now have the technology to be more in touch with their community and past than ever before. Internet sites, like the aforementioned books, reproduce nostalgic images of the past, re-create Algerian communities, and join together testimonies of the shared past. The sites simultaneously provide an amazing texture of histories and a unified image of the past. The Internet serves as perhaps the most appropriate receptacle for all of these memories because it is searchable, it creates a virtual network, and the pages disappear when there is no one left to maintain them. Such is the case of Stora's personal web page, which was available in 2005 but is not today, and of the site *Piedsnoirs.net II — le retour*, which, although in version 2.0, is already apparently outdated.[19] Stories intertwine and deconstruct themselves through the immediacy and instability

of the medium, until finally, through reproductions and repetitions, all that is left are, like the title of another Pied-Noir
web page, "Photos de souvenirs" [Pictures of Memories].[20]

In 2007 Solange de Martini created a board game to be
advertised and sold to the Pied-Noir community. Le Parcours
du Pied-Noir [The Route of the Pied-Noir] is intended to be
fun and educational for the whole family, with representations
on the board of little black feet moving from town to town,
from Khenchela to Constantine. Martini invites us to "have
some quality family time with your grandchildren, for ages
10 and up. [. . .] 450 questions (and answers, naturally!) about
the history, cuisine, cities, language [. . .] of our Algeria before
the exodus. 50 token cards illustrated with photos from over
there" (Jeune Pied-Noir Information). Perhaps this interac-
tive type of visual return is the future frontier of Pied-Noir
memory. Playful re-creations may deconstruct nostalgia for
the past, but returning will remain the perpetual game of the
Pieds-Noirs.

NOTES

1. See Jordi's works 1962 and De l'exode à l'exil for a thorough account
of the arrival of the Pieds-Noirs in France. Domergue, in L'Intégration
des Pieds-Noirs dans les villages du Midi, also provides a fascinating
sociological view of the difficult integration of the Pieds-Noirs in the
south of France.

2. Cardinal's Écoutez la mer [Listen to the Sea], the story of a love
affair between a Pied-Noir woman and a German man, was published in
1962. Francine Dessaigne's Journal d'une mère de famille pied-noir [Diary
of a Pied-Noir Mother] appeared in the same year, and in 1963 Anne
Loesch published La Valise et le cercueil [The Suitcase and the Coffin].

3. Special thanks are offered to Benjamin Stora, among others, on
the copyright page of Les Pieds-Noirs.

4. Writing on behalf of the community is common for Pied-Noir
authors, as the members tend to subscribe to a unified version of the

past. Through their repeated retelling, many memories have melded into one version of the past, but the underlying diversity of the individuals remains. Since 2006 divergent accounts of the past, including increasingly violent memories, have begun emerging in Internet resources such as listservs and websites.

5. She names her Algerian "fathers"—Barisien, Barded, Aoued, and Youssef—who appear in other texts in which Cardinal remembers her childhood.

6. This passage is particularly troubling and potentially subversive: "In Algeria, some believe in the promises of emancipation" (227). But as quickly as the uprising is recounted, it is absorbed into the larger story of the Pieds-Noirs.

7. See Stora's *La Gangrène et l'oubli* [Gangrene and Forgetting] as well as his more recent work *La Guerre des mémoires: La France face à son passé colonial* [The War of Memories: France Confronted with Its Colonial Past], which is a published interview with Thierry Leclère.

8. See, for example, Patrick Rotman's documentary *Ennemi intime* [Intimate Enemy], a special edition of the magazine *Le Point* titled "Quand l'Algérie était française" [When Algeria Was French], and the historical works *Les Crimes de l'armée française: Algérie, 1954–1962* [The Crimes of the French Army: Algeria, 1954–1962] by Pierre Vidal-Naquet, Benjamin Stora and Mohammed Harbi's *La Guerre d'Algérie* [The Algerian War], and Stora's aforementioned *La Guerre des mémoires*.

9. Fechner continues, "For them, as for all Pieds-Noirs, first there was the coffin and the suitcase, *with nothing left*, then forgetting, and finally, the passing to an appeased memory that allows them today to finally establish a warm rapport with the sites in which they were born. How? By the intermediary of an incredible chain of friendship, which through 350 clubs and more than 1,000 small groups methodically maintains the charm rediscovered in the past" (9).

10. Included is an account of a personal visit from Charles de Gaulle, who promised Laugier that they would no longer be betrayed (14).

11. While en route to places of Derrida's past, Cixous writes, "No cemetery? Oh! Everything has become cemetery for fifteen minutes" (174).

12. See, for example, "Souvenirs d'Algérie." As quoted on the site's homepage, *"Memories of Algeria* is a French organization specializing

in the maintenance and renovation of tombs and vaults of the Français d'Algérie." Film clips from Pied-Noir return voyages have been appearing on sites such as *Dailymotion* and *YouTube* since 2006. See, for example, "Cimetière catholique Algérie," which depicts the cemetery of Beaumarché in 1997. Viewers' comments reflect how outraged they are by the condition of the graves.

13. I wish to thank the Northeast Modern Language Association and Kansas State University for summer research fellowships that allowed me to attend Pied-Noir gatherings throughout France in 2007 in commemoration of the forty-fifth anniversary of their exile.

14. See *Impressions de voyage* (93). Cardinal produces something similar in her return travelogue *Au pays de mes racines*, in which she visits the Université d'Alger and is moved to tears that young Algerian women are reading her novels.

15. The authors call nostalgia "this lullaby for memory" (13).

16. See the photo of the tile. In *Tourner les mots* Derrida captions a similar image "Who is this tile [. . .] poorly adjusted, disjointed, disadjusted, displaced, or poorly placed?" (between page 80 and page 81).

17. Having never been to Algeria, I had my own disjointed experience while being returned to Saïda through film. Many places were familiar to me from my research, but the overall effect of the film was nauseating. The multiple images spliced together and the many unsteady hands on the cameras forced me to look away sometimes to regain my equilibrium. As I soon came to understand that those around me were viewing not the film on the screen but their own memories of the places they recognized, another sort of nausea took hold.

18. The selected quote comes from the original manuscript sent to me directly from the author, Marie-Claude San Juan. The editors of *Mémoire plurielle* cut this section from their final publication.

19. The Internet is powerful in "preserving the past," but without fact-checking measures in place, some sites propagate myth as easily as fact.

20. See Bartolini, "Photos de souvenirs." Bartolini, the webmaster for *bone.piednoir.net*, announced to his mailing list in August 2008 that he would no longer continue as the administrator of these memories, and that his readers could expect even the *photos de souvenirs* to soon disappear. "My decision is to no longer be involved in anything

currently related to the Pied-Noir community, neither to the living, nor the dead, nor to the missing, to whom I remain profoundly attached" ("Ma décision"). Later that year Bartolini began the arduous process of disassembling the site for the cemeteries of Bône, among others, and intended to go on removing memories (and thereby freeing up memory on his server) ("FW: La Seybouse 76"). While the site now indicates all of the memories that have been erased, Bartolini continues to administer his newsletter and website, and in April 2009 expressed restored faith in at least part of his community.

WORKS CITED

Bartolini, Jean-Pierre. "FW: La Seybouse 76." E-mail to subscribers of *Echo des Français d'AFN*. 30 Sept. 2008.

———. "Ma décision." E-mail to subscribers of *Echo des Français d'AFN*. 1 Aug. 2008.

———. "Photos de souvenirs." *bone.piednoir.net*. (5 Oct. 2008.)

Boym, Svetlana. *The Future of Nostalgia*. New York: Basic Books, 2001.

Cardinal, Marie. *Au pays de mes racines*. Paris: Grasset, 1980.

———. *Ecoutez la mer*. Paris: Julliard, 1962.

———. *Les Mots pour le dire*. Paris: Grasset, 1975.

———. *Les Pieds-Noirs*. Paris: Belfond, 1988.

"Cimetière catholique Algérie." Online video clip. Posted by Comite-6-fevrier on *Dailymotion.com*. Sept. 2007. (7 Oct. 2008.)

Cixous, Hélène. *Si près*. Paris: Galilée, 2007.

D'ailleurs, Derrida. Dir. Safaa Fathy. Perf. Jacques Derrida. Videocassette. France Arte, 1999.

Derrida, Jacques, and Safaa Fathy. *Tourner les mots: Au bord d'un film*. Paris: Galilée-Arte, 2000.

Dessaigne, Francine. *Journal d'une mère de famille pied-noir*. Paris: L'Esprit Nouveau, 1962.

Domergue, René. *L'Intégration des Pieds-Noirs dans les villages du Midi*. Paris: Harmattan, 2005.

Ennemi intime. Dir. Patrick Rotman. France Télévisions Editions, 2001.

Fechner, Elisabeth. *Alger et les Algérois*. Paris: Calmann-Lévy, 2002.

———. *Constantine et les Constantinois*. Paris: Calmann-Lévy, 2002.

———. *La Gloire de l'Algérie: Ecrivains et photographes de Flaubert à Camus*. Paris: Calmann-Lévy, 2000.

―――. *Le Pays d'où je viens*. Paris: Calmann-Lévy, 1999.

Guicheteau, Gérard, and Marc Combier. *L'Algérie oubliée: Images d'Algérie (1910–1954)*. Preface by Benjamin Stora. Paris: Acropole, 2004.

Haverkamp, Anselm. "The Memory of Pictures: Roland Barthes and Augustine on Photography." *Comparative Literature* 45.3 (1993): 258–79.

Jeune Pied-Noir Information. "Jeu 'Le Parcours du Pied-Noir' de Solange de Martini." *Jeune Pied-Noir Information*. (10 Feb. 2008.)

Jordi, Jean-Jacques. *De l'exode à l'exil: Rapatriés et Pieds-Noirs en France, l'exemple marseillais, 1954–1992*. Paris: Harmattan, 1993.

―――. *1962: L'Arrivée des Pieds-Noirs*. Paris: Autrement, 1995.

Laugier, Lucien. Preface. *Souvenirs d'Oranie*. By René Bail. Paris: Trésor du Patrimoine, 2003. 5–16.

Leclère, Thierry, and Benjamin Stora. *La Guerre des mémoires: La France face à son passé colonial*. Paris: Broché, 2007.

Loesch, Anne. *La Valise et le cercueil*. Paris: Plon, 1963.

"Quand l'Algérie était française." *Le Point* 22 May 2008.

Saïda . . . On revient! Sur les pas de notre enfance. Dir. Bernard Allène and Amicie Allène. 2007.

San Juan, Marie-Claude. "Souk-Ahras, mes villes . . ." *Mémoire plurielle: Les Cahiers d'Afrique du Nord* 52 (September 2007): 12–14.

"Souvenirs d'Algérie." *www.souvenirs-algerie.com*. (28 Sept. 2008.)

Stora, Benjamin. *Algérie: Formation d'une nation* suivi de *Impressions de voyage*. Biarritz: Atlantica, 1998.

―――. *La Gangrène et l'oubli: La mémoire de la guerre d'Algérie*. Paris: La Découverte, 1998.

Stora, Benjamin, and Mohammed Harbi. *La Guerre d'Algérie*. Paris: Pluriel, 2005.

Vidal-Naquet, Pierre. *Les Crimes de l'armée française, Algérie, 1954–1962*. Paris: La Découverte, 2006.

GEORGES PEREC, MEMORY,
AND PHOTOGRAPHY

Peter Wagstaff

Peter Wagstaff

A CRISIS OF REPRESENTATION

Georges Perec's texts are characterized by a preoccupation with the themes of absence, loss, and emptiness; this may appear at odds with the ludic nature of much of his writing. Yet it is the unsettling tension between, on the one hand, his cryptic ingenuity and playfulness and, on the other, the void at the center of the narratives that underscores both a personal trauma and a more widely applicable crisis of expression and representation. In exploring ways to resolve that crisis of representation, Perec does more than confront the personal trauma; his narrative strategies, focusing on the delineation of emptiness, oscillate between the verbal and the visual and, thereby, offer one possible solution to a problem that, through the latter half of the twentieth century and beyond, has beset all those attempting to come to terms with Theodor Adorno's aporetic dictum "to write poetry after Auschwitz is barbaric" (30). Examples abound in Perec's work of the leitmotiv of absence: the lipogrammatic omission of the letter "e" from *La Disparition* [*A Void*] and the missing final piece of the jigsaw puzzle in *La Vie mode d'emploi* [*Life: A User's Manual*] exemplify a strategy that seeks to isolate his core concerns through a refusal to spell out the details, inviting the reader instead to pierce the opaque screen of allusion and metaphor.

Perec is confronted with a twofold problem of representation, both facets of which are rooted in an awareness of the limitations of language and give full weight to the complexity of Adorno's observation, with its insistence on the "moral peril" of attempting to give aesthetic expression to mass extermination (Martin 2). The first, common to all who have sought a means to describe the Holocaust, poses the challenge of expressing the inexpressible or, rather, of acknowledging the chasm that separates the event and the language available to describe it.[1] The second facet of Perec's problem of representation both exacerbates the challenge and offers an oblique resolution in the context of the conjunction of the unsayable and the unknowable: the uncertainty surrounding the fate of his mother at Auschwitz, ignorance of the language and culture of his forebears, incomprehension of his Jewish identity. At stake is a sense of selfhood: hence the profoundly autobiographical nature of his writing, even when the texts offer no obvious autobiographical substance. It is of course the negation of the autonomous subject—itself at the heart of the autobiographical project—that is the aim of the Nazi ideology that found its most extreme expression in the extermination camps.

Perec's preoccupation with absence and the challenge of expression is one that lends itself to analysis by reference to the term "postmemory," proposed by Marianne Hirsch to describe "the experience of those who grow up dominated by narratives that preceded their birth, whose own belated stories are evacuated by the stories of the previous generation shaped by traumatic events that can neither be understood nor recreated." Hirsch's principal interest related to the children of Holocaust survivors, although she suggests that the term might be appropriate for "other second generation memories of cultural or collective traumatic events and experiences" (22). The problematical status of memory, as it is enshrined in this formulation, seems apposite in the case of Perec who, denied access to generational memory by the deaths of his parents, in violent circumstances, in his early childhood and to a wider cultural memory by their migration to France from their native Poland before his birth, defines his relationship to the past by oblique reference to the one faculty that can provide access to it.

It is in this context that I want to examine Perec's auto-biographical work and, in particular, two works from the last decade of his life. The first, *W ou le souvenir d'enfance* [*W or the Memory of Childhood*], with its two alternating and menacingly convergent narratives, one fictional, the other referential but marked by hesitation and lack of memory, is described by Philippe Lejeune as "a new autobiography" and "one of the very few books that have seemed to me to be doing something completely new in a genre—the childhood narrative—endlessly devoted to repeating the same procedures" (*La Mémoire et l'oblique* 71). The other is the less well-known documentary film written by Perec and made in collaboration with director Robert Bober, *Récits d'Ellis Island: Histoires d'errance et d'espoir* [*Ellis Island: Tales of Vagrancy and Hope*], which traces the phenomenon of European mass migration to the United States at the turn of the nineteenth century from the perspective of those arriving by steamship, steerage class, at the Ellis Island reception center at the mouth of the Hudson River.

These two texts constitute, in complementary fashion, a response by Perec to the challenge of representing the absence of memory. They also embody, in complex and mutually reinforcing ways, approaches to the exploration of memory processes that recognize both the temporal and spatial aspects of those processes. In each case textual narratives that trace and attempt to reconstruct the passage of time as a continuum engage with the existence—and reflect upon the significance—of photographic images that cut across that continuum, fixing the instantaneous moment. The resulting counterpoint of text and image thus provides an insight into the construction and expression of autobiographical memory, its evident uncertainties and unformulated desires.

AUTOBIOGRAPHICAL MEMORY AND PHOTOGRAPHY

If autobiographical writing is motivated by the quest for an understanding of selfhood, and if selfhood is inconceivable without the faculty of memory, then the evidence of past existence provided by photographs seems, at the very least, to offer a powerful tool and aide-mémoire for the autobiographer. The uniquely corroborative function of the photograph needs no underlining. Barthes's "ça-a-été" [this has been] (*La Chambre* 121) is merely the most lapidary modern expression of an evidential awareness that has its origins in the earliest examples of photographic experimentation, from Fox Talbot's *Lattice Window* (1835) to Daguerre's *Boulevard du Temple* (1838). There is little evidence of theorization of the status of the photograph, however, before the mid-twentieth century.[2] It has an early advocate in André Bazin who, in elaborating, largely for aesthetic purposes, an "ontology of the photographic image" (Wollen 125), adopts a categorization not dissimilar to that developed earlier by Charles Sanders Peirce as a semiological ordering of classes of sign. In his well-known tripartite division of icon, index, and symbol Peirce offers a key to the multiple ways in which a photograph may signify. A photograph has representative force: it looks like what it represents (icon); it is existentially dependent on its subject, carrying its referent, palimpsest-like, within itself (index); it may, of course, also symbolize. Seen in this triple perspective, the photographic image is challenging, as it ensures both presence and absence of the referent; it becomes a site of mourning. The photograph's role as key to the functioning of memory is further exemplified by Walter Benjamin, whose juxtaposition of photography, forms of reproduction, the archive and historical memory suggests the centrality of the photographic image to the operation of memory and thought in the modern era (see, for example, Cadava xvii–xxx). Further, the work of Roland Barthes and Susan Sontag has stimulated interest in the ways autobiographers make use of the photograph as a crucial element in the reconstruction or invention of selfhood. More recently, Laura Mulvey, citing Rosalind Kraus, has underlined what should have been long evident, that the still photograph is located at a strange crossroads between science and a form of spiritualism, as it combines, for the first time in history, the "mechanized imprint of reality" with "associations of life after death" (54). The rapid spread of the technology of photography in the nineteenth century, as both an amateur and a professional activity, is easily understood in terms of a fascination with a determinist and positivist worldview, combined with the ever-present awareness of the precariousness of human existence: what was, demonstrably, there, and is no more. This is photography as the seal of mortality. In similar terms, Tom Gunning emphasizes that while in its earliest form, "photography emerged as the material support for a new positivism, it was also experienced as an uncanny phenomenon, one which seemed to undermine the unique identity of objects, creating a parallel world of phantasmatic doubles alongside the concrete world of the senses verified by positivism" (42–43). In contrast, the celebrated nineteenth-century photographer Nadar relates in his solipsistic autobiography *Quand j'étais photographe* (1900) [When I Was a Photographer], that Balzac, for whom human personality was built up, onionlike, of successive layers, feared the erosion of that personality, layer by layer, by the act of being photographed (17–18). Clearly, the relationship between the photograph and its referent is unstable and open to reevaluation.

In considering Perec's autobiographical project, as reflected in *W ou le souvenir d'enfance* and *Récits d'Ellis Island*, I want to refer in particular to the writings on photography and history, and the relation between them, by the Czech philosopher Vilém Flusser, whose attempt to elaborate a philosophy of photography seems to me to refine previous attempts to develop an "ontology of the photographic image" (Bazin) and to cast an interesting light on Perec's insistent, often despairing search for a past that has meaning: in short, for evidence of an autonomous selfhood. Flusser sees photography, and the uses to which it is put, as both a problem and a challenge. The relative newness of the photographic image and its ubiquity are seen as a threat in a culture that takes for granted the analytical, progressive, and explicatory function of language. Photographs, by contrast, convey information in apparently incontrovertible, instantaneous form; they constitute, in Barthes's formulation, a "message without a code" ("Le Message" 939; see also "Rhétorique de l'image" 1419).

Echoing Plato's metaphor of the shadowy silhouettes on the wall of the cave, Flusser warns of the danger—exacerbated by the seductive relationship of camera apparatus and photographer—of a visual illiteracy that takes image for reality. He argues instead for a constant awareness of the disjuncture between the two and, in consequence, of the ways in which a linear historical narrative unrolling in time is cut across by the photograph, punctual in its impact, stopping the historical process. In freezing time, it becomes timeless, offering a form of utopian alternative to that seemingly unstoppable process. It is the prospect of this utopian alternative that, I argue, underlies Perec's preoccupation with the photographic image.

PEREC AND THE PROBLEM OF MEMORY

The relationship between Georges Perec and the faculty of memory is an intimate and a troubled one. His writing is a constant interrogation of the ways in which the past hovers inescapably over the present, casting its shadow but—for him, at least—resisting attempts to follow its traces, to uncover its secrets. The relationship takes on an added depth and complexity with the incorporation of photographs, often alluded to and used as source material in his writing. For Perec, whose motivation as a writer is founded on—and founders on—the tension between the need to remember and the impossibility of memory, photographs are seductive. In 1970, searching for an appropriate form and stimulus for the work that was to become *W; ou, Le Souvenir d'enfance*, Perec sought inspiration in an album of family photographs, hoping to find clues to the world of his parents, of relations, an entire culture and ethnicity from which he was excluded by historical circumstance; by what, in a typically ambivalent and ironic phrase, he described as "l'Histoire avec sa grande hache" [History with a capital H] (13).[3] In a note unpublished in his lifetime he writes, "Where should I start? On the point of giving up, I finally came across, in my files, a photograph album, from which I selected the seven oldest photos. I studied them for ages, even enlarging some of the details with a magnifying glass, then I went to watch the athletics on the television" (qtd. in Delage and Guigeno 124).[4] Notwithstanding Perec's recourse to visual evidence as a foundation for the reconstitution of memory, *W ou le souvenir d'enfance* contains no actual photographs. There are, however, references to a small number of crucially significant photographs—"I have one photo of my father and five of my mother" (41)—some of which are described in detail, only for the descriptions to be queried, modified, undermined in a series of equally detailed endnoted emendations. It is clear that these are photographs to be read, analyzed, in all their detailed discrepancies, rather than viewed, although their physical existence is attested by subsequent biographical study.[5]

It would appear, therefore, that in *W ou le souvenir d'enfance* Perec betrays an ambivalent attitude to the status of the photographic image. The text predates the publication of Barthes's *Chambre claire* by some five years, but for Perec the debate about the indexicality of the image, prefigured by Bazin as early as 1945 and encapsulated in Barthes's "ça-a-été," is precisely appropriate. The meager evidence of his family album offers incontrovertible proof, Barthes's "certificate of presence" (135) that is also an incontrovertible "certificate of absence." Just as Barthes, annotating a photograph of a nineteenth-century American assassin awaiting execution with the words "he is dead and he is going to die" (149), captures the temporal conundrum implicit in the image, so Perec is faced with the conundrum that the photographs he possesses offer simultaneous proof of presence and absence. The photographs of his father and mother, in attesting to their lives, are an incontrovertible guarantee of their mortality. Perec's dilemma is encapsulated in Barthes's "photography tells me of future death" (150), with its hint of an elusive future anterior tense.

In *W ou le souvenir d'enfance*, Perec's reticence in relation to this photographic evidence is matched by a reluctance to concede that what he writes about the images, or about anything else, might be in some way more worthy of credence. The text is marked by hesitation and uncertainty; the prevalence, throughout the referential, autobiographical chapters, of phrases such as "I don't know," "perhaps," "I'm not sure, it seems to me that," is inescapable (passim, particularly 21, 53, 58, 69, 73, 77, 94, 104, 117, 126). His lack of confidence in presenting a version of the past is clear: not only does he undermine the indexicality or even the iconicity of the images by failing to show them, in addition he refuses to present an unambiguous commentary on them. Instead he offers a commentary on an earlier written version, calling into question, point by point, a description written—it would seem—fifteen years previously: "The father in the photo poses like a father. He is tall. He is bareheaded, holding his kepi in his hand. His greatcoat comes down very low" (42). Seven pages later he adds a corrective, or destabilizing, note: "No, in fact, my father's greatcoat does not come down very low: it goes down to the knee. [. . .] Between the polished military boots—it is Sunday—and the hem of the greatcoat you can just make out the interminable puttees" (49). Describing the same photograph, Perec comments, first: "The father is smiling. He is a private. He is on leave in Paris; it is the end of winter, in the Bois de Vincennes" (42), only to revise his interpretation in the subsequent note: "Sunday, leave, Bois de Vincennes: there's no basis for any of this" (49). It is not memory of the event that is at issue here but memory of an earlier exegesis of the photographic record, and thus the validity of the written interpretation. Why this need, first to distrust the photographic evidence, and then to distrust and destabilize the written commentary? It is important to Perec that he invalidate the guarantee represented by the visual image; in undermining the evidential truth of the photographs, he disputes their status as "certificates of presence/absence" and therefore refutes the mortality that their unchallenged existence represents.

Flusser suggests that the age of photography—what he calls "the invention of technical images" (*Towards a Philosophy* 7)—marks a decisive turning point in the way we understand our relationship to the world around us, to the processes of history, to the structure of our culture. For Flusser, "[P]hotographs are simply the first among the posthistorical images" (*Writings* 131); they break the sequence of historical process. Conversely, "[L]inear texts explain images, they roll out their scenes into processes, and they order things into irreversible chains of causality" (127). This, I think, explains why Perec, whose every written word fails to address in direct terms the only subject that concerns him—the loss of his closest family, an entire cultural history, and therefore a sense of his own selfhood in the midcentury Holocaust—mistrusts the causality of the written word. This is why this most articulate of writers is always faced with the challenge of finding ways to say the unsayable, the "indicible," and why every text by Perec is authentically different from every other, except in the sense that each of his works is a fresh approach to the articulation of absence and loss. It explains, too, why the void at the heart of the childhood story in *W ou le souvenir d'enfance*, encapsulated in the admission that "I have no childhood memories" (13), is balanced, or matched, by the parallel fictional narrative of a regimented, dystopian society founded on an unending if improbable sequence of sporting competitions that move toward a nightmarish conclusion of random exterminations. Perec has no need to explain the purpose of this bizarre and unnerving fiction: as readers we are ensnared by the cold, precise, unemotional logic of his description, forced to make the connections as the two narratives converge but never quite meet, and to understand the necessary absence of memory, as Flusser's "irreversible chains of causality" come into their own.

Georges Perec, then, is defeated by History, the inevitability of which is only confirmed by the causal linearity of the written text. And photographs serve only as intimations of mortality. Yet Vilém Flusser suggests that photographs cut across the chain of causality that is historical process.

> Structurally speaking, [the image] is anti-historical. We do not experience our environment through images as a process, but as a scene. Even when we order images into rows (as in film or video), we experience the environment not as a process but as a sequence of scenes. For we are able to cut and paste the rows; not acting historically, but magically. Certainly, the photograph has succeeded in carrying the image into history; but, in doing so, it has interrupted the stream of history. Photographs are dams placed in the way of the stream of history, jamming historical happenings. (*Writings* 128)

What resources are available, then, to Perec, to exploit the anti- or posthistorical nature of the photographic image without succumbing to the countervailing impact of the photograph as, in Sontag's words, *"memento mori"* (15)?

In an interview conducted in 1979 and published under the title "Le Travail de la mémoire" [The Work of Memory], Perec speaks about the processes of memory and about his new project:

> I'm starting work with Robert Bober on a film about Ellis Island, in New York, near the Statue of Liberty. It was the reception center for emigrants between 1880 and 1940 and is now a museum. Millions upon millions of Europeans, especially Italians [and] Russian and Polish Jews, came through there. So it's more or less the melting pot of America, and we are going to make a film that will try to convey something of this movement that neither Robert nor I knew (because we stayed in France) but that we might have known and that was, as it were, a possibility for us, since Robert Bober came from Berlin and my parents came from a small town near Warsaw. So it's a study of memory, and of a memory that concerns us, even though it is not our own memory; it is—what shall I say?—very close to our own, and determines who we are almost as much as our own history. (85–86)

Perec has glimpsed, then, in this project for a film on the plight of the migrant facing the need to construct a new existence and a new identity the possibility of a narrative that runs parallel to that of his own life while at the same time remaining utterly unrelated to it. Perec's reference in *Récits d'Ellis Island* to "a probable autobiography" (55) suggests a note of wistful regret hard to reconcile with the negative-positive polarity that throws into sharp definition the distance between his experience and that of the millions of arrivals in the New World. There is a shift of tenses here: the future anterior embedded in the photograph as death foretold becomes a past conditional in the subjunctive mood: what might have been or could have been. There are perhaps comparisons to be made here with the suggestion of "negative" autobiography hinted at by Jacques Derrida in an essay titled "Comment ne pas parler: Dénégations" [How Not to Speak: Denials]. For Derrida, like Perec of Jewish origin, it would seem that the need to avoid speaking of himself springs from the realization that to do so would leave him vulnerable to being defined by others: "how can one do so without letting oneself be invented by others?" (Baker) but for Perec, the existence of the Other holds none of the same threat. It is instead the impossibility of situating himself in relation to the other—any other—that prompts the search for a narrative that explores what, but for the randomness of chance, might have been his narrative, and one that can be structured in such a way that the fog of a history pertinent to him might be pierced. Quotations from Raymond Queneau used as epigraphs in *W ou le souvenir d'enfance* foreshadow the theme of an impenetrable mist: "That mindless mist where shadows swirl, how could I pierce it? [. . .] This mindless mist where shadows swirl—is this then my future?" (7, 87). A preoccupation with the ways in which we relate to physical space and, in particular, empty, undifferentiated space where there is nothing to focus on, recurs throughout Perec's writing and suggests the limits of comprehension and the sense of impotence that results. Perec crossed the Atlantic by container ship on his way to film *Récits d'Ellis Island*. The several dozen Polaroid photos he took on the crossing show little but the blank expanse of the ocean receding in the mist and the minimal geometry of the vessel. Neefs and Hartje comment of these images that "the space is bare, open, captured in the slowness of time" (170) and point to the similarity with Perec's observation in

Espèces d'espaces [Species of Spaces]: "When there is nothing to arrest our gaze, our gaze is far-reaching. But if it meets nothing, it sees nothing. It can only see what it meets: space is that which halts the gaze, that which sight comes up against: an obstacle: some bricks, an angle, a vanishing point" (109). In similar vein, Reggiani describes "the referential evacuation" of these minimalist images where "a dissolution of form [. . .] appears to be a real aesthetic choice" (2).

As we have noted, no photographs are reproduced in *W ou le souvenir d'enfance*. In contrast, still photographs feature prominently in *Récits d'Ellis Island*. A brief opening sequence shows Perec turning the pages of an album containing a mixture of historic images of Ellis Island, of the Statue of Liberty, of turn-of-the-century migrants and photographs of Perec and Bober themselves involved in filming. The album is, in effect, a preamble, a sort of working plan or rudimentary index for the film, yet its format is precisely that of the family photo album that is the traditional repository of individual and collective memories. In contemplating this factitious album at the start of the film, Perec is highlighting his lack of those memories whose absence constitutes the motivation at the heart of the enterprise. The sequence is accompanied by Perec's voice-over reflections on that motivation:

> Whenever we told people in Paris that we were planning a film on Ellis Island, the question nearly everyone asked was: what is it about? In New York, the usual question was why—not why a film on Ellis Island, but why us? What did the subject have to do with the two of us, with either Robert Bober or Georges Perec?
>
> It would be forcing the truth to say that our aim in making this film was to find out why we wanted and needed to make it. All the same, the images and text that follow will

be obliged to deal not only with Ellis Island and what it was but with our own itinerary in getting there. (5)

From the start, then, the film is identified as a meditation on the motives of the filmmakers rather than a descriptive account of the experiences of European migrants arriving in their millions in the New World. The frustration of attempting to convey a sense of a site long fallen into disuse and disrepair, of even being able to imagine the lived human reality within the derelict buildings, is evident throughout Perec's commentary: "how can things be described? or talked about? or looked at?" (37). The most distinctive feature of the film's mise-en-scène, and one clearly intended as a strategy to bridge the gap between the present of filming and the historical reality, is the use of enlarged still photographs. They are not, however, exploited in the traditional documentary mode of the rostrum camera that simply scans and pans across mounted photographs; they are, rather, enlarged images of individual migrants, or groups of migrants, placed on the benches or against the railings of the deserted Ellis Island reception halls, caught from time to time by the filming camera as it wanders around the abandoned site, mute reminders of both presence and absence. These images function as punctuation marks in the camera's narrative journey, accentuating the emptiness and dereliction of their surroundings and evoking what Robert Desnos called "the irreducible relation between life and death that structures the photographic event" (qtd. in Cadava 11). In this way Perec and Bober were able to destabilize the distance from their subject in both temporal and spatial terms: historical evidence but also vivid reminders of a living presence rendered more vivid still by the mise-en-scène — dilapidation as a marker of the passage of time framing images that proclaim "ça-a-été": this has been. Perec, who is prominent not just as voice-over commentator but as visible participant in the film's narrative, watches traces of the past in the present of filming, so that the viewer is constantly confronted with the constructed, ironic nature of the images on view.

The photographs filmed by Perec and Bober, selected from a well-known collection of work by Lewis Hine held in the New York Public Library, are of individuals or in one or two instances family groups—mother, father, child, waiting patiently to be assessed for entry, or gazing in awe toward the Statue of Liberty across the water. The spoken narrative, however, is in sharp contrast to the images of hope and expectation. It tells of the triage process of medical assessment to which steerage-class arrivals were subjected, the swift demarcation, by a chalked, coded letter on the lapel, of those deemed unfit for entry by virtue of disability or suspected infectious diseases—often contracted in the insanitary conditions of the Atlantic crossing—such as tuberculosis and trachoma. It tells, too, of the three thousand suicides on Ellis Island in the thirty years from 1890 to 1920. The final sequence of the film is a slow, hesitant traveling shot along the disused, narrow, dark-timbered walkway leading to the ferry for Battery Park and Manhattan, silent but for the eerie clanging of the boat's mooring chains, eloquent in its evocation of the unknown, and of fear.

It now becomes clear that, as in *W ou le souvenir d'enfance*, Perec has constructed a narrative—a history—that, in failing to converge with his own personal history, leaves an imaginative space for that history to be glimpsed or felt. While it is clearly inappropriate to suggest that Perec is proposing a simple comparison between one view of Ellis Island and the extermination camps, the visual parallels with Alain Resnais's filmic exploration of memory in relation to camps such as Auschwitz in *Nuit et brouillard* are striking: the same slow traveling shots along dark, deserted corridors, the same understated, unemotional commentary that thrusts onto the viewer the responsibility to comprehend and to judge.

CONCLUSION: THE UTOPIC IMAGE

One still photograph in particular—the last in a long sequence as the camera pans slowly across the empty Ellis Island reception hall—seems to possess a resonance that goes beyond the purely historical. It is of a small girl—perhaps nine or ten years old, clutching a coin, an American penny—a symbolic right of entry to the New World. She is more or less the age that Perec's mother would have been if she had left Europe

8. Italian child finds first penny, 1926, Ellis Island. Series of photographic documents of social conditions, 1905–39. Photograph by Lewis W. Hine. Photography Collection, Miriam and Ira D. Wallach Division of Art, Prints and Photographs, The New York Public Library, Astor, Lennox and Tilden Foundations.

instead of staying in France and, subsequently, being deported to Auschwitz. The camera lingers on this photograph, accentuating its frozen moment in space and in time.

Flusser writes, "This space and time peculiar to the image is none other than the world of magic, a world in which everything is repeated and in which everything participates in a significant context. Such a world is structurally different from that of the linear world of history in which nothing is repeated and in which everything has causes, and will have consequences" (*Towards a Philosophy* 9). This "world of magic," endlessly repeated, represented by the photographic image, then, makes it possible to break free from the chain of causality to reveal what Flusser calls "the dormant utopic virtualities of photographs" (*Writings* 131). For Flusser, "the task of a philosophy of photography is to reflect upon this possibility of freedom [and upon] the way in which, despite everything, it is possible for human beings to give significance to their lives in the face of the chance necessity of death" (*Towards a Philosophy* 82). For Perec, the photograph seems to offer a similar possibility. First, in subverting the evidential nature of the photographic image in *W ou le souvenir d'enfance* by refusing to show it and by casting doubt on his memory of what it shows, he negates its association with mortality. Second, in exploiting the story of Ellis Island immigration to create a history that is parallel but unrelated to his own, supported by images that both embody and transcend the historical process, he taps into an alternative, utopian narrative devoid of both causes and consequences, hinting at the freedom of an endlessly repeated present.

NOTES

1. See, for example, Rancière for an analysis of the incommensurability of representation and reality in this context: "It could even

be said that unrepresentability lies precisely in the impossibility of an experience to be expressed in a language proper to itself" (142).

2. The obvious exception is Charles Baudelaire, although his comments were limited to its reception.

3. The English translation loses the menacing ambiguity of "sa grande hache," which, as well as indicating "its capital H," means "its great ax."

4. A reader familiar with the text will have observed that the casual reference to "athlétisme" in Perec's note carries an uncomfortable premonition of the "athlétisme" narrative that forms one strand of *W ou le souvenir d'enfance*, with its perverted aims and catastrophic consequences.

5. See, for example, Bellos. Also Lejeune, "La Genèse."

WORKS CITED

Adorno, Theodor W. *Gesammelte Schriften*. Ed. Rolf Tiedemann. *Kulturkritik und Gesellschaft* 10.1. Frankfurt am Main: SuhrkampVerlag, 1977.

Baker, Peter. *Georges Perec's "Negative" Autobiography*. (10 Feb. 2009.)

Barthes, Roland. *La Chambre claire: Note sur la photographie*. Paris: Gallimard Seuil, Cahiers du Cinéma, 1980. (*Camera Lucida*. Trans. Richard Howard. London: Jonathan Cape, 1982.)

———. "Le Message photographique." *Œuvres complètes*. Paris: Seuil, 1993. 1:938–48.

———."Rhétorique de l'image." *Œuvres complètes*. Paris: Seuil, 1993. 1:1417–29.

Baudelaire, Charles. "Le Public moderne et la photographie." *Salon de 1859. Œuvres complètes*. Paris: Seuil, 1968. 394–96.

Bazin, André. *Qu'est-ce que le cinéma?* Paris: Cerf, 1985.

Bellos, David. *Georges Perec: A Life in Words*. London: Harvill, 1993.

Cadava, Eduardo. *Words of Light: Theses on the Photography of History*. Princeton NJ: Princeton University Press, 1998.

Delage, Christian, and Vincent Guigeno. "Ce qui est donné à voir, ce que nous pouvons montrer: Georges Perec, Robert Bober et la rue Vilin." *Etudes photographiques* 3 (1997): 121–40.

Derrida, Jacques. "Comment ne pas parler: Dénégations." *Psyché: Inventions de l'autre*. Paris: Galilée, 1987. 535–95.

Flusser, Vilém. *Towards a Philosophy of Photography*. London: Reaktion, 2000.

————. *Writings*. Ed. Andreas Ströhl. Minneapolis: University of Minnesota Press, 2002.

Gunning, Tom. "Phantom Images and Modern Manifestations: Spirit Photography, Magic Theater, Trick Films, and Photograph's Uncanny." *Fugitive Images: From Photography to Video*. Ed. Patrice Petro. Bloomington: Indiana University Press, 1995. 42–71.

Hirsch, Marianne. *Family Frames: Photography, Narrative and Postmemory*. Cambridge MA: Harvard University Press, 1997.

Lejeune, Philippe. "La Genèse de *W ou le souvenir d'enfance*." *Textuel* (*Cahiers Georges Perec* 2) 21 (1988): 119–55.

————. *La Mémoire et l'oblique: Georges Perec autobiographe*. Paris: POL, 1991.

Martin, Elaine. "Re-reading Adorno: The 'After-Auschwitz' Aporia." *Forum* 2 (Spring 2006): 1–13.

Mulvey, Laura. *Death 24x a Second: Stillness and the Moving Image*. London: Reaktion, 2006.

Nadar. *Quand j'étais photographe*. Paris: Babel / Actes Sud, 1998.

Neefs, Jacques, and Hans Hartje. *Georges Perec: Images*. Paris: Seuil, 1993.

Nuit et brouillard. Dir. Alain Resnais. Argos Films, 1955.

Perec, Georges. *La Disparition*. Paris: Denoël, 1969.

————. *Espèces d'espaces*. Paris: Galilée, 1974.

————. "Le Travail de la mémoire (entretien avec Frank Venaille)." *Je suis né*. Paris: Seuil, 1990. 81–93.

————. *La Vie mode d'emploi: Romans*. Paris: Hachette / POL, 1978.

————. *W ou le souvenir d'enfance*. Paris: Denoël, 1975. (*W or the Memory of Childhood*. Trans. David Bellos. London: Harvill, 1989.)

Rancière, Jacques. *Le Destin des images*. Paris: La Fabrique, 2003.

Récits d'Ellis Island: Histoires d'errance et d'espoir. Dir. Georges Perec and Robert Bober. Paris: Institut National de l'Audiovisuel / Seuil, 1980. Illustrated screenplay, Paris: Hachette / Le Sorbier, 1981. New ed., Paris: POL, 1994. (*Ellis Island: Tales of Vagrancy and Hope*. Trans. Harry Mathews. New York: New Press, 1995.)

Reggiani, Christelle. "Perec: Une Poétique de la photographie." *Cabinet d'amateur* (March 2001): 1–32.

Sontag, Susan. *On Photography*. London: Penguin, 1979.

Wollen, Peter. *Signs and Meaning in the Cinema*. 3rd ed. London: Secker & Warburg /BFI, 1972.

THE SELF-PORTRAIT IN FRENCH CINEMA

REFLECTIONS ON THEORY AND ON AGNÈS VARDA'S
LES GLANEURS ET LA GLANEUSE

Agnès Calatayud

> Our lives are a series of self-portraits. We're constantly
> appraising ourselves, analyzing ourselves, but in a low-key
> and unassuming way.
> · AGNÈS VARDA, "Ciné-brocante"

"Intimate cinema," "personal cinema," "cinema of the 'I,'"
"cinema of the Self": all these closely related terms have been
used by film critics to categorize a diverse group of films over
the course of the last decade, a time when questions of identity
were more urgently posed than ever before. Suddenly, in the
1990s, "an interest in genealogy took hold of people. [. . .]
From all sides the need to know one's roots grew. Identity [. . .]
was becoming a major concern. [. . .] It was something that
people had to possess, rediscover, conquer, assert, express.
A precious and supreme asset," remembers Annie Ernaux

in *Les Années* [The Years] (152). This obsession with identity did not bypass French cinema: soon a wave of self-reflexive films embracing miscellaneous cinematic practices such as intimate visual diaries, genealogical quests, home movies, travelogues, personal essays, mockumentaries, fictions of the real, even "haiku portraits" was beginning to emerge. At the junction of these different introspective film practices, the self-portrait—once believed to be all but impossible in cinema—progressively developed into a film genre in its own right, probing the nebulous territory of the Self where personal experiences are interwoven with social, political, and cultural events. Some are "parallel films," or "UFOS" (unidentified filmic objects), strange experimental outputs of the "third cinema genre" championed by Vincent Dieutre, running in a continuous loop in modern art galleries and not shown in traditional cinemas. Others, which I will discuss in this chapter, are personal works, favorites of documentary festivals around the globe and generally shown in French art house cinemas or on French cultural TV channels (although lately they have been relegated to late-evening slots or have disappeared altogether from TV programs).

Building on the skilful and intuitive theories of Jean-Luc Godard, one of the few filmmakers to have reflected upon this genre, this chapter will outline the strategies employed by filmmakers to represent the embodied self on-screen. It will then propose a flexible interpretative grid in a bid to understand the creativity and the limits of these eclectic self-reflexive films. The chapter then goes on to apply the grid to key sequences of Varda's seminal documentary *Les Glaneurs et la glaneuse* [The Gleaners and I] (2000) which, apart from documenting the nearly forgotten practice of gleaning, is also an engaging, well-crafted, and revelatory self-portrait.

The self-portrait genre made its breakthrough in French cinema history in 1995 with Jean-Luc Godard's *JLG/JLG—Autoportrait de décembre* [JLG/JLG-Self-Portrait in December]. Godard explained at the time his wish to find out "how far he could push the limits of cinema and up to what point cinema would accept this" (Danel 30). It is interesting but hardly surprising to note that both Godard and Varda, whose long film careers started at the same time, have tried their hands at this type of filmmaking. Moreover, they are the only two directors to this day to have purposefully included the word "self-portrait" in the title of their respective films. Both are rightly conscious that their "signature"—their names, works, bodies, voices, and general fame—have long been familiar to filmgoers: Varda has always played a significant part in her films and Godard has often cast himself as "*Oncle Jean ou l'idiot*" [Uncle Jean or the idiot] in his (Baecque). Philippe Lejeune calls the awe that arises in the spectators when they recognize the artist's face "the self-portrait effect" (75).

At the other end of the spectrum, we find budding film-makers who, in their very first film, are also moved by the compulsion to test and prove their desire to make films, trying in the process to answer the eternal question of the true nature of cinema through a family anecdote. Antony Cordier's *Beau comme un camion* [As Beautiful as a Truck] (1999), in which he explores a working-class milieu from within and asks himself why he has become a filmmaker instead of following in the footsteps of his truck driver father, is a case in point. These new filmmakers are able to find their feet within the film world through a self-portrait before envisaging a career in cinema. They try to "take an interest in others by creating their own path, by escaping from the media and from fashion, by marking their own rhythm in the way they approach their subject matter," to quote Henri-François Imbert, a filmmaker with his own array of films all closely linked to his life story. Often accused of navel-gazing, self-portraits are in fact the exact opposite: a filmmaker who says "I" "engages the spectator in conversation" (Gheerbrandt) and then the filmmaker-character and his spectator-witnesses end up by discovering their "common emotions" (Kendall). In Jean-Luc Godard's own words: "After fifty years of cinema behind me, it is only natural that I should end up merging cinema with my own life and that of my contemporaries. Only cinema can bind together this 'I' and this 'we'" (Baecque).

Not all autobiographical films are self-portraits, and especially not those in which a filmmaker adapts his or her life or an episode of it for the screen, while handing over his or her own part to an actor, as in the case of the fruitful collaboration between François Truffaut and Jean-Pierre Léaud, for instance. Unlike an autobiography, the self-portrait is not a continuous narrative: "its main form is that of discontinuity, of anachronistic juxtaposition, of fragmented elements brought together" (Beaujour 9). Consequently, no scandalous personal details are revealed: in *JLG/JLG*, Godard anticipates that his spectators will be disappointed by the absence of revelations from his supposed "miserable little pile of secrets"—to use André Malraux's famous and disdainful expression. However, as Godard grumbles: "What you are watching is not an autobiography, but a self-portrait!" Against all odds, self-portraitists represent themselves "with humility and cautiously," warns Godard in *JLG/JLG*; "with discretion but objectively," specifies Agnès Varda ("Ciné-brocante" 32); with "tact and decency," adds the filmmaker Emmanuel Carrère in the moving *Retour à Kotelnitch* [Return to Kotelnitch] (2003). Paradoxically, the filmmaker's identity does not emerge unscathed from the making of a self-portrait: to represent oneself is a "painful and useless" quest (Belzane 3) that never reaches its aim, no matter who embarks upon it.

THE MAKING OF A SELF-PORTRAIT

According to Jean-Luc Godard, one creates a self-portrait first and foremost to "show oneself to others" (306) — "to make oneself public" said Montaigne in his time. For Nicolas Philibert, author of *Retour en Normandie* [Back to Normandy] (2007), it is to list and then make public the contents of one's "living memory": all past events mentioned in *Retour en Normandie* are taken from photos, various film clips such as home movies on Super-8 or digital camera, and the like. They are pulled out of oblivion, reworked by editing, and commentated upon here and now by a first-person voice-over, weaving in the process the fabric of a new film. Several generations encounter and question one another on-screen, and the confrontation of these different memories, corresponding to images of contrasting grain, interrogates the handing down of values, of know-how, of traditions within a family, a group, or society itself.

"To show oneself to others" also means to cross over the line and slip in front of the camera under one's own identity. But how can one be in front of and behind the camera at the same time? Filmmakers dodge this difficult question by playing hide-and-seek with their reflection, their shadow, their silhouette, which they track in multiple mirrors, windows, screens, magnifying glasses, even rearview mirrors, chanced upon while filming or opportunely placed in their path. The "I" desperately seeks its place in the world around it, but the image that the mirror reflects — the "indispensable tool" (Poiron 11) of the self-portrait — is never clear; its surroundings interfere with it; it is partial, deceptive, and disturbing.

The Other can also be embodied by an ancestor, as in Sabine Franel's *Le Premier du nom* [The First of the Name] (2000), or by a missing friend, as in Henri-François Imbert's *Doulaye: Une saison des pluies* [Doulaye: A Rainy Season] (2000), or even by a whole category of people, such as the various gleaners in *Les Glaneurs et la glaneuse*. This double is the focus of attention in the film, it is the mask behind which the filmmaker hides: the self-portrait thereby produced is oblique or indirect.

The making of one's self-portrait can also allow one to "examine one's own painting of oneself" continues Godard—that is to say, to consider with a certain critical distance the "films that were made" and the "films not [yet] made" (287) (that is, films that remain in drawers or that did not meet with public success, or even work in process, in particular the self-portrait we are watching). To compose her recent self-portrait *Les*

9. Agnès Varda: the artist in the mirror. Still from Agnès Varda's *Les Plages d'Agnès*.

Plages d'Agnès, Varda says she used all her other films "as a database" (Interview). A self-portrait is also a counterpoint, or an echo to one's own work, an "exercise in admiration" that allows its author to allude to the works of particular directors he or she considers as his or her masters or to those of inspirational figures like painters, writers, or philosophers. The filmmaker can then question his or her work, his or her art, and determine what pleasure he or she draws from making a film. Like painters who represent themselves in a studio surrounded by their own artistic accomplishments—standing in front of a canvas, brandishing a paintbrush, a palette in their hands—filmmakers portray themselves in the practice of their craft that Godard calls "his daily routine" (287): location scouting, filming, sitting at an editing table, receiving praise from their crew on the last day of filming or from the public during a preview, or even walking the red carpet at a film festival.

"To examine one's own painting of oneself" reminds us that *the body* of the artist in a self-portrait is primarily a fabricated image made out of paint or, when it comes to cinema, shadows and light. This invites us also to look at the film in terms of texture, of flesh, of the grain of the skin, of frames and forms, of colors and outlines, as if the artist portrayed in the film were standing in front of us. Finally, "to examine one's own painting of oneself" is to contemplate, long after, the timeless image that one has made of oneself at a precise moment of one's life: this film-mirror is an additional image to add to one's gallery of personal portraits. To juxtapose in the course of the film two or more self-portraits of oneself taken at various points in time is a common feature of self-portraits and a telling way, both for filmmakers and spectators, to assess the time that has passed between the two images and to revisit the "landscapes traveled through" (Godard 287).

The evocative titles of self-portraits in cinema are revealing of their author's concerns at the time of their making: *Corps étrangers* [Foreign Bodies] (Sophie Bredier, 2004), *Demain et encore demain* [Tomorrow and Again Tomorrow] (Dominique Cabrera, 1998), *Doulaye: Une saison des pluies, Histoire d'un secret* [Story of a Secret] (Mariana Otero, 2002), *JLG/JLG—Autoportrait de décembre, Le Filmeur* [The Man with a Camera] (Alain Cavalier, 2005), *Le Premier du nom, Les Glaneurs et la glaneuse, Mes toits et moi* [My Roofs and I] (Anne Morin, 2003), *Nos traces silencieuses* [Our Silent Traces] (Sophie Bredier, 1998), *Petite conversation familiale* [A Little Family Conversation] (Hélène Lapiower, 1999), *Racines* [Roots] (Richard Copans, 2002), *Retour à Kotelnitch, Séparées* [Separated] (Sophie Bredier, 2000), *Substitute* (Vikash Dhorasoo, 2006), to name just a few examples. Time (its inescapable passage, with death looming on the horizon, but also more prosaically the seasons and the weather), the past (its traces and memories), roots (filiation, origins, the family home, a family secret), the body and its double (the Other, the foreigner, separation), absence (the loss and the resulting pain) and, above all, the filmmaker's craft and passion for cinema are the threads from which a self-portrait is woven.

AGNÈS VARDA AND THE SELF-PORTRAIT GENRE

Agnès Varda's self-portrait, *Les Glaneurs et la glaneuse*, was "born out of her emotions at the sight of social deprivation in society around her, was spurred by the recent availability of a small digital camera and by her desire to film what [she] sees of herself: [her] aging hands and [her] graying hair. [Her] love of painting was also key. All of this had to match up and overlap in the film without betraying the subject that [she] wished to present: waste and junk" (Varda, "Glaneurs"). Here she underlines, among other things, the similarities between "forgotten, shriveled, and re-sprouting potatoes" (Barillet) and her own life, between their rebirth as works of art and her mocking of old age (she was seventy-two at the time of filming). Her wish to turn heart-shaped potatoes and junk into works of art through cinema echoes one of the characteristics of the self-portrait: a "found object [. . .] is turned into a self-portrait as the film develops. [. . .] The self-portraitist never knows where he or she goes, what he or she is making" (Beaujour 10).

This documentary received such a sympathetic reception that in 2002 Varda returned to get news of the gleaners whom she had filmed two years previously. The result of this trip is *Les Glaneurs et la glaneuse: Deux ans après* [The Gleaners and I: Two Years Later] (2002). One year later, at the Venice Biennale and then at a Parisian art gallery, Varda offered another variation on this theme: exchanging her director's hat for that of a conceptual artist, she presented the installation *Patatutopia*: at the entrance to the exhibition, a giant potato topped with an image of Varda's face welcomed the visitors, thus taking to its limit her identification with the "heart-shaped potatoes," stars of her initial documentary. If *Les Glaneurs et la glaneuse* caused such a surge of affection in its audience and unleashed such creativity in its director, it is indeed for its highly topical subject matter, undertaken from an original point of view, and for the charm of its poignant characters. But would she have received so many public accolades and so many awards around the world if the film had not gone beyond a narcissistic project and tackled a subject "bigger, more general, more important, more universal, even" (Varda, "En ligne")?

Agnès Varda has been interested in self-portraiture for a long time. This is evident from two early items featured in her 1994 autobiographical experimental book, *Varda par*

Agnès [Varda by Agnès]. Like a Byzantine mosaic—doubt-less a tribute to her Greek ancestors—her *Autoportrait 1954* [Self-Portrait 1954] (*Varda par Agnès* 10) gives us a foretaste of the "portrait-puzzles" of Mona in *Sans toit ni loi* [Vagabond] (1985) and of Jane Birkin in *Jane B. par Agnès V.* [Jane B. by Agnès V.] (1986–87). It also anticipates the mosaic and kalei-doscopic self-portrait obtained with her small digital camera in *Les Glaneurs et la glaneuse*. Playing with the features of this camera, she amuses herself by zooming in on a part of her face, fragmenting it, adding double exposures to it, and making it disappear. This reinforces the fact that "any portrait [is] impossible to make. [. . .] Through the play of attractions, through the exchange of glances, through different points of view, and through fragmentary information, one never stops moving the pieces of the puzzle, reconstituting an image made with fragments that fit together. One seeks the pieces one by one, as if in an investigation" (*Varda par Agnès* 159).

In her *Autoportrait à Venise, parmi quelques hommes de Gentile Bellini* [Self-Portrait in Venice, among Some of Gentile Bellini's Men] (1960), Varda takes a photograph of herself in profile in front of Bellini's painting. Everything about her—the way she is posing, the color of her skin, the way her hair is done, the cut and fabric of her jacket—gives her the air of one of those important Venetians. She repeats this procedure in *Les Glaneurs et la glaneuse*: she has herself filmed with a sheaf on her shoulder in the pose of Jules Breton's *La Glaneuse* [Woman Gleaning], which hangs in the Arras Museum of Fine Art. She admits that, so far as the title of her film is concerned, "*la glaneuse*, that other gleaner, is me. I'm willing to relinquish a few ears of corn in order to hold the camera" (*La Glaneurs*). In 2006 she used this device again in her exhibition L'Ile et elle [The Isle and Her] at the Cartier Foundation in Paris for her installation *Les Veuves de Noirmoutier* [The Widows of

Noirmoutier].[1] This time, Agnès Varda appropriates for herself one of the fourteen small screens that show continuous footage of different widows of Noirmoutier. But unlike the other widows, whose testimony we can hear through headphones, Varda remains mute, her cheeks bathed in tears, seated next to an empty chair marking the absence, one can surmise, of her dead husband, the filmmaker Jacques Demy. In her self-portraits Varda manages both to blend into the scenery and to highlight what makes her so distinctive.

LES GLANEURS ET LA GLANEUSE: THE BEAUNE ALTARPIECE SEQUENCE

This staging takes a more complex turn in the solemn sequence of the Beaune Altarpiece in Burgundy that features in *Les Glaneurs et la glaneuse*. Varda films the principal side of Rogier van der Weyden's *The Last Judgment* (1443–50). Through this scene, Varda highlights *Les Glaneurs et la glaneuse*'s inner clockwork and metronomelike rhythm: as the title of the film indicates, the camera swings regularly from the gleaners to Varda to the point that they become confused in our thoughts. This sequence is also a nod to the self-portraits in *assistenza* of the painters of the past who signed their paintings by including themselves in the guise of a saint or of an anonymous member of the crowd, one whose penetrating look, calling to the viewers, reveals his or her real identity.

First of all, Varda's camera sweeps across the altarpiece and shows us the men and women who "rise up out of a dried and cracked brown landscape" (Gondinet-Wallstein 18), leaving their tombs, their arms raised toward the sky, their hands together in a sign of entreaty or gratitude. We cannot help but make a connection between this "brown landscape" painted by van der Weyden and the wintry scenes in *Les Glaneurs et la glaneuse* or in *Sans toit ni loi*, between the destiny of those who rose from the dead in *The Last Judgment* and the destiny of the different gleaners in the film. Then the camera lingers on the long silhouette of the Archangel Michael in the center of the altarpiece. The enormous magnifying glass moves across it, stopping here and there to bring certain details to the attention of the visitors, returning regularly to his serene face. Likewise, in the film, between two sequences on the gleaners the camera pauses on the face of the filmmaker and films her in close-up. Like the angel who holds the horizontal bar of the scales of Judgment in his right hand, Varda makes the same gesture when she holds her camera at eye level. She deliberately accentuates her resemblance to this angel as if filming herself in a mirror, a facial shot strikingly resembling that of a *photomaton* [passport photo], as I will discuss later. Moreover, the archangel maintains, according to a specialist of this painting, a "strictly neutral stance [. . .] as indicated by his expressionless face and by his left hand, which carefully moves away so as not to exercise any undue influence on the weighing of the scales" (Gondinet-Wallstein 19). Varda does not weight her judgment either in her interviews with the gleaners; "she keeps emotion at bay" (Varda, "C'était si beau" 58), as the playwright Jean Vilar taught her at the beginning of her career: her questions to the gleaners are always direct and free of prejudice. Varda identifies with the angel who is perched on top of a hill against a pastoral background right in the middle of the picture. Like him, she has a slightly "raised" position in comparison with the other gleaners whose group she has infiltrated: "I slipped in and out between [the gleaners] as if, by virtue of the act of filming, I, too, were a gleaner" (Varda, "Glaneurs").

In the past, the glorious scenes of the Beaune Altarpiece were displayed only on Sundays and on religious festivals. When the altarpiece was closed, it revealed somber scenes aimed at frightening van der Weyden's contemporaries in times of raging wars and plagues when people feared the end of the world and divine punishment. Similarly, Varda shows the camera her own "dark side" in the following sequence, called "Vieillesse. Cheveux. Mains. Prendre la route" [Old Age. Hair. Hands. Hit the Road], a title that precisely summarizes her journey in *Les Glaneurs et la glaneuse*. It is a rather disturbingly intimate scene: she combs her hair harshly and exposes the white roots that hair dye cannot hide. The digital camera allows such intimacy because it eliminates distance: without pity it captures the slightest wrinkle on Varda's bare face and erases any illusion of youthfulness.

LES GLANEURS ET LA GLANEUSE AS AN "AUTO FILM FESTIVAL"

The dissonant music of Joanna Bruzdowicz, with its haunting cello, softly accompanies the film and Agnès Varda's varying moods. The director has also "physically permeated" the music just as she has the film by signing her initials on the score and naming it "Agnès-Vieillesse" [Agnès Aging]. Made up of "sounds that were juxtaposed but that never truly resolved themselves into harmony" (*Varda par Agnès* 270), the music reinforces the idea of the impossible portrait, of the identity forever "unformed and unresolved" (Montaigne book 3, chapter 2). But the other sizeable section of music in the film, which also expresses a variety of emotions, is called *Rap de Récup* [Scavengers' Rap]. Much of it is sung by Agnès Varda, whose voice on the soundtrack denotes her ownership of the music in the same way as her initials on Joanna Bruzdowicz's score. Listening to the music, we become aware of its many disparate constituent parts; it "samples" Joanna Bruzdowicz's music in that it "recycles" or has "gleaned" its notes from Agnès-Vieillesse. The rap enables her to give vent to her "hatred" of a society that "discards people just as it discards things" (Varda, "Le Journal"). Most important, it is a means of expression commonly linked with an inner-city world of deprivation and marginalization: in other words, the kind of environment that the gleaners themselves come from. One of the distinguishing features of rap music is the very specific way it speaks, combining different forms of inner-city slang, plays on words, and the bringing together of different sounds. Against the film's staccato rap rhythm, unusual words are united to form unusual, whimsical images. When Varda encourages us to put different images together, she makes us create a "mental rap" of these images: the traveling director and the homeless, her disquiet and the social unease, the *restos du cœur* [soup kitchens, called "restaurants of the heart"] and the heart-shaped potatoes, the furrows and the wrinkles, the mildew and the old age, the translucent flesh of the potatoes and the skin, death and the agricultural harvesting machine, gleaning and filming, recycling and editing. This "flow," this rhythm, calls forth images from her previous films: the gleaners and the grape pickers of *Mur murs* [Mural Murals] (1981) or Mona in *Sans toit ni loi* who is picking grapes in the vineyards; the shellfish gatherers in *La Pointe courte* (named after a small Mediterranean village) (1954); the down-and-outs in *L'Opéra mouffe* [Diary of a Pregnant Woman] (1958) wandering through Paris's rue Mouffetard; the island of Noirmoutier as it appeared in *Les Créatures* [The Creatures] (1966) and in *Jacquot de Nantes* (1991). The endless sunflower fields seem to come straight out of *Le Bonheur* [Happiness] (1964); the image of the dead sheep lying in a field resonates with the corpse of the goat in *Ulysse* (1982); when on her return home Varda exclaims, referring to her plants: "One has dried up, the other hasn't," it evokes the title of her film *L'Une chante, l'autre pas* [One Sings, the Other Doesn't] (1977). When she marvels, looking at her hand, that she had also filmed the hand of Jacques Demy in close-up in *Jacquot de Nantes*—"I am an animal that I don't understand"—she quotes word for word a line from her *Documenteur* [Documenteur: An Emotion Picture] (1981). One also remembers, though, the hands of the rue Daguerre shopkeepers and the agile hands of Mystag the magician in *Daguerréotypes* (1976). When Varda says of a group of young homeless people that they are "without a roof in the face of the law," she only uses the literal meaning of the title of her own *Sans toit ni loi*. In the anguish that torments her throughout the film, one recognizes Cléo's in *Cléo de 5 à 7* [Cléo from 5 to 7] (1962). The facetious tone of the commentary, the choice of picturesque characters, the successive road signs that turn this film into a kind of treasure hunt, the music that hesitates between jazz and cacophony, all these features were already present in her two very first documentaries, *O saisons, ô châteaux* [Oh Seasons, Oh Castles] (1958) and *Du côté de la côte* [Over on the Coast] (1958).

Thus from allusion to quotation, *Les Glaneurs et la glaneuse* resembles a career-summarizing film, a kind of "auto film festival." However, even though Agnès Varda's style and her pet concerns are clearly recognizable in this film, what is even clearer is the unexpected way in which she tackles them. A self-portrait should be seen "among other works from the same painter" confirms Philippe Lejeune; "it is there that it breathes, that it comes alive, that it truly means something, through likeness and difference, through reminders or breaks" (84). *Les Glaneurs et la glaneuse* thus distinguishes itself from other Varda films inasmuch as it seeks to make us share the chances, the opportunities—she calls chance her "first assistant"—and the enchantments that are at the origin of the film's sequences. The film is interspersed with unforeseen encounters; traffic diversions direct the protagonists onto uncharted territory and byroads; the filmmaker shares with us in wonderment the special features of her small digital camera. We therefore constantly see at play the mysterious and unexplained "truth of inspiration" (Varda, "7P"), which uplifts an artist—Varda in this case—and renews her art. In other words, in the making of *Les Glaneurs et la glaneuse*, Agnès Varda manages successfully to catch a glimpse of her true self and to expose it to us.

While *Les Glaneurs et la glaneuse* fits perfectly into Varda's filmography, it also inscribes itself into the history of cinema. To emphasize this filiation, Varda takes us to the Domaine de la folie, Etienne-Jules Marey's home near Beaune. According to her, he was the "absolute forefather of filmmakers" and it was in this house that Marey experimented with his photographic rifle. In the Domaine de la folie, Varda meets Jean Noël-Bouton, one of Marey's descendants and "the only wine grower to show any concern for what would become of the gleaners. [. . .] We are proud to be a part of the Marey family," she says, as if cinema itself encourages people to take the first step toward reaching out to others. In the juxtaposition of the images obtained by Marey's camera and the digital camera, the complete history of cinema unfolds, from the inspired inventions of "the eleventh hour workers," as Laurent Mannoni calls them, to today's high-tech developments that facilitate introspection and direct contact with the real. In her homage to Marey, Varda slips in the name of his assistant Georges Demenÿ as well as several images from a little film he made with a *chronophotographe* (a camera perfected by Marey in 1888). Demenÿ films himself for several seconds in close-up: he laughs while curling his moustache. In other clips not shown here, he plays the violin, he laboriously writes his name, he smokes. These close-ups could be considered as the first filmed self-portraits, of which *Les Glaneurs and la glaneuse* is the worthy heir.

In 1957, while filming *O saisons, ô châteaux*, her documentary
on the Loire Valley castles, Agnès Varda visited Chambord,
Francis I's Renaissance abode. In the royal wing of the castle
there is a mysterious little room whose purpose is still disputed by historians and which they call, for lack of a better
word, an oratory. On the oratory's wooden door there appears
the king's monogram and his emblem, the salamander, has
pride of place. These symbols, as well as the fleur-de-lis and
the three-knot strings—revealing the eternal bond between
the king, his mother, and his sister—cover the walls and the
vaulted ceiling. Maybe when Varda visited the place, the guide
pointed out to her what only a trained eye can notice: the
imperial crown—not the expected royal crown—hanging over
the monogram of Francis I. Yet Francis I was never to become
an emperor, unlike his archenemy the Holy Roman Emperor
Charles V. Historians have maintained that this room is both a
summary of the king's actual life and of his hostile, undeclared
dreams. Francis I therefore had good reason to call Chambord
his "true home." In *Les Glaneurs et la glaneuse* the sequence
filmed in rue Daguerre in the fourteenth arrondissement of
Paris, where Varda returns after a trip to Japan, can be seen
in the light of the Renaissance king's self-portrait, carved in
the white stone of his castle. The house in rue Daguerre, hers
since 1951, serves also as her production office, her editing
studio, and her shop for selling her DVDs. It is thus the ideal
place, as symbolic as one could find, where the pieces of the
puzzle can be assembled, where the different facets of Varda's
"I" crystallize, even if the portrait still remains fragmented.
As she retakes possession of her domain, one soon notices
that it is her own "state of conservation" that she assesses. In

this "beehive," as she nicknames it, where cinema and daily life make good companions, the mistress of the house, in perfect osmosis, ages like her walls and fades like her plants: her destiny, written on her own skin, is also engraved on and between these four walls.

In *Les Glaneurs et la glaneuse* Varda also chronicles one of her trips to Japan. For a European, traveling to Japan can be truly disorientating. In Japan a European tourist is confronted with a world he or she is unable to unlock, and in which he or she has lost his or her bearings. The customs and traditions, the language, the writing, the food, everything is something else; it is all a source of wonder and discovery. The journey therefore leads us to question everything we had previously taken for granted. This sequence is an aside whose length and style—the house is plunged into a darkness that is redolent of Varda's absence from it—tells us that this is something more than a mere return from a journey. We realize that this is a return that concerns herself, the distinction between her private and public life, her *cinécriture*.

From the moment Varda opens the door to her den, she films an inventory of its contents: the need to take stock, to establish lists, is one of the characteristics of self-portraiture. She checks to see what kind of state her house is in, comparing its present condition with how she remembered it when she set out on her travels. It is also a way of assessing the difference between two films, to compare their themes and treatment. Varda has already tackled the theme of the gleaners, or poverty, in her other films; how does this latest film differ from the rest of her work?

Her journey toward a new understanding of herself leads her to a frame hanging on a wall containing the black-and-white photograph of two children, a boy and a girl. Who are they? Do they share a family likeness? She tries with difficulty to film their faces and her own simultaneously and to get them into the same picture. This produces a series of images similar to the contact-sheet effect in *Varda par Agnès*, a photomontage on the life of the novelist Elsa Triolet (85). The children seemed from their photograph as though they were looking after the house in Varda's absence. She returns to them to check that they are there, as if their disappearance would automatically bring about her own.

This journey has brought us to her "workshop." Her little red case is the equivalent of the little digital camera packed full of images. She unpacks her red suitcase like Mary Poppins, randomly pulling out the souvenirs she has brought back from Japan. They serve to "reanimate" this trip—an expression Varda uses to refer to the photographs that make up her film *Salut les Cubains* [Hello, Cubans] (1963)—in just the same way as the fortune-teller's tarot cards foretold Cléo's Paris itinerary. Furthermore, when Varda opens her suitcase, our eyes are immediately attracted to a walking map of Tokyo resting clearly on top. Little lacquered boxes, paper decorations, a piece of material depicting the *maneki-neko* (a Japanese cat used as a good-luck charm, a wink at Zgougou, Varda's beloved cat seen in the opening credits of the film), an assortment of postcards showing sumo wrestlers, different types of sushi, Mount Fuji, Hokusaï's famous "Wave," portraits of Utamaro's actresses, a Zen garden. This Prévert-like inventory is what any tourist having just returned from Japan would be likely to unpack. Therefore, the following sequence is all the more personal when, leaving aside the Japanese clichés and brandishing a book on which we manage to distinguish a famous photo of the actor Gérard Philipe once taken by her, Varda, in a tone of hushed confidentiality, takes us back to the beginnings of her career: from 1948 to 1960 she worked with Jean Vilar as the official photographer for the Avignon Theatre Festival.

Continuing with her great unpacking, she shows a series of *photomatons* of herself to the camera, in which she maintains a similar, familiar pose. It is this type of photo—in which she seems to have always worn the same haircut, the same style of clothing, sometimes with a camera in her hands—which over the years has illustrated the numerous articles and book covers about her around the world, including the recent DVD *Varda tous courts* [Varda Shorts/Just Varda] (2007), which playfully features a selection of these photos on its cover. These passport photos "paint her in imperishable colors" (to paraphrase the formula that Albrecht Dürer inscribed on his self-portrait in 1500) and give the impression that time has no hold on her. In *Jane B. par Agnès V.*, she had told Jane Birkin the story of the death mask of *L'Inconnue de la Seine*, an unknown woman who was found drowned in the 1930s. Then she had already wondered whether "the only true portrait [was perhaps] a death mask [. . .] the face completely still, looking straight ahead. That's essentially what remains of a person. [. . .] Or maybe what remains of a person is a passport photo, always motionless, always looking straight ahead" (voice-over). Thus this fixed face, frozen, that she has fashioned for herself will forever represent her. By contrast, the film seems to us to be entirely directed toward life, toward movement; it remains as a work in progress: it is forever in a state of becoming. Two such disparate means of "immortalizing oneself" create a doubt in the spectator: who is the real Agnès Varda, which image truly represents her?

She next pulls from her suitcase a Japanese article on the film *Jeanne et le garçon formidable* [Jeanne and the Perfect Guy] by Olivier Ducastel and Jacques Martineau (1998), slipping in a photo of her son Mathieu Demy, one of the lead actors of *Jeanne et le garçon formidable*. Further articles pulled from the suitcase show us the face of her daughter Rosalie, a cinema costume maker, and again of Mathieu, in vignette under the portrait of their mother: like Marey's descendant, she presents her family tree—a family tree that is intertwined with the history of cinema. The display of these press clippings—her life related in indecipherable signs for those who don't read Japanese—reminds us, if there was a need, that every portrait remains enigmatic and obscure. Finally, Agnès Varda distractedly leafs through the program from the Japanese film festival from which she has just returned, as if while turning the pages, the memories linked to her trip and to her life in general were escaping.

At the end of this sequence, Agnès Varda films her hand, "which is old as [she is] old" (Varda, "Ciné-brocante"), and comments with delight, "What was so amazing was that in this large store in Tokyo, there were Rembrandts [. . .] and then, here is my hand in all its detail. In other words, that was my project, to film one hand with the other hand, to go into the horror of it. That's what I find so amazing. I feel as if I'm an animal. Actually, it's worse than that. I'm an animal I don't recognize. And here's Rembrandt's self-portrait. But it all comes down to the same thing—it's always a self-portrait."

Rembrandt, who used himself as a model hundreds of times in paintings, etchings, and drawings, is the tutelary figure of filmmakers who indulge in self-portraits: they always seem to find one way or another to refer to him in their films. In effect, in a self-portrait, nothing should stop the artist from substituting

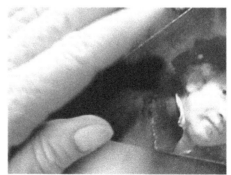

10. Agnès Varda: I'm an animal I don't recognize. Still from Agnès Varda's *Les Glaneurs et la glaneuse*.

the hands for the face, even if the latter is the one body part that is commonly used. The hand here is representative of Agnès Varda in her entirety just as she portrayed herself: she reunites in one image both the woman who ages and the filmmaker in the exercise of her art in a way reminiscent of Louise Bourgeois in the photograph titled "The Artist's Hands Placed over One of Her Etchings" (2003), for instance. Additionally, unlike the hair or the face, hands cannot be so readily disguised or made up. They are therefore more expressive than the face of their owner's age, of the harshness or ease of his or her personal and working life. And, in the case of artists, it is clearly their hands that are the primary tool of their work. Agnès Varda, who loves filming long shots of the characters' hands, often compares her work as a filmmaker to that of an artisan and her films to craftwork.

When one discovers the impossibility of knowing oneself, except in fleeting moments, what, then, can a self-portrait represent if not a whirlwind of questions, a collection of diverse and contrasting representations that simply deepen the examination of oneself? According to Pascal Bonafoux, author of a book on Rembrandt: "Rembrandt's series of self-portraits [. . .] do not offer us a resemblance, but a challenge. Rembrandt [. . .] represents a worried and perhaps disenchanted consciousness that is facing up to the irreparable." Similarly, Agnès Varda, following the example of the prolific Dutch painter, wants to "face up to death" with this self-portrait. Thus, if *Les Glaneurs et la glaneuse* is a memento mori, it is also and above all a challenge thrown at the grim reaper by a gatherer of images.

A self-portrait in cinema is a complex work, difficult to put together. It highlights the place of a filmmaker and of cinema in general at a particular point in time. It takes stock of the evolution of film techniques and of the ways a given society views questions of identity. Self-portraitists do their utmost to cast an objective, almost forensic eye on themselves, examining the ruthless work of time on them and in them. A self-portrait forces filmmakers to unravel the strands of their lives and their inspiration, to weigh up what they have achieved, and to prove to themselves that their desire to make films has not dulled. "An exercise in virtuosity" (Poiron 8), for budding directors, the self-portrait serves as a calling card; for those more seasoned filmmakers, it circumscribes their territory and looks back upon the furrows they have ploughed in cinema.

CONCLUSION

Self-portraits in cinema are incredible pieces of work and cannot by their nature be formatted. In a world where films tend to be funded only if they follow a tried and tested pattern, which brings in viewers and therefore financial rewards, the future of the self-portrait in French cinema may well be threatened. However, for aficionados of the self-portrait in cinema there does remain at least one country purveying such works of art: Japan. For example, Naomi Kawase, author of many personal films such as *Sky, Wind, Fire, Water, Earth* (2001), and the great Takeshi Kitano have been successful. His recent self-portrait trilogy (*Takeshis'* [2005], *Glory to the Filmmaker!* [2007], and *Achilles and the Tortoise* [2008]) is hilarious and refreshing and an indication that this young film genre is not yet heading for marginalization.

NOTES

1. *Ile* is a homophone for *il* [him].

WORKS CITED

Baecque, Antoine de. "Godard: Le cinéma a été l'art des âmes qui ont vécu intimement dans l'Histoire." *Libération* 6 Apr. 2002.
Barillet, Anaïs. "Agnès Varda." *Kuntaspekte*. (30 Dec. 2010.)

Beaujour, Michel. *Miroirs d'encre: Rhétorique de l'autoportrait.* Paris: Seuil, 1980.

Belzane, Guy. "Le Même et l'autre." *Textes et documents pour la classe: L'Autoportrait* 853 (2003): 3.

Bonafoux, Pascal. "L'Enigme de Rembrandt." *Le Monde de Clio.* 1999. (30 June 2008.)

Danel, Isabelle. "Une Bouleversante expérience intérieure." *Télérama* 8 Mar. 1995: 30–31.

Ernaux, Annie. *Les Années.* Paris: Gallimard, 2008.

Gheerbrandt, Denis. "Alter Ego." *France inter radio* 2 Jan. 2004.

Les Glaneurs et la glaneuse. Dir. Agnès Varda. Paris: Ciné-Tamaris, 2000.

Les Glaneurs et la glaneuse: Deux ans après. Dir. Agnès Varda. Paris: Ciné-Tamaris, 2002.

Godard, Jean-Luc. *Jean-Luc Godard par Jean-Luc Godard.* Vol. 2, 1984–98. Paris: Cahiers du Cinéma, 1998.

———. *JLG/JLG—Autoportrait de décembre.* Paris: Gaumont, 1995.

Gondinet-Wallstein, Eliane. "Le Jugement dernier." *Hors-Série Beaux Arts Magazine: Hôtel-Dieu-Hospices de Beaune* (Sept. 2000): 18–21.

Imbert, Henri-François. "Autour d'Henri-François Imbert: Hommage et rencontre." *www.abc-toulouse.net.* 2003. (12 Nov. 2003.)

Kendall Anna-Célia. "Le Partage des larmes." *www.lussasdoc.com.* 2004. (5 Jan. 2004.)

Lejeune, Philippe. "Regarder un autoportrait." *Moi aussi.* Paris: Seuil, 1986. 73–86.

Malraux, André. *Antimémoires.* Paris: Gallimard, 1967.

Mannoni, Laurent. *Le Grand art de la lumière et de l'ombre.* Paris: Nathan, 1994.

Montaigne, Michel de. *Essais.* 1582.

Poiron, Jean-Marc. "Narcisse peintre." *Textes et documents pour la classe: L'Autoportrait* 853 (2003): 6–12.

Retour à Kotelnitch. Dir. Emmanuel Carrère. Paris: TF1 Vidéo, 2003.

Retour en Normandie. Dir. Nicolas Philibert. Les Films du Losange, 2007.

Varda, Agnès. "C'était si beau, le théâtre populaire!" *Nouvel observateur* 5–11 July 2007: 56–59.

———. "Ciné-brocante." Interview with Frédéric Bonnaud and Serge Kaganski. *Inrockuptibles* 4 July 2000: 28–32.

———. "En ligne avec Agnès Varda." *www.cahiersducinema.com.* 12 June 2008. (30 Dec. 2010.)

————. "Les Glaneurs et la glaneuse." *www.cinema-de-recherche.org.* 18 Sept. 2000. (5 Jan. 2004.)

————. Interview by Virginie Apiou. ARTE 9 Sept. 2008.

————. "Le Journal des spectacles." *Europe 1 radio* 26 Sept. 2000.

————. Presentation of "7P., cuis., s.de b." 1984. *Varda tous courts: Intégrale des courts métrages d'Agnès Varda.* Ciné-Tamaris Vidéo et Screen, 2007. DVD.

————. *Varda par Agnès.* Paris: Cahiers du Cinéma et Ciné-Tamaris, 1994.

10

AUTOBIOGRAPHY IN *BANDE DESSINÉE*

Ann Miller

Since the 1990s, autobiography has been an increasingly important genre in *bande dessinée*, or French-language comic art.[1]
This chapter will begin by tracing the origins of this tendency
and the publishing context within which it has flourished, that
of the emergence of alternative comics presses in France since
the 1990s. It will go on to consider Lejeune's pact in relation
to *bande dessinée* autobiography, and then to focus on three
aspects of the resources of the medium that are relevant to
an analysis of autobiographical work: the inscription of subjectivity, the rendering of temporality by spatial means, and
the proliferation of the self. It will finally look at some critical
responses, personal and political, to the emergence of this
genre in *bande dessinée*.

THE ORIGINS OF THE AUTOBIOGRAPHICAL
TENDENCY IN *BANDE DESSINÉE*

If we take a wide definition of autobiography, then the most obvious candidate for the first example produced in the medium of *bande dessinée* is probably Hergé's *Tintin au Tibet*, written in 1960. In *Le Pacte autobiographique* [The Autobiographical Pact], Philippe Lejeune uses the term "autobiographical space" in a discussion of the claims made by certain authors, such as André Gide and François Mauriac, who have produced both autobiographical and fictional work and who have asserted that it is in the latter that the essential and deeper truths about themselves are to be found (41).[2] They thereby, according to Lejeune, indirectly extend the autobiographical pact, which becomes a "fantasmatic pact" inviting readers to read all their works as situated in the space between autobiography and novel (42–43). Hergé did not write an autobiography, but he did give a book-length interview to Numa Sadoul between 1971 and 1972, and was very actively involved in the production of the final typescript, making numerous amendments, as Sadoul explains in *Entretiens avec Hergé: Edition définitive* [Conversations with Hergé: Definitive Edition], an augmented version of his original book that came out in 1989 (10–12). In a discussion about *Tintin au Tibet*, Hergé explains how, at the time of its writing, he was suffering from extreme anxiety, which appeared in his dreams as a terrifying whiteness (178). A rather more frank interview with Benoît Peeters is published in Peeters's *Le Monde d'Hergé* [Hergé's World]. The interview took place in 1982, the year before Hergé's death, and in it he attributed these dreams to the anguish and guilt occasioned by his separation from his first wife, describing the album as a way of exorcising the "demon of purity" that was haunting him (212). Certain critics have chosen to read other works by Hergé according to the terms of the "fantasmatic pact." Pierre Assouline, in his biography titled *Hergé*, attributes the creation of the monstrous and castratory diva Castafiore to Hergé's need to settle scores with his first wife (317–18).

If, however, we take the narrower definition of autobiography as outlined in Lejeune's original formulation of the pact, as implying the identity of author, narrator, and character (14), then the first example of *bande dessinée* autobiography would be an interview with the artist Jean Giraud (also known as Moebius) in 1974 in the fanzine *Schtroumpf* [Smurf]. The interview, drawn by Giraud in *bande dessinée* format, consists of questions from his out-of-frame interviewer, Sadoul, about his childhood, early career, and artistic influences, which are answered by the artist in the speech balloons that he gives to his drawn self. Giraud offers a highly interesting visual take on preoccupations that surface in autobiographies across all media and that would persist in the work of later *bande dessinée* autobiographers. The head of the Giraud character is portrayed in the opening panel as a skull, onto which he puts a mask in the form of his own head with its immediately recognizable long hair and hippie glasses (8). One could have imagined the opposite: a removal of the mask and a laying bare of the "real" Giraud beneath the appearance of the cult figure. Instead, Giraud chooses to put the mask on and so calls into question the notion that there is an essential self that can be portrayed. In the remainder of the interview, the character appears at his drawing board before adopting various other forms: as a rock (complete with its own speech balloon), as a dapper-looking man with an intriguing sticking plaster on his forehead (suggesting that any psychic wound will be well hidden) (15), and in women's clothes (more housewife than vamp, offering improbably steamy revelations about the "burning kisses" of his fellow artist Mézières) (13). The notion of self-exposure is further derided when the character shows his buttocks but refuses to discuss his inner life (13, 15). The interview stages a mutually disparaging encounter with his younger self, who has no vocation as a *bande dessinée* artist, professing instead his ambition to become a knife grinder (10–11). This emphasis on the less than prestigious career prospects offered by the medium prefigures the concern over status that would become a preoccupation of later *bande dessinée* autobiographers.

Giraud's example remained an isolated one, in spite of the fact that at around the same period autobiographical comics were flourishing in the American underground. In *Alternative Comics: An Emerging Literature*, American comics theorist Charles Hatfield speaks of "a new level of adult and achingly personal content" in work such as Harvey Pekar's *American Splendor*, which began in 1976, scripted by Pekar and drawn by several artists including Robert Crumb. The textual Harvey, with his acerbic observations and resolutely blue-collar outlook, was a radical departure from what Hatfield calls the "corporate comics hero" churned out in various superpowered guises by the comics industry (111). In France, though, autobiography played little part in the adult *bande dessinée* culture that thrived in the political and social ferment of the post-1968 period.

Moreover, by the end of the 1970s, many of the collectives set up by artists had been bought out by mainstream publishers, and during the 1980s much of *bande dessinée* became (re)infantilized and conservative, devoted to escapist genres like heroic fantasy. Among a few significant exceptions was the work of Edmond Baudoin, who may be credited with inaugurating the tendency that would become so conspicuous in the next decade. Baudoin produced his first autobiographical album, *Passe le temps* [Time Passes], in 1982 for the one noncommercial *bande dessinée* publishing house that still existed in the 1980s, Futuropolis, and he continued in this vein through the 1990s and beyond. His work has none of the derisiveness and evasiveness characteristic of Giraud. He uses an unfinished graphic line to convey emotional rawness, and he obsessively draws places, often places from his childhood, that are filtered through nostalgia and loss.[3]

The 1990s saw the advent of a number of small presses that were determined to contest the dominance of the mainstream.[4] The first of these was L'Association, based in Paris and founded in 1990. Some of the earliest autobiographical work was produced by members of the Association collective. Mattt Konture, who had already produced autobiographical texts for various magazines including *Psykopat* in the late 1980s,[5] continued to give graphic form to his sense of his own abjection and to his death wish in a prolific output that included *Ivan Morve* [a play on words from "mort-vivant," zombie] in 1996. Jean-Christophe Menu's *Livret de phamille* [Family Record Book], which focuses on the tensions of marriage and fatherhood, appeared in 1995, while the first volume of David B.'s six-volume *L'Ascension du haut mal* [translated into English as *Epileptic*] came out in 1996, and the sixth and final volume in 2003. In it he recounts a childhood and adolescence dominated by his brother's increasingly severe illness.[6] L'Association has also published much work by other artists, including Joann Sfar's freewheeling notebooks, beginning with *Harmonica* in 2002, and, most famously, between 2000 and 2003, Marjane Satrapi's *Persepolis*. These four volumes, subsequently made into an animated film, chronicle the artist's childhood in Iran: born into a liberal professional family, she saw the revolution against the shah usurped by the ayatollahs, spent her adolescence in a French school in Austria, and then returned to Iran to find her country devastated by the war with Iraq and still in the grip of the fundamentalists.

L'Association were followed in 1991 by Cornélius, also based in Paris, which published Lewis Trondheim's *Approximative-ment* [Approximately] in 1995, a confessional portrayal of his own neuroses and an ironic take on the *bande dessinée* milieu.[7] In 1994 Ego comme X, set up in Angoulême, devoted itself exclusively to autobiography, including Fabrice Neaud's remarkable *Journal*, the first volume of which came out in 1996 and the fourth in 2002, and which documents the arduous-ness of struggling against socioeconomic marginality and homophobia. In the same year Amok appeared in Paris and Fréon in Brussels: they went on to merge into Frémok in 2002, and their catalogue includes avant-garde autobiographical work like Kamel Khélif's *Ce pays qui est le vôtre* [This Country Which Is Yours], which at times verges on abstraction. The number of independent publishers that have come into being since the 1990s has been estimated at around forty (Ratier, "2005: L'Année de la mangalisation" 6–7). Apart from Ego comme X, their output is not restricted to autobiography: it has included other nonfictional genres such as reportage as well as fictional work, often experimental. However, autobi-ography has loomed large in most of their catalogues.

Thierry Groensteen attributes the sudden surge in autobio-graphical *bande dessinée* to a reaction against the formulaic work of the 1980s, which incited young artists to produce more personal material. He also points to the influence of the American forerunners as well as a general cultural climate marked by "the flourishing of a narcissistic sensibility and the multiplication of works about the Self" (61). The Canadian *bande dessinée* theorist Bart Beaty proposes a further develop-ment of Groensteen's first point, arguing in *Unpopular Culture* that autobiography legitimizes cartoonists as auteurs rather than as mass-cultural hacks. He emphasizes that, while auteur theory may no longer be fashionable in film studies, back in the 1950s and 1960s it had legitimized film as an object of academic study. He acknowledges that *bande dessinée* artists may be "arriving late to the party" in relation to the status of auteur, but suggests that their adoption of autobiography to valorize their underrated art form may be compared to the use of the genre by certain minority groups who only attain subjecthood when the concept itself becomes contested (143).

Conversely, in his discussion of the American branch of the autobiographical genre, Hatfield points to a blurring of the boundaries between countercultural and mainstream production. He claims that, paradoxically, autobiography is highly adapted to the marketplace since it possesses some of the very features that make for the commercial success of mainstream comics: a continuing character and the possibility of sequels and series. Hatfield refers to a "collusion of mainstream commercial habits and countercultural sensibility" (112). In France the paradox has become particularly apparent in the case of *Persepolis*. The first volume was originally published with a print run of 3,000, as attested by an editorial by Menu in the Association's magazine *Lapin* [Rabbit] in 2002 (9). The official website for the film version states that the series as a whole has now sold 400,000 copies in France and 1,200,000 in the rest of the world. It is responsible for over 60 percent of the turnover of L'Association, according to a 2007 web article by *bande dessinée* journalist Gilles Ratier, but the organizational adjustment needed to manage the Satrapi operation has been considerable on the part of a publishing house that has never prioritized commercial success.

For some, autobiography has ceased to represent an artistically ambitious current in the medium. Neaud has announced in a published exchange of correspondence with Menu that he intends to cease working within a genre that has become as formulaic as any other,[8] appropriated by a plethora of thirty-somethings uniformly, if vaguely, leftish, recounting pseudo-intimate anecdotes, often in the form of *bande dessinée* blogs

(454–55),[9] for the benefit of the same group of "pimply male virgins" who used to read heroic fantasy (460). For Neaud, autobiography has no value unless it puts the author in danger (460). Menu suggests that it would be better to call these examples "sociobiographies," because they do not express the relationship that one individual has with the social world, but simply correspond to the profile of the target readership (457).

THE PACT: THE NAME, THE FACE, AND THE ARTIST'S HAND

In *bande dessinée* a verbal/visual medium, the identity of the extratextual author (whose name is on the cover), the narrating "I," and the character can be, and almost invariably is, established verbally. This can happen either through dialogue—in *Approximativement*, Trondheim is greeted by "Bonjour Lewis!" as he arrives in a restaurant (6)—or in some other way: Vincent Vanoli includes his own name in the Vanoli family tree in *Pour une poignée de polenta* [For a Handful of Polenta] (15), a meditation on the relations between different generations in a family of Italian immigrant origin. The issue becomes more complicated in the case of Konture, who, in his early work, embodies different aspects of himself in variously named characters. However, in *Ivan Morve* the eponymous character, angered by the artist's decision to change his features (on the grounds that the post-punk graphic style in which he is drawn has become outdated), rips off a mask, revealing himself as an identical double of the artist's own drawn character, shouting, "I-van Morve is Mattt Kontu-reu!"[10]

The *bande dessinée* reader is, though, likely to seek further evidence of identity in the form of a resemblance between the drawn character and its extratextual model. In his discussion of textual autobiography, Lejeune makes a distinction between identity, the factual basis of the pact, and resemblance, "a secondary aspect," arguing that the authenticity of a first-person account is not annulled by distortion and forgetting (39–40). In a medium where the self is represented visually, however, the question of resemblance, in the narrowly defined sense of physical likeness, necessarily becomes salient. In "Photosfictions," an article on first-person cinema, Roger-Yves Roche articulates the spectator's sense that, in that medium at least, reference and resemblance are interdependent: "What help is a proper name in cinema, what can I do with it if I can't match it up with a reference, a referent? So it would seem that in cinema it is the face that acts as the proper name" (192).

Roche's question about cinema seems pertinent to *bande dessinée*, even if, in a medium that is not based on mechanical recording, resemblance is a matter of degree, and artists may be concerned to give shape to an inner sense of self as much as, or more than, to outward features. At one end of the scale, Neaud draws himself, like his entourage, with an almost photographic realism. He does, nonetheless, sometimes depart from this: for example, in the first volume of the *Journal*, after the departure of his lover, Stéphane, who is unable to reciprocate his feelings, Neaud, diminished, draws his own face as scratched over and blurred (65). This loss of definition, occasional in Neaud's work, is systematic in Manu Larcenet's *Presque* [Almost], which recounts the horror and brutality of events that occurred during his military service, and in which the artist draws himself and others as not much more than circles on sticks, or as smudgy and indistinct. Trondheim, whose chosen title "Approximativement" is significant, avoids grappling directly with the question of physical likeness by drawing himself and his entourage as birds and animals. In an (unpaginated) epilogue, they are invited to comment on how far a resemblance has been achieved. Fellow *bande dessinée* artist Charles Berberian says that he would not have seen Lewis as a cockatoo, or himself as a badger, but admits that "Lewis's vision of things is accurate."

Any visual equivalence established between drawn character and extratextual model does not of itself guarantee that the latter has produced the image: in an online article, Jan Baetens has pointed out that, given the relative autonomy of verbal narrator and visual "graphiateur," which we can anglicize as "graphiator," these two functions could be split, allowing for an autobiographical *bande dessinée* to be drawn by an artist other than the subject. As we have seen, this possibility is actualized in the work of Harvey Pekar. Pekar's case is exceptional, though, and in the French examples that we will discuss, the extratextual model is invariably also the graphiator. The question remains as to how this identity is established.

In "Regarder un autoportrait" [Looking at a Self-Portrait], Lejeune argues that there is nothing in a self-portrait to distinguish it from a portrait of the painter done by a fellow artist: only the name on the label can do this. However, he concedes that an image of an artist holding a brush and facing a canvas will induce a "self-portrait effect" (137–40). *Bande dessinée* autobiography includes many such metarepresentative panels showing the character at the drawing board or, in some cases, simply the metonym of the drawing hand, with previous and subsequent panels confirming that the hand belongs to the artist/character.

It would seem, then, that the pact can be both visually and verbally realized in autobiographical *bande dessinée*, which allows not only for the identification of the extratextual model with the drawn character and as the source of the dialogue in speech balloons, but also with both the verbal narrator of voice-overs and the graphiator responsible for graphic line, composition, framing, and layout. The medium therefore escapes the difficulties outlined by Elizabeth Bruss in a famous article, "Eye for I: Making and Unmaking Autobiography in Film," in which she set out to demonstrate that there was no cinematic equivalent of autobiography. Bruss asserted that the identity of author, narrator, and protagonist is "shattered" by film, which "forbids that the same person can be both the figure on the screen and the one whose consciousness is registering that figure" (297).[11] In *bande dessinée*, a nonmechanical (and so nonsimultaneous) means of reproduction, the artist's view of events, remembered and re-created, can include the artist him- or herself without giving rise to the logical inconsistency that worries Bruss when the person thought to be behind the camera suddenly appears in the frame. Moreover, the artist's perspective cannot be equated with the mere optical positioning of the camera. The "impersonality of the cinematic eye," a further concern for Bruss (308), is replaced by a subjective vision, traced on the paper by the artist's hand. In the following section we will discuss some of the ways in which subjectivity enters into *bande dessinée* autobiography.

SELECTIVITY AND MODALIZATION

Bruss develops her argument by cataloguing various resources of language, essential in her view to the construction of an autobiographical self, and lacked by film. We will begin this section by taking some of Bruss's comparisons and applying them to *bande dessinée*. She makes the point that "truth-value" cannot be achieved by the mere imprint of external reality on the screen and claims that "images lack the articulation and hence the selectivity of sentences; they do not distinguish between subject and predicates in a way that allows us to discriminate between the essential and the accidental" (301–02). It is true that in the *bande dessinée* panel people or objects cannot be separated from their attributes, as they can in language (a drawn person is simultaneously both a person and a tall or short person), but selectivity is nonetheless a key resource of a medium whose representational system is based on metonymy: in Dupuy and Berberian's *Journal d'un album* [Journal of an Album] Berberian's Beirut childhood is conveyed by a few palm trees overshadowed by war planes (2).[12] The background may be omitted altogether, as in a panel from Morvandiau's *D'Algérie* [From/About Algeria] showing a telephone that brings the news of the shooting of his uncle and three fellow Catholic priests in Tizi Ouzo. The details of the surroundings, suddenly irrelevant, are faded out to white.

Bruss pursues the question of truth-value by contending that it must be assessed in relation not only to veracity but also to sincerity. She asks what in the image would allow for gradations of commitment: voice-over can cast doubt on the image, but nothing within the shot itself can be identified as an expression of doubt (303). Not only can *bande dessinée* employ a textual equivalent of voice-over, it also has just such a modalizing capacity within the images. In *Journal 4* Neaud varies levels of iconicity within a single panel, drawing a landscape with careful precision at the edges but rendering the central section as mere outlines, and comments explicitly on this gradation in detail, referring to *bande dessinée* as "a new way of hierarchizing memories" (109). In *D'Algérie*, concerned with public as well as private memories, Morvandiau introduces a recurring motif of a small village by a river, the palm trees and buildings repeated more imprecisely as they are reflected in the water. The reappearance of both the bold and the murkier image at various points in the album evokes the more troubled recollections and *non-dits* underneath the official narratives.

11. The fading of memory. From *Sentiers battus*. © 2002 Vincent Vanoli and
Ego comme X.

Degrees of doubt or certitude, and the fading of memory, may also be registered by the lowering of iconicity from one panel to the next. In *Sentiers battus* [Well-Trodden Paths], Vanoli depicts his childhood exploration of the forest beyond the fenced-in boundary of his parents' garden before returning to the security of the house as evening falls. In the final image, he suddenly distances himself: the house appears as a mere sketch above a caption saying, "And I make everything disappear into the white of the paper" (24).

Bruss also raises more generally the question of the inscription of subjectivity into the image, using the example of grieving: she argues that while it is possible to film a grieving person, there is no filmic equivalent of the expression of grief by the filmmaker (303). *Bande dessinée*, in contrast, has a variety of ways of suffusing the image with emotion. In general, the medium allows for considerable permeability of inner and outer worlds. Less dependent than film on the realist illusion, it can simply introduce conscious or unconscious elements of mental life into the external reality of the scene. In *Journal 3* Neaud can draw whirling dancers, birds, and angels in the background to convey the ecstasy of a prolonged conversation in a café with Dominique, the object of his passion (43–47), just as in the first volume of *L'Ascension du haut mal*, David B. can show his childhood self swept out of his bed by a typhoon, as the terror of a nightmare spills over into his waking life (4).

In some cases, subjectivity is expressed through the breakdown of representation. Line drawings dissolve into a scribbled jumble to portray Dupuy's mental disintegration during a crisis in his marriage (11). Elsewhere, the collapse of representation may be still more radical: as he approaches Dominique's flat, Neaud's extreme apprehension is expressed through a large expanse of white on the page, spattered with traces of ink and, within the panels, by streaks of white paint against a black background (290–91).

If the creation of an autobiographical self depends on the potential of the medium for selectivity and modalization, then, we hope in this section to have shown that *bande dessinée* has resources that can be compared to those of language. We will go on in the next two sections to look at the complex effects that can be achieved first in relation to time, and second in relation to the sense of the self as discontinuous or split.

TIME AND SPACE

The emotional expressivity of the medium is increased by the necessity of representing time through spatial means, and in particular by the indeterminacy of the temporal value of the interframe space, allowing for the speeding up or slowing down of the rhythm of recounting. Very marked ellipsis can have a potent effect. In *Pour une poignée de polenta*, Vanoli begins an account of a visit home to his parents by a sequence in which time is excised unobtrusively between panels, in a *bande dessinée* version of continuity editing: he arrives at the station, is next seen in his father's car, and then inside the house. Suddenly, though, there is an abrupt change of both direction and rhythm. A chasm opens up between panels as the story plunges back into the past: Vanoli is a child and his parents are once more youthful and vigorous (42–44).

Temporal indeterminacy can operate not only between but also within panels. We have referred above to the possibility of varying the level of iconicity in a single panel to imply greater or lesser clarity of recollection. The graphic resources of the medium can also invest the layers of time and memory with affective force. In one of the episodes of *Le Côté obscur du dimanche après-midi* [The Dark Side of Sunday Afternoon], Vanoli draws a walk with an artist friend across a wasteland on the edge of a formerly industrial suburb of Nancy, past an abandoned factory and derelict houses. The title of the episode, "Commémoration," alludes to the fact that the walk took place on 11 November, but it also refers to the merging of time frames: "I feel sensations that I have already experienced rising in me." These sensations arise not from the events depicted, which are indistinct, but from the materiality of the swirling lines and the shadow play on the page.[13] To borrow terms from Deleuze's discussion of Francis Bacon, Vanoli creates here the intensity of the "figure" rather than the merely illustrative or narrative "figurative" (12).

Baudoin, who led the way in *bande dessinée* autobiography, also creates a sense of the overlapping of past and present through the material qualities of the image: this often involves a collage method, where fragments of a sketchbook are pasted onto the surface of the page. The spatialization of memory carries a strong erotic charge in Baudoin's work: in *Terrains vagues* [Wastelands], a landscape is not only pervaded with nostalgia but identified with the sensuality of the woman's body that is juxtaposed to it on the page.

CONTINUITY AND METAMORPHOSIS,
BETWEEN AND WITHIN PANELS

The sense of continuing identity is precarious for any *bande dessinée* character, given that it is drawn anew in each panel. This very instability makes the medium peculiarly apt for the portrayal of the autobiographical self. The dialectic between iteration and transformation, on which the medium depends, may be compared to the simultaneous will-to-form and the desire for open-endedness alluded to by Michael Sheringham in relation to literary examples of autobiography. Sheringham says that in order to redress a sense of amorphousness, the autobiographer may fetishize a particular manifestation of selfhood, a kind of scale model, and make it stand for totality. He refers to this as a "homunculus," and says that it may, for example, be a nickname, like Sartre's "Poulou" (6–7). The term seems very apposite in designating the drawn selves of *bande dessinée* autobiographers: Menu's character always wears a striped jersey, Konture's has his dreadlocks, and Trondheim not only always draws himself as a cockatoo, but as one with a permanent frown. However, notwithstanding any unvarying visual traits, Neaud insists in his correspondence with Menu that the subject of an autobiography never simply coincides with a "character": the subject is never a finished essence but "a process, a becoming that is under construction" (472).

The discontinuity of the subject that is built into the medium offers a powerful resource for expressing this open-endedness. In autobiography, the potential for metamorphosis from one panel to the next may be exacerbated.[14] Hatfield argues that the display of successive, and disparate, versions of the self in comic books amounts to what he calls "ironic authentification" precisely because of its denial of any authentic and irrefutable identity (125). The transformation may take the form of an idealized self-image: when, in *Pour une poignée de polenta*, Vanoli goes to Italy, where some of his family members still live, he likes to imagine himself as a predatory Latin womanizer for the duration of four panels (33), a fantasy that becomes altogether more persistent in Guillaume Bouzard's auto-derisive *The Autobiography of Me Too* (an English title for a work written in French), in which the character repeatedly mutates into the persona of the irresistible stud Ramón.

Elsewhere, the self may suddenly appear as it is seen by others; in *Krokodile Comix II* Konture is preoccupied by how he is seen by women and more sexually successful men: he becomes a woodlouse (10) when his wife rejects him for a hard-line ecologist and, in *Cinq heure du Mattt* [Five O'Clock

in the Morning/Five: Mattt's Time], some kind of indeterminate vegetable when a woman appraises him as a potential
partner.

A number of *bande dessinée* autobiographies express the
notion of split identity in another way: not by the transfor-
matory mechanism of the interframe space, but by allowing
successive selves to inhabit a single panel. The sequential
mechanism of the medium operates according to the convention that the character remains unaware of his or her past and
future selves in adjacent panels, although this is a mechanism
that has been disrupted since the 1970s by artists like Fred
and Gotlib, who allow their characters to climb back into
previous frames (see Gravett). Autobiographies may similarly
transgress the convention that different versions of the self
do not meet. Following the example of Moebius, they may
stage an encounter between child and adult selves: this happens when Berberian's childhood self turns up to reproach
him for using his itinerant childhood as a pretext to justify
his need to hoard old *bande dessinée* albums (9–10).

The conceit of the child as conscience may be replaced by

12. The proliferation of the self within the panel. From *Approximativement*. ©
2001 Lewis Trondheim and Cornélius.

a simple doubling of the self. This is the case of Julie Doucet, whose conscience makes an appearance in *Ciboire de Criss!* [Christ's Ciborium! a Québécois expletive] to rebuke her not for the squalid state of her flat, as a terrifying superhousewife figure had done previously, but rather for being too inhibited and straight. Trondheim takes the principle of multiplicity considerably further in *Approximativement*, splitting into two initially, to admonish himself for his lack of culture, but subsequently splitting again as he finds more and more aspects of his character to deplore, including his paranoia and his vindictiveness, until these versions of himself turn collectively against the conscience-figure, claiming that he has no right to judge them (84–85).

In the case of Killoffer, in *Six cent soixante-seize apparitions de Killoffer* [Six Hundred and Seventy-six Apparitions of Killoffer], it is not the superego that initiates the doubling but rather the id unconstrained. It remains held in check for the first part of the book, while there is still a verbal voice-over: it is still possible here to suppose that the different Killoffers represent the artist at different moments in time, even if these are not demarcated by frame boundaries, as he engages in various unremarkable everyday activities such as working and cooking. Once the voice-over has died away, though, the character starts to proliferate in an alarming way, with numerous versions of itself trashing his flat and engaging in bouts of complicated group sex, before they are overcome by food poisoning and the ensuing violent explosions of various bodily substances.

THE POLITICS OF EXPOSURE AND SELF-EXPOSURE

We will conclude this essay by considering some issues raised by the deployment of *bande dessinée* as a medium for autobiography: firstly, the offense that may be taken by the artist's real-life entourage and secondly, the adverse reactions aroused by what has been taken to be a retreat into self-obsession.

All autobiographers are likely to have to confront the extra-textual consequences of working in a genre that, according to the terms of the pact, is read as referential. For *bande dessinée*, the recognizability of family and acquaintants is a further difficulty. A literary autobiography can be sparing of descriptive details, and film has the possibility of re-creation using actors. The problem is treated with inventive disdain by Konture, who draws his wife's new partner, angered by previous portrayals, with a balaclava over his head in *Tombe* [Tomb/Fall] and, for good measure, replaces his name with "God." He does, though, later recount in *Cinq heure du Mattt* how he had changed certain physical details of his wife and daughter in *Headbanger* in order to respect their anonymity. Boulet, in his autofictional *Notes: Le Petit Théâtre de la rue* [Notes: The Little Street Theater], draws his parents as the "Barbapapas" cartoon characters "in order to respect their privacy," and for the same reason draws his former Spanish teacher as Bernadette Chirac and an ex-girlfriend as Lucy Liu (65–67). Neaud steadfastly refuses any such solution. *Journal 3* offers a mise en abyme of the issue, showing Dominique's embarrassment when some of his friends come across a series of drawings of him by Neaud, in which he figures as the object of the artist's desiring gaze (146), and subsequently his fury when he discovers that his image has been reproduced and circulated as the target of Neaud's scorn in a short *bande dessinée* titled *Le Doumé: Vers un machismo cultivé* [Doumé: Toward a Cultivated Machismo] (213). Neaud's response to the torrent of rage unleashed by his subject is to draw him over and over again in a long sequence of *Journal 3*, every indignant expression and posture carefully delineated or, in some cases, the eyes covered by a cache, parts of the image not inked in, or the panel simply left blank. The arbitrariness with which Neaud makes these selective omissions seems to announce that these images do not belong to Dominique: they belong to the artist (292–310).

While individuals have charged the *bande dessinée* version of the genre with invading their privacy, it has elsewhere been criticized for the absence of a wider referentialism. In his correspondence with Menu, Neaud alludes to the reception of *bande dessinée* autobiography, claiming that it has been relegated to the journalistic categories of "narcissism," "navel-gazing," "egocentrism," "self-exposure" (461–62). Some *bande dessinée* autobiographers feel vulnerable to this accusation. Konture in particular is appalled by his own narcissism. In *Printemps automnes* [Spring Autumns], he draws a speech balloon containing only the letter "j" for "je" [I], blocking his drawn character off from the world of politics, culture, and life itself, and in one page of *Cinq heure du Mattt*, in a section that details his parallel work as a musician and his taste in rock music, he systematically blanks out all first-person pronouns

13. The graphiator deplores the need to exhibit himself as character. From *Cinq heure du Mattt*. © 2001 Mattt Konture and L'Association.

and possessive adjectives from the text. In the same album, he shows himself waking at night, screaming, "Aagh! How can I exhibit myself as much as this?!? It's grotesque!"

He goes on to lament his weariness at drawing himself over and over again in keeping with the conventions of the medium, even experimenting with the replacement of his undeniably good-looking face with an older, craggier version. However, he pleads that writing is the only way that he can stay alive; having felt himself to be a zombie since his mother's death when he was a child, *nombrilisme*, or navel-gazing, is his only link with her. Killoffer, on the other hand, feels no need for any such justification and he goes as far as to dedicate his book to himself, "Without whom this Work would not have been possible."

The reproach of "egocentrism" is, in any case, surely unfounded. It is quite simply inapplicable to certain *bande dessinée* autobiographies that are overtly political: this is clearly the case of Satrapi's *Persepolis*, which takes in not only contemporary Iranian politics but centuries of Iranian history, and of Morvandiau's attempt to understand how his own family history is related to official narratives of colonization and decolonization in Algeria. Although more muted in tone, Vanoli's work is haunted by its sociopolitical context, the loss of a tradition of industrial labor in northeastern France. Neaud's own journals are implicitly political through their challenge to heteronormativity, which is all the more striking because of the elegance of the graphic line that he brings not only to his detailing of his experience of homophobia, including gay-bashing incidents, but also to his portrayal of various aspects of his lifestyle such as cruising. More generally, as Menu has argued, the adoption of autobiography as a genre by the small presses was in itself political because it defied the mainstream publishers by opening up new territory for the medium ("Avant-garde" 176).

Unlike the journalists referred to by Neaud, Hatfield has a positive take on the idea of autobiography as self-exposure. He refers to the "radical intimacy" of autobiographical comics, including psychosexual and scatological details, as part of an authenticating strategy that can validate their social and political observations (114). Examples abound in the work that we have discussed and, arguably, the disregard for the conventional boundaries of what can be shown is part of a more general refusal of orthodoxies. Neaud's emotionally resonant depiction of his sexual encounters and fantasies has been contrasted by Loïc Néhou of Ego comme X with the "impersonal, formulaic fantasies" marketed by traditional "adult" *bande dessinée* (2). Doucet similarly disturbs normative representations of the female body, celebrating not only embodiment but bodily fluids, to the extent that in *Ciboire de Criss!* she floods the street with her menstrual blood when she runs out of Tampax. "Radical intimacy" is by no means guaranteed by the display of sexual acts and body parts and functions, of course. A trek through *bande dessinée* blogs currently available may well involve a few unrewarding detours around bedrooms and bathrooms, but artistic experimentation and personal and political questioning are very much alive, particularly among female artists. Caroline Sury's exploration of the deep resentments and renunciations generated by the taking up of parental roles, *Bébé 2000* [Baby 2000], and Dominique Goblet's portrayal of the silences and emotional violence within family life, *Faire semblant, c'est mentir* [Pretending Is Lying] offer the rawest kind of self-exposure.

CONCLUSION

This chapter began by surveying instances of the autobiographical turn that has marked *bande dessinée* production since the 1990s before assessing the resources that the medium can mobilize in the construction of an autobiographical self. It was noted that identity between the *bande dessinée* artist and character is normally established through face as well as name, even if identity does not presuppose photographic resemblance, and that metarepresentative panels habitually testify to the implication of the artist's own hand and eye in the production of the drawings. The inherent selectivity of the medium was considered, along with its capacity for modalization, allowing the narrating instance to register varying degrees of certainty or uncertainty, and to imbue the visual as well as the verbal narrative with subjectivity. The potential for distending or collapsing time, between and within panels, can have a strong affective charge, while the discontinuous nature of the medium makes it particularly suited to the expression of a sense of self that is fragmented and never definitive: the built-in multiplicity of the self works against any fixity of the autobiographical subject.

Although certain artists have explicitly linked their own life stories to larger historical narratives, it was suggested, following Menu, that the political dimension of this apparently self-regarding genre may lie in its challenge to the limitations imposed on the medium by the stranglehold of the mainstream and, following Hatfield, a link was made between radical self-exposure and the disturbance to sociopolitical conformity. We noted the concern expressed in some quarters that groundbreaking artistic and personal exploration, with all its risks, may have given way to banal exhibitionism. However, we would contend that, within a medium that has received scant critical attention, a body of work of astonishing originality and quality has been produced, and we would urge readers who are unfamiliar with the primary texts to discover them for themselves.

1. I will use the French term here to preserve the cultural specificity of the French-language texts that I discuss, even though work of similar ambition and depth produced in English (mainly by American artists) is categorized as "comic strip," "comics," or "commix."

2. The original references are to Gide (278) and Mauriac (14).

3. See Groensteen's "Les Petites Cases du moi: L'Autobiographie en bande dessinée" [The Little Me Panels: Autobiography in Comic Strip] for a detailed discussion of the antecedents of autobiographical *bande dessinée* in France and an analysis of the examples published by independent publishing houses in the early 1990s.

4. The setting up of alternative comic strip presses was not confined to France but was a Europe-wide phenomenon in the 1990s. Bart Beaty's *Unpopular Culture* surveys and analyzes the whole range of European small-press output.

5. Collected together in *Printemps automnes* [Spring Autumns] in 1993 and reprinted in an expanded version in 2001.

6. David B. left the Association collective in 2005.

7. Trondheim was a member of the Association collective, which published some of his subsequent autobiographical work in the form of four *Carnets* [Notebooks] between 2002 and 2004. He left L'Association in 2006.

8. Neaud argues that the word "genre" should not apply to autobiography, implying as it does a code and "autobiographemes," but goes on to say that, for this very reason, it is entirely appropriate for much of the current output (Neaud and Menu 455).

9. The website *annuaireblogbd.com* listed 723 *bande dessinée* blogs when consulted on 2 August 2008.

10. Most of Mattt Konture's albums, like some others of those to which we will refer, are unpaginated. Where no page reference is given, this is the reason.

11. Bruss's contention has, as one would expect, been widely disputed: see, for example, Bellour, who specifically takes issue with Bruss's argument, and Esquenazi and Gardies, the title of whose edited collection, *Le Je à l'écran* [The I on the Screen], asserts the existence of the cinematic first-person that she calls into question.

12. Dupuy and Berberian, who usually write as a team, departed from this practice in this book, which takes the form of a *bande dessinée* diary, the "making of" one of their fictional albums and, ultimately, of the *Journal* itself. Each writes separate episodes, each of which is paginated separately.

13. Vanoli has spoken of the importance of the physical substance of his drawing materials in achieving affect—'materials that suited me on an affective level"—and he has described drawing as "an eminently carnal exercise" ("Conversation" 95).

14. Radical metamorphosis is not, of course, confined to autobiography: in Moebius's *Arzach* (1976), the eponymous character changed his appearance and the spelling of his name from one panel to the next.

WORKS CITED

Assouline, Pierre. *Hergé*. Paris: Plon, 1996.

Baetens, Jan. "Autobiographies et bandes dessinées." *Belphégor* 4.1 (2004).

Baudoin, Edmond. *Passe le temps*. Paris: Futuropolis, 1982.

——. *Terrains vagues*. Paris: Asssociation, 1996.

Beaty, Bart. *Unpopular Culture: Transforming the European Comic Book in the 1990s*. Toronto: University of Toronto Press, 2007.

Bellour, Raymond. "Autoportraits." *Communications* 48 (1988): 327–88.

Berberian, Charles. "Les Confessions d'un adolescent attardé." *Journal d'un album*. Ed. Philippe Dupuy and Charles Berberian. Paris: Association, 1994.

Boulet. *Notes: Le Petit Théâtre de la rue*. Paris: Delcourt, 2009.

Bouzard, Guillaume. *The Autobiography of Me Too*. Albi: Requins Marteaux, 2004.

Bruss, Elizabeth. "Eye for I: Making and Unmaking Autobiography in Film." *Autobiography: Essays Theoretical and Critical*. Ed. James Olney. Princeton NJ: Princeton University Press, 1980. 296–320.

David B. *L'Ascension du haut mal*. 6 vols. Paris: Association, 1996–2003. (*Epilectic*. Trans. Kim Thompson. New York: Pantheon, 2005.)

Deleuze, Gilles. *Francis Bacon: Logique de la sensation*. Paris: Seuil, 2002.

Doucet, Julie. *Ciboire de Criss!* Paris: Association, 1996.

Dupuy, Philippe. "L'Année dernière." *Journal d'un album*. Ed. Philippe Dupuy and Charles Berberian. Paris: Association, 1994.

Esquenazi, Jean-Pierre, and André Gardies, eds. *Le Je à l'écran*. Paris: Harmattan, 2006.

Gide, André. *Si le grain ne meurt*. Paris: Denoël, 1972.

Giraud, Jean. "Entretien avec Jean Giraud." *Schtroumpf: Les Cahiers de la bande dessinée* 25 (1974): 8–16.

Goblet, Dominique. *Faire semblant, c'est mentir*. Paris: Association, 2008.

Gravett, Paul. "De Luca and Hamlet: Thinking Outside the Box." *European Comic Art* 1.1 (2008): 21–35.

Groensteen, Thierry. "Les Petites Cases du moi: L'Autobiographie en bande dessinée." *9e art* 1 (1996): 58–69.

Hatfield, Charles. *Alternative Comics: An Emerging Literature*. Jackson: University of Mississippi Press, 2005.

Hergé. *Tintin au Tibet*. Tournai: Casterman, 1960.

Khélif, Kamel. *Ce pays qui est le vôtre*. Montreuil: Frémok, 2003.

Killoffer. *Six cent soixante-seize apparitions de Killoffer*. Paris: Association, 2002.

Konture, Mattt. *Cinq heure du Mattt*. Paris: Association, 2001.

———. *Headbanger*. Paris: Association, 2000.

———. *Ivan Morve*. Paris: Association, 1996.

———. *Krokodile Comix II*. Paris: Association, 1999.

———. *Printemps automnes*. Paris: Association, 2001.

———. *Tombe: Auto-psy d'un mort-vivant*. Paris: Association, 1999.

Larcenet, Manu. *Presque*. Montreuil: Rêveurs, 1998.

Lejeune, Philippe. *Le Pacte autobiographique*. Rev. ed. Paris: Seuil, 1996.

———. "Regarder un autoportrait." *Corps écrit* 5 (1983): 135–46.

Mauriac, François. *Ecrits intimes*. Geneva: Palatine, 1953.

Menu, Jean-Christophe. "Avant-garde et ultra-critique." *Eprouvette* 1 (2006): 173–86.

———. Editorial. *Lapin* 33 (2002): 6–9.

———. *Livret de phamille*. Paris: Association, 1995.

Moebius. *Arzach*. Paris: Humanoïdes Associés, 1976.

Morvandiau. *D'Algérie*. Rennes: Œil Electrique, 2007.

Neaud, Fabrice. *Journal*. 4 vols. Angoulême: Ego comme X, 1996–2002.

Neaud, Fabrice, and Jean-Christophe Menu. "Autopsie de l'autobiographie." *Eprouvette* 3 (2007): 450–72.

Néhou, Loïc. Interview. *Jadecomix*. 2001. (6 Mar. 2006.)

Peeters, Benoît. *Le Monde d'Hergé*. Tournai: Casterman, 1990.

Pekar, Harvey. *The New American Splendor Anthology*. New York: Four Walls Eight Windows, 1991.

Ratier, G. "2005: L'Année de la mangalisation." *ToutenBD*. 21 Dec. 2005. (13 Apr. 2006.)

———. "Zoom sur les meilleures ventes de BD no 135." *BDzoom.com*. 2007. (10 Nov. 2007.)

Roche, Roger-Yves. "Photos-fictions." *Le Je à l'écran*. Ed. Jean-Pierre Esquenazi and André Gardies. Paris: Harmattan, 2006. 189–200.

Sadoul, Numa. *Entretiens avec Hergé: Edition définitive*. Tournai: Casterman, 1989.

Satrapi, Marjane. *Persepolis*. 4 vols. Paris: Association, 2000–2003.

Sfar, Joann. *Harmonica*. Paris: Association, 2002.

Sheringham, Michael. *French Autobiography: Devices and Desires; Rousseau to Perec*. Oxford: Clarendon, 1993.

Sury, Caroline. *Bébé 2000*. Paris: Association, 2006.

Trondheim, Lewis. *Approximativement*. Paris: Cornélius, 1995.

———. *Carnets de bord*. 4 vols. Paris: Association, 2002–04.

Vanoli, Vincent. "Conversation avec Erwin Dejasse." *Artistes de bande dessinée*. Ed. Thierry Groensteen. Angoulême: Editions de l'an 2, 2003. 78–100.

———. *Le Côté obscur du dimanche après-midi*. Paris: Association, 2006.

———. *Pour une poignée de polenta*. Angoulême: Ego comme X, 2004.

———. *Sentiers battus*. Angoulême: Ego comme X, 2002.

AGNÈS CALATAYUD is a lecturer in French in the School of Arts (Department of European Culture and Languages) at Birkbeck College, University of London. She has two research interests: contemporary French cinema and representations of France's colonial past in contemporary popular culture. She has published in French and in English on Agnès Varda, Dominique Cabrera, and Henri-François Imbert, among others and on various productions such as French colonial songs and postcolonial cinema. Her articles have been featured in *Studies in French Cinema, Studies in European Cinema*, and *Dalhousie French Studies*.

NATALIE EDWARDS specializes in twentieth-century women's writing in French, particularly in autobiography and francophone studies. She has published articles on Hélène Cixous, Simone de Beauvoir, Paule Constant, Ken Bugul, Buchi Emecheta, and Aminata Sow Fall. She is the author of *Shifting Subjects: Plural Subjectivity in Francophone Women's Autobiography* (2011) and coeditor (with Christopher Hogarth) of *This "Self" Which Is Not One: Women's Life Writing in French* (2010) and *Gender and Displacement: "Home" in Contemporary Francophone Women's Autobiography* (2008).

JOHNNIE GRATTON is holder of the 1776 Chair of French at Trinity College, Dublin. He is the author of *Expressivism: The Vicissitudes of a Theory in the Writing of Proust and Barthes* and coeditor of five books, including *The Art of the Project: Projects and Experiments in Modern French Culture* and *L'Œil écrit: Etudes sur les rapports entre texte et image, 1800–1940*. He has published articles on Roland Barthes, André Breton, Sophie Calle, Colette, Michel Foucault, Patrick Modiano, Marcel Proust, and Nathalie Sarraute, among others.

AMY L. HUBBELL is associate professor of French at Kansas State University, where she teaches twentieth-century French and francophone literature and is assistant editor of *Studies in Twentieth and Twenty-first Century Literatures*. She is a specialist in Pied-Noir studies and has published articles on their literature and cinema in journals such as *Life Writing, Dalhousie French Studies, CELAAN Review*, and the *Revue diasporas*. Amy has contributed to several volumes on contemporary francophone women's autobiography and published a French business textbook, *A la recherche d'un emploi*, in 2010. In 2011 Amy became a lecturer in French at the University of Queensland.

ERICA L. JOHNSON holds a PhD in comparative literature and is an associate professor of English at Wagner College in New York City. She specializes in Caribbean literature and is the author of two books: *Caribbean Ghostwriting* (forthcoming) and *Home, Maison, Casa: The Politics of Location in Works by Jean Rhys, Marguerite Duras, and Erminia Dell'Oro*. She has also published articles on a range of twentieth-century women writers in such journals as *Modern Fiction Studies, Journal of Narrative Theory, Biography, Meridians, Journal of Caribbean Literatures*, and *Texas Studies in Language and Literature*.

SHIRLEY JORDAN is professor in French at Queen Mary, University of London. She specializes in contemporary French women's writing and visual culture and has published articles and chapters on Christine Angot, Sophie Calle, Annie Ernaux, Marie Darrieussecq, Virginie Despentes, Amélie Nothomb, Marie NDiaye, and Agnès Varda. Her publications include the monograph *Contemporary French Women's Writing* and articles on photography and installation art within autobiographical and autofictional projects. Dr. Jordan is currently completing a monograph titled *Private Lives, Public Display: Women and Exposure in Contemporary French Culture*.

ANN MILLER began her career as a teacher and teacher trainer before moving to an academic post at the University of Leicester in 1997, where she is now a senior lecturer. She teaches French cinema, comic art, textual analysis, and language. She has published widely on film and on *bande dessinée*, including *Reading Bande Dessinée: Critical Approaches to French-Language Comic Strip*, and she is joint editor of *European Comic Art*, published biannually by Liverpool University Press.

VÉRONIQUE MONTÉMONT teaches at the Université Henri Poincaré in Nancy. She has published numerous articles on the poets Jacques Garelli, Lorand Gaspar, and Jacques Roubaud as well as a book on the latter called *Jacques Roubaud: L'Amour du nombre*. She has also published on the statistical analysis of the markers of identity in autobiographical work and on the relationship between literature and photography.

FLORIANE PLACE-VERGHNES is a lecturer in French at the University of Manchester. She has published two books, *Tex Avery: An MGM Legacy, 1942–1955* and *Jeux pragmatiques dans les contes et nouvelles de Guy de Maupassant* [Pragmatic Games in the Tales and Short Stories of Guy de Maupassant], and is currently working on a monograph on photobiography. She jointly guest-edited, with Catherine Dousteyssier-Khoze, two issues of *Image [&] Narrative*: *L'Affiche fin-de-siècle* [The Turn-of-the-Century Poster] and *L'Affiche contemporaine: Discours, supports, stratégies* [The Contemporary Poster: Discourses, Contents, Strategies].

PETER WAGSTAFF lectures in French and European studies at the University of Bath. He has published extensively on French autobiographical writers—notably Georges Perec—and has edited the books *Cultures of Exile, Border Crossings, European Regionalism*, and *War and Society in 20th-Century France*. His research interests focus on memory and identity, cross-border themes, and film and visual culture. He is currently leading the Leverhulme Trust–funded international collaboration network Cultural Continuity in the Diaspora: Russian Jews in Paris and Berlin, 1917–1937.

INDEX

Acconci, Vito, 147, 148, 149, 150,
  164n3
Adams, Timothy Dow, 7, 8, 117
Adorno, Theodor, 190
agency, 10, 21, 133
albums: *bande dessinée*, 236, 238,
  246, 252, 256, 259n10, 260n12;
  photographic, 19, 30, 40, 55,
  59–60, 63, 71, 75, 82, 84, 90,
  175, 195–96, 202
Algeria, 20, 23, 80, 82, 90,
  100, 111, 175, 176, 256; and

Franco-Algerian identity, 101,
  175. *See also* Algerian War;
  Pieds-Noirs
Algerian War, 22, 173
Algiers, 170, 173–74, 176, 182
Allison, Dorothy, 39
Annaud, Jean-Jacques, 21, 116,
  122–35
anxiety, 54, 60, 236
Arbus, Diane, 54
Assouline, Pierre, 237
Auslander, Philippe, 163

authenticity: in autobiography, 2–3, 12, 39, 130, 198, 243, 251, 257; in film, 21–22, 123–27, 134; in performance, 163; in photography, 5, 44–45, 148

autobiography, 1–4, 7–12, 14–15, 17, 19–20, 24–26, 30–31, 33, 35, 40, 42–44, 45–46, 47, 53, 63, 75, 79–81, 83–84, 86, 88, 92–95, 100, 105, 110, 112n1, 117–18, 122, 126, 135–36, 143, 169, 177–78, 191, 194, 200–201, 211–12, 235–38, 240–42, 244–46, 248, 250–60; in *bande dessinée*, 15–16, 25, 235–62; definitions of, 2–5; diaries as, 41, 43, 61–62, 88, 100, 152–53, 222, 260n12; filmic, 4, 11–15, 25, 126, 204, 209–33; history of, 2–5; pacts in, 2, 3, 13, 15, 16, 18, 25, 34, 42, 43, 44, 45, 46, 64, 74, 80, 81, 94n2, 235, 236, 237, 242, 243, 244, 254; and photoautobiography, 52; and photobiography, 6, 18, 20, 22, 32, 35, 100, 101, 109

autofiction, 14, 30, 52–54, 56–58, 74, 112n1, 155, 254; definitions of, 3, 39; and distinction from autobiography, 60

autoportrait, 18, 24, 52, 60–62, 64, 100, 104, 211, 216, 218, 244

Baetens, Jan, 244
Bajac, Quentin, 44
Barthes, Roland, 7, 8, 9, 18, 19, 30, 32, 55, 74–75, 76n1, 193,

194; *Camera Lucida*, 5, 31, 37, 106–07, 127, 192, 196–97; *Roland Barthes sur Roland Barthes*, 2–3, 5–6, 8, 12, 36, 80, 99; and the Winter Garden photograph, 17, 37, 69, 118–19

Baudoin, Edmond, 238, 250
Baudrillard, Jean, 153
Bazin, André, 125, 192, 194, 196
Beaty, Bart, 240, 259n4
Bellour, Raymond, 13, 259n11
Benjamin, Walter, 10, 193
Berberian, Charles, 244, 246, 252, 260n12
biography, 2, 44, 79, 143, 151, 171, 237
Bober, Robert, 191, 200, 202–04
Bois, Yve-Alain, 41
Boltanski, Christian, 30, 39, 40, 44, 70
Bon, François, 30, 44
Bonnetto, Jérôme, 101, 103
Boulet, 254
Bouzard, Guillaume, 251
Boyle, Claire, 4
Boym, Svetlana, 170–71, 180
Brochet, Anne, 16–18, 37–38, 52, 55–56, 65–70, 74, 100
Bruss, Elizabeth, 6, 11–14, 245–46, 248, 259n11
Buskirk, Martha, 146, 147, 148, 149, 150, 151, 157, 164n3

Calatayud, Agnès, 24–25
Calle, Sophie, 16, 30, 40–42, 44, 56, 66, 70, 72, 100; *Douleur exquise*, 41–42; *M'as-tu vue?*,

41, 150–52, 155; *Suite véniti-enne*, 21–22, 139–64
Camart, Cécile, 29, 164n7
Canguilhem, Denis, 44
Cardinal, Marie, 169–71, 173, 175–76, 179–80, 184n5, 185n14
Cartier-Bresson, Henri, 20, 112n6
catharsis, 55
childhood, 21, 23, 31–32, 36, 39–40, 44–45, 79–80, 115, 120, 124, 135, 169, 173, 178, 184n5, 191, 198–99, 237, 239, 246, 248, 252
Chodorow, Nancy, 112n8
Cixous, Hélène, 17, 19, 30, 79–82, 84, 86–91, 93–94, 176, 182, 184n11
collage, 43, 101–02, 106–07, 111, 250
collection, 11, 26, 30, 56, 106–07, 111–12, 179, 204–05, 230, 259n7
collective identity, 1, 11, 15–16, 22–23, 40, 55, 101, 103, 110–12, 126, 168–69, 171, 191, 202–03
concealment, 18, 20, 155
Constantine, 172–74, 176, 182–83

Daguerre, Louis-Jacques-Mandé, 7, 223, 225
David B., 239, 248, 259n6
death, 5, 7, 17, 19, 24, 25, 59, 71–72, 74, 81, 85–86, 90–91,

100, 103, 107, 118, 121, 130, 132, 172, 178, 193, 197, 201, 203, 206, 216, 222, 228, 230, 236, 239, 256
Deleuze, Gilles, 250
Delory-Momberger, Christine, 35, 45
Depardon, Raymond, 6, 29–30, 32, 36, 43, 80, 108, 156
Derrida, Jacques, 23, 82, 92, 167, 176, 178, 180–81, 185n16, 201
desire, 3–4, 14, 17, 53–57, 74, 88, 112, 119, 121, 127, 131, 135, 179, 211, 216, 231, 250
Desplechin, Marie, 30
Didi-Huberman, Georges, 109
Dilasser, Antoinette, 30
Djebar, Assia, 80, 111
documentary: and autobiog-raphy, 41, 47, 157, 163; film, 24, 173, 176–77, 191, 210, 217, 225; photography, 6, 13, 22, 65–66, 144–45, 148, 156, 159, 161, 203. *See also* photodocumentary
Doucet, Julie, 253, 257
Dubois, Philippe, 112n1
Duperey, Anny, 33
Dupuy, Philippe, 246, 248, 260n12
Duras, Marguerite, 17, 21, 69, 80, 115–25, 127, 129–36

Eakin, Paul John, 8
Edwards, Natalie, 19
ekphrasis, 31–32, 37, 46, 59, 135n1

embodiment, 10, 19, 89, 257

Ernaux, Annie: *Les Années*, 31–32, 94, 107–08, 210; *L'Evénément*, 79; *Une femme*, 79; *La Place*, 79; *L'Usage de la photo*, 18–19, 30, 32, 52, 70–74, 79–94, 100, 104, 105, 107–08, 111

Evans, Walker, 159

Everett, Wendy, 14

exile, 169, 171–73, 179–80, 182, 185n13

family, 14, 19, 23, 24, 33, 47, 55, 58, 60–61, 70, 82, 99, 108, 111, 120, 122, 124, 129, 131, 170, 176, 183, 195, 196, 198, 202, 204, 211, 213, 216, 224, 226, 229, 239, 242, 251, 254, 256, 257

Fathy, Safaa, 23, 176, 180

Felman, Shoshana, 110

feminism, French, 79

Flusser, Vilém, 24, 194–95, 198–99, 206

Fox Talbot, William Henry, 192

fragmentation, 6–7, 13, 20, 23, 24, 55, 61, 65, 75, 82, 88, 92, 101, 102, 106–10, 180, 212, 218, 225, 250, 258

Frank, Robert, 7

Friday, Jonathan, 143

Gardies, André, 14–15, 259n11

Gasparini, Philippe, 39

Gide, André, 236, 259n2

Giraud, Jean, 237, 238, 239

Goblet, Dominique, 257

Godard, Jean-Luc, 24, 210, 211–15

Goldin, Nan, 6, 66

Gratton, Johnnie, 21–22

Grenier, Roger, 30, 40

Groensteen, Thierry, 240, 259n3

Guibert, Hervé, 9, 30, 35, 55, 80, 95n3, 99, 100

Guichard, Jean-Paul, 42

guilt, 14, 236

Hatfield, Charles, 15, 238, 241, 251, 257–58

Hergé, 236, 237

Hine, Lewis W., 204, 205

Hirsch, Marianne, 63, 116, 134, 191

historiography, 79

Hollander, John, 31

Holocaust, 23, 190–91, 198

Hubbell, Amy L., 22–23

Hughes, Alex, 8, 9

hybridity, 62, 101

illustration, 21–22, 65, 81, 110, 139–66

immigration, 206

individual identity, 4–5, 12, 16, 20, 33, 45, 61, 62, 94n2, 101, 103, 108, 122, 169, 171, 173, 202–03, 242

intersubjectivity, 121, 126

intertextuality, 135

intimacy, 6, 8, 51, 53–55, 58, 66–67, 69, 72–74, 104, 130, 221, 257

Jameson, Frederic, 20, 105
Johnson, Erica L., 20–21
Jones, Elizabeth H., 3
Jordan, Shirley, 18–19
journalism, 108–09, 144, 145
Judaism, 23, 82, 176, 178, 190, 200, 201

Khélif, Kamel, 240
Killoffer, 253, 256
Konture, Mattt, 239, 242, 251, 254, 255, 259n10
Krauss, Rosalind, 8
Kress, Gunther, 144

Lacan, Jacques, 12, 53, 121
Larcenet, Manu, 243
Laurens, Camille, 16–18, 51, 55–62, 65, 74, 80, 106, 109, 111
Le Clézio, J. M. G., 30
Legendre, Claire, 20, 100, 101, 103
Lejeune, Philippe, 2–3, 12–13, 18, 25, 34, 42–43, 45–46, 94n2, 191, 211, 223, 235–37, 242, 244
life writing, 2, 3, 116, 117
Lionnet, Françoise, 4
loss, 10, 17, 18, 23–24, 54, 55, 57, 59, 67, 69, 73, 74–75, 104, 109, 127, 168, 171, 177, 189, 198, 216, 239, 243, 256
love, 20, 130, 216; maternal, 54; patriotic, 170; romantic, 41, 54, 56, 57–58, 65, 69, 71, 72, 82, 123, 134, 183n2, 243

Marey, Étienne-Jules, 25, 224, 229
Marie, Marc, 18, 19, 20, 30, 32, 52, 55–56, 67, 69–70, 72–74, 79, 82, 85, 87–90, 100
Mauriac, François, 236, 259n1
Maynard, Patrick, 145
Méaux, Danièle, 55
memory, 10, 23, 34, 36, 47, 51, 69, 72, 109, 189, 191, 193, 200, 204, 206, 249, 250; collective, 11, 22, 112, 126, 167, 171, 174, 182, 193; loss of, 55, 58, 122, 180, 192, 195, 198–99, 248; of loved ones, 58, 70; of place, 181; of self, 14, 18, 24, 45, 101, 213
Menu, Jean-Christophe, 239, 241, 242, 251, 255, 256, 258, 259n8
Miller, Ann, 25
Miller, Nancy K., 4
Mitchell, W. J. T., 139, 140, 141, 142, 149
Moebius, 237, 252, 260n14
Montandon, Alain, 42
Montémont, Véronique, 17–18
Mora, Gilles, 6–7, 29–30, 32, 35, 45
Morvandiau, 246, 256
mother-child relationships, 5, 9, 31, 33, 61–63, 82, 85, 107, 118, 120–22, 131–34, 196–97, 225, 229, 256
mourning, 193
Mulvey, Laura, 193

Nadar, Félix, 118, 194
NDiaye, Marie, 17, 18, 52, 56, 60–65, 80, 100
Neaud, Fabrice, 240, 241, 242, 243, 246, 248, 251, 254, 255, 256, 257, 259n8
Néhou, Loïc, 257
Nerlich, Michael, 42
Nora, Pierre, 109, 111
Nori, Claude, 29–30
nostalgia, 125, 168, 170–71, 174–75, 178, 180, 183, 185n15, 239, 250

obsession, 65, 108, 210, 254

Pachet, Pierre, 44
Peeters, Benoît, 236
Peirce, Charles S., 6, 31, 193
Pekar, Harvey, 238, 244
Perec, Georges, 3, 4, 16, 17, 23–24, 30, 31, 45, 189–206
performativity, 10, 69
phantomization, 9, 58, 84, 119, 127, 129
photodocumentary, 22, 158–59, 167–69, 172, 174
photo essay, 140
phototext, 8, 21, 51, 52, 54, 55, 59, 69, 71, 73, 74, 75, 108, 139, 147, 149, 151, 155
Pieds-Noirs, 16, 22, 167–87
Place-Verghnes, Floriane, 20
Plato, 195
postcolonialism, 20, 101, 126
postmodernism, 67, 102, 104, 112n5, 119, 124, 135n4

post-structuralism, 8
prototype, 21–22, 140–46, 149, 154, 163n1
publishing industry, 25, 105, 168, 235, 238, 241, 259n3

Queneau, Raymond, 201

referentiality, 7–10, 15, 34, 39, 84, 117
resistance, 4, 7, 10, 21, 63, 139–40, 148, 164n4
Roche, Denis, 7, 29–30, 32, 35, 36, 43, 44, 100
Roche, Roger-Yves, 243
Rosenstone, Robert, 11
Roubaud, Alix Cléo, 43, 45
Rouillé, André, 103
Rugg, Linda Haverty, 9–10, 81, 89

Sadoul, Numa, 236, 237
Satrapi, Marjane, 239, 241, 256
Schaeffer, Jean-Marie, 31, 34
Sebald, W. G., 99
Sebbar, Leïla, 20, 80, 100–101, 108, 110, 111
self-portrait: in film, 24–25, 124, 209–31; in literature, 21, 60, 64, 135; in painting, 127, 211, 223, 229–30; in photography, 43–44, 116, 119, 127, 155
semiotics, 118
sexuality, 56, 88, 110, 126, 131–32, 257
Sfar, Joann, 239

Sheringham, Michael, 3, 4, 71, 116, 117, 119, 250

Smith, Sidonie, 4, 10, 81, 83, 135n5

Sontag, Susan, 8, 71, 72, 81, 106, 193, 199

Soulages, François, 34, 35, 41, 42

Spence, Jo, 43, 44

Stora, Benjamin, 23, 167, 170–71, 176, 178–80, 182, 183n3, 184n7

Strand, Paul, 158

subjectivity, 2, 10, 11, 12, 14, 15, 25, 86, 93, 100, 116, 119, 125–26, 130, 135, 135n5, 235, 245, 248, 258

subversion, 15, 82, 156–57

suffering, 41, 100, 125, 135, 168, 236

Sury, Caroline, 257

testimonial narrative, 95n4, 106, 178, 182, 219

Tisseron, Serge, 19, 53, 54, 65, 73–74

traces: filmic, 24, 204, 216; literary, 89, 195; photographic, 12, 17, 18, 19, 20, 22, 31, 33, 34, 55, 65–66, 70–71, 75, 80, 144. *See also* memory

trauma, 19, 80, 93, 168, 178, 189, 191

Trondheim, Lewis, 240, 242, 243, 251, 252, 253, 259n7

truth, 2–3, 7, 11, 12, 13, 15, 25, 33–35, 47, 61, 69, 102, 118, 122, 149, 171, 198, 202, 224, 236, 245–46. *See also* autofiction

Van Leeuwen, Theo, 144

Vanoli, Vincent, 242, 247, 248, 249, 250, 251, 256, 260n13

Varda, Agnès, 17, 25, 209–33

Vray, Jean-Bernard, 55

Wagstaff, Peter, 23–24

Watson, Julia, 10, 135n5

Wolf, Christa, 10

Milton Keynes UK
Ingram Content Group UK Ltd.
UKHW010704280324
439889UK00010B/124